The Closing of the Auditor's Mind?

In *The Closing of the Auditor's Mind?*, author David J. O'Regan describes internal auditing as an important "binding agent" of social cohesion, for the accountability of individuals and organizations and also at aggregated levels of social trust. However, O'Regan also reveals that internal auditing faces two severe challenges – an external challenge of adaptation and an internal challenge of fundamental reform.

The adaptation challenge arises from ongoing, paradigmatic shifts in accountability and social trust. The command-and-control, vertical hierarchies of traditional bureaucracies are being replaced in importance by networked, flattened patterns of accountability. The most challenging assurance demands of the modern era are increasingly located in three institutional domains – in the inner workings of organizations; in intermediary spaces at organizational boundaries; and in extra-mural locations. Internal auditing continues to cling, barnacle-like, to the inner workings of traditional, bureaucratic structures, and it has little to offer the emerging assurance demands on or beyond institutional boundaries. The reform challenge arises from internal auditing's prevailing tendency toward a rigid, algorithmic, checklist mindset that suppresses practitioners' creativity and critical thinking. This trend is increasingly narrowing internal auditing's intellectual and moral horizons. Under the pressures of these challenges, internal auditing is struggling to fulfil its primary purpose of serving the public interest.

O'Regan's powerful book focuses on:

- The redistribution of social trust from traditional, hierarchical institutions to diffuse, horizontally distributed networks
- The perennial validity of the classical virtues as the humane foundation of professional activity
- The role of creative expertise in promoting professional wisdom

The Closing of the Auditor's Mind? is a philosophical audit of a profession on the threshold of crisis. The book presupposes no prior knowledge of philosophy, nor indeed of auditing. Philosophical technicalities are contained in an Appendix, leaving the main text jargon-free. O'Regan provides original and striking perspectives on the malaise of modern internal auditing, and he proposes radical remedies. This captivating and well-informed book is a must-read for all who are concerned with our collective socio-economic and political well-being.

Security, Audit and Leadership Series
Series Editor: Dan Swanson, Dan Swanson and Associates, Ltd., Winnipeg, Manitoba, Canada.

The ***Security, Audit and Leadership Series*** publishes leading-edge books on critical subjects facing security and audit executives as well as business leaders. Key topics addressed include Leadership, Cybersecurity, Security Leadership, Privacy, Strategic Risk Management, Auditing IT, Audit Management and Leadership

Why CISOs Fail (Second Edition)
Barak Engel

Riding the Wave: Applying Project Management Science in the Field of Emergency Management
Andrew Boyarsky

The Shortest Hour: An Applied Approach to Boardroom Governance of Cybersecurity
Lee Parrish

Global Audit Leadership: A Practical Approach to Leading a Global Internal Audit (GIA) Function in a Constantly Changing Internal and External Landscape
Audley L. Bell

Construction Audit: Building a Solid Foundation
Denise Cicchella

Continuous Auditing with AI in the Public Sector
Lourens Erasmus and Sezer Bozkus Kahyaoglu

Ironwill 360° Leadership: Moving Forward: Unlock Twelve Emerging Trends for Forward Thinking Leaders
Douglas P. Pflug

The CISO Playbook
Andres Andreu

Leveraging Blockchain Technology: Governance, Risk, Compliance, Security, and Benevolent Use Cases
Shaun Aghili

The Closing of the Auditor's Mind?: How to Reverse the Erosion of Trust, Virtue, and Wisdom in Modern Auditing
David J. O'Regan

For more information about this series, please visit: https://www.routledge.com/Internal-Audit-and-IT-Audit/book-series/CRCINTAUDITA

The Closing of the Auditor's Mind?

How to Reverse the Erosion of Trust, Virtue, and Wisdom in Modern Auditing

David J. O'Regan

Foreword by Michael Power

CRC Press
Taylor & Francis Group
Boca Raton London New York

CRC Press is an imprint of the
Taylor & Francis Group, an **informa** business

Author biography

David J. O'Regan has authored nine books on auditing and related themes. His interests include the application of Aristotelian logic to the auditing process, and he is the author of the *Auditor's Companion: Concepts and Terms from A to Z* (Georgetown University Press, 2024). He earned a doctorate in accounting and finance from the University of Liverpool and is a Fellow of the Institute of Chartered Accountants in England and Wales. His auditing experience covers more than three decades, spanning the private, public, and academic sectors. He commenced his career in the United Kingdom with Price Waterhouse, a forerunner firm to today's PricewaterhouseCoopers, and subsequently worked in industry before heading the internal audit function at Oxford University Press. He then entered public service in the United Nations system, initially at the Organisation for the Prohibition of Chemical Weapons in The Hague, the Netherlands. From 2009 he has served as Auditor General to the Pan American Health Organization in Washington, D.C.

Foreword

It is rare for accomplished audit and accounting professionals to write books. It is even rarer for them to write books which reflect critically and expansively on their practice. Yet, this is just such a study and David J. O'Regan has synthesized the wisdom of his many years as an internal auditor with an array of insights from philosophy and other disciplines. The result is a compelling exploration not just of auditing but also of the changing fabric of organizational life in the digital age. His distinctive combination of the operational and concrete with more abstract deliberations reminds us that theory and practice are not worlds apart. If we look closely and carefully enough, we see that practice is infused with theoretical elements and ethical assumptions, which require attention and reflection.

This book and its many insights are especially timely as auditing finds itself at a crucial inflection point. Auditors, both internal and external, have always encountered developments in technology somewhat ambivalently. On the one hand technology advances have promised both increased efficiency and enhanced possibilities for assurance. On the other hand, to the extent that they make incursions into the professional "craft" of audit, the judgement of the individual auditor has been increasingly circumscribed. While this dialectic of technology and judgement has been going on for many decades, in both auditing and other areas of professional activity, the stakes have been raised by what is now called the fourth industrial revolution. Is technology and, more precisely, the rise of the algorithm, a friend or foe for the auditor? There is already much debate about these matters, both on the use of algorithms to augment the audit process as a decision aid, and also on the very possibility of being able to audit algorithms themselves as they pervade organizations and information systems. What indeed is the future of human auditor judgment when the outputs of machine-learning algorithms to support the audit cannot themselves be readily understood by the human auditor but must be taken on trust?

These questions matter because now more than ever society, in the form of multiple and diverse stakeholders, demands trust and security from audit and related practices of oversight at a time when they are facing significant changes and disruption. Indeed, it can be said that the intellectual framework of governance and assurance is being turned upside down as algorithm-based technologies are not so much enhancing auditing, but also challenging the nature of what it is to audit and to provide assurance. And, as this book demonstrates, the internal auditor is a critical actor at the center of these developments and cannot ignore them.

David J. O'Regan situates these new challenges in its broader historical and philosophical context, taking us back to the fundamentals of the audit craft in order to reveal the tensions and pathologies of restricted judgment and a compliance mentality which have always existed but which now have intensified. Indeed, when audit and assurance processes are increasingly fragmented and piecemeal, it is not so fanciful to imagine that only an algorithm can audit another algorithm. At this point, the mind of the human auditor, and the very possibility of skepticism, judgement and virtue, is "closed" because it is increasingly marginalized.

While this fully automated governance order is not yet with us, the arguments of this book remind us that professional auditors are not well-prepared for it. They need to be more vigilant than ever to renew and sustain the ethics of their craft, not to engage in a Luddite rejection of new technology but to govern it for the public good which has always been their purpose. The reader will be taken on a rich and wide-ranging journey which provides both a compelling diagnosis of the closing of the auditor's mind and also hope in the form of prescriptions for a reconstruction of the ethical mission of the internal auditor. I therefore commend this excellent work; it should be read both by auditors and professionals more generally since it speaks to their very identity and purpose.

Michael Power
July 2024
London School of Economics and Political Science

Preface

As the playwright Alan Bennett once remarked, "you don't put yourself into what you write – you find yourself there" (Bennett, 2015, 5). He was right: The articulation of the arguments in this book has been central to my understanding of them. In our age of increasing conformity and regimentation, not least in internal auditing, it has been both refreshing and troubling to venture into largely unnavigated territory, in which to ponder things many prefer not to consider.

This book summarizes an internal audit practitioner's attempt to grasp the contours of a new era of accountability and social trust, and to assess the uncomfortable implications for the future of internal auditing. I also describe the nature and scale of internal auditing's current limitations, and I stake out a long hard road to overdue and necessary changes. If my ringing of warning bells and the results of my inquiries are sometimes at odds with official discourse, it is because I have sought to look at internal auditing in fresh ways and, where appropriate, challenge official narratives.

All opinions expressed in this book – be they sagacious or misguided – are my responsibility alone and do not necessarily reflect the views of any of the organizations with which I have been associated. In setting out the outlines of the battle for the soul of modern internal auditing, my aim has not been to debunk. Any debunking that takes place along the journey is an unavoidable by-product of my main purpose, which is to connect internal auditing to enduring truths of the human condition. Nor do I seek to be a modern-day Jeremiah, lamenting internal auditing's failings amid widespread institutional decay and the erosion of social trust. But the implications of the challenges facing internal auditing for our future socio-economic well-being are too important to be explained away or softened by euphemism or understatement.

My approach in this book is not one of traditional social science. It is, instead, a philosophical inquiry. Or, perhaps, a philosophical audit. I approach the problem from a range of viewpoints, as though measuring the aesthetic worth of a statue by approaching it from various angles. To explain my eclectic approach, I have included a brief *Note on methodology* at the start of the book, while Appendix A sets out my methods in greater detail. The material I shall cover is wide, ranging from the cardinal virtues of classical Greece to the superstitions of numerology, and from neuroscience to the sociology of professions.

My inclusion of cultural and literary references in the text illustrates internal auditing's role as an important component of the human condition. I do not see internal auditing as a dry, algorithmic specialism, nor as a charmless outgrowth of bureaucratic proceduralism that is removed from our basic humanity. On the contrary, internal auditing is a socially constructed yet remarkably consistent phenomenon intertwined with our collective well-being. In this book I shall refer to Homer, Plato, Aristotle, and Shakespeare; to Hans Sachs and Richard Wagner; to the gentle nostalgia of Matthew Arnold and Marcel Proust; to the chilling, dystopian visions of Aldous Huxley; and to many more besides, including non-Western sources, from Confucius to the *Ramayana* to Rabindranath Tagore. In so doing, I aim to show that internal auditing is as much a global humane endeavor as a scientific activity, and that it is intertwined with perennial aspects of our social existence.

I have not hesitated to embed historical observations in the text. Too often, internal auditing seeks to leap forward without a prudent awareness of past experiences, and modern internal auditors tend to treat their activities ahistorically, as though the sequence of events that led us to the current day were unimportant or obsolete. As Allan Bloom warned us, our impulse is generally "toward the future, and tradition seems more of a shackle to it than an inspiration" (Bloom, 1987, 244). Internal auditing did not come to us gift-wrapped: It has evolved over time, it continues to develop, and it is on the brink of a new era to which it may or may not successfully adapt. A tendency by internal auditors to ignore all but the most recent history of their subject can lead to gaps in understanding and losses of perspective. History suggests that auditing of various types matters for our shared well-being, and for this reason the current state of internal auditing is of grave concern. I intend this text to be a corrective to some of internal auditing's harmful ahistorical tendencies.

Owing to the complexity of the topics I have compressed as tightly as possible into this book, the presentation of my arguments might best be viewed as provisional rather than completed. Indeed, given the dangers inherent in sketching significant complexity within the constraints of a modestly sized volume, I hope that my arguments' broad strokes might offset any abridgements of detail in what follows. I do not claim to occupy any privileged position of interpretation, and I welcome correction of (or supplementation to) my arguments. In this spirit I invite readers' comments and criticisms that I might put to constructive use for the development of a possible future edition of the book.

I dedicate this book to all internal auditors who sense that internal auditing is not only failing to adapt to emerging patterns of accountability and social trust but also forfeiting characteristics of enduring importance.

David J O'Regan
Falls Church, Virginia, May 2024
www.davidoregan.com

Acknowledgments

My gratitude goes above all to my editor Dan Swanson, who set the ball rolling and supported this book from the time its central themes were first taking shape, like glowing fragments, in my thoughts. At Routledge/CRC Press, I thank Gabriella Williams and Radhika Gupta who saw the book through to publication with friendly enthusiasm and artful competence. My gratitude also goes to anonymous reviewers for their perceptive criticism at the proposal stage, and to Dr. Sara I. James, Dr. Rainer Lenz, Dr. Hernan Murdock, and Professor Jeffrey Ridley for reviewing parts of the draft manuscript. Section 4.2 draws on some of the ideas presented in my co-authored article with Dr. Rainer Lenz, "The *Global Internal Audit Standards* – old wine in new bottles?" (Lenz and O'Regan, 2024). In addition, Professor Michael Power provided comments on an early draft of Chapter 3, and Dr. Mark Dooley, Ireland's great philosopher, kindly made suggestions for the discussion of philosophical hermeneutics in Appendix A. Their comments yielded many suggestions I was compelled to consider, yet I alone am responsible for the text, including any infelicities. An individual's involvement in reviewing the draft manuscript doesn't suggest any endorsement of my ideas.

More broadly, my encounters over more than three decades in internal auditing have furnished me with a seemingly inexhaustible reservoir of information. I have appreciated and valued the opinions of countless individuals: Most have made internal auditing delightful for me, and only a very small number have tried to make it an ordeal, but all have enriched my views. These innumerable interactions have underwritten many of my reflections on the issues discussed in this book. I am grateful for the support of many friends along the auditing way, and I hope this book conveys my gratitude to people too numerous to count.

I also thank the Institute of Internal Auditors (IIA). The IIA has published four of my previous books, three of which ran to second editions, and I am a former contributing editor of the IIA's magazine *Internal Auditor*. My critique in this book encompasses some of the directions the IIA has taken in recent years, but it is as a friendly critic that I address the problems that beset modern internal auditing. The IIA is currently carrying a heavy burden of responsibility for the future health of internal auditing, amid revolutionary shifts in the patterns of accountability and social trust. My awareness of the magnitude of the IIA's current and future challenges is matched only by my admiration for the IIA's many past and current achievements.

Abbreviations

BBC	British Broadcasting Corporation
BRICS	Traditionally: Brazil, Russia, India, China, and South Africa. At the time of writing (early 2024) the current BRICS organization has four member states in addition to the initial five countries: Egypt, Ethiopia, Iran, and the United Arab Emirates.
CBOK	Common Body of Knowledge (of the IIA)
ERM	Enterprise Risk Management
ESG	Environmental, Social and Governance practices
GIAS	*Global Internal Audit Standards* (issued by the IIA in 2024)
GPS	Global Positioning System
IIA	Institute of Internal Auditors
IMF	International Monetary Fund
PMC	Professional–Managerial Class

A note on methodology

There are many ways to interpret a social activity like internal auditing. We may, for example, seek to understand internal auditing through the lenses of economics, politics, or history, or via the methodologies of logic. Social sciences typically test their hypotheses through surveys, observations, and experiments. In this book, I take a different approach – I undertake a philosophical inquiry. One might, perhaps, describe it as a philosophical audit. It is certainly not an exercise in social science. I have unashamedly adopted philosophical methods like analogy, conceptual clarification, and the spelling out of speculative and counterfactual alternatives to current internal auditing practices. The book does not presuppose any philosophical background for its readership, and it is largely devoid of philosophical terms. For those interested in my approach, I have included, in addition to this introductory note, a more detailed discussion in Appendix A. I have also gathered examples of aphoristic wisdom applicable to internal auditing in Appendix B, and a glossary of the principal philosophical (and auditing) terms used in the text.

At the core of my arguments in this book is a differentiation between two broad understandings of internal auditing – the phenomenological and the scientistic. We should at the outset clarify our terminology, and I shall use the analogy of a smile to illuminate the differences between phenomenology and scientism. When I see my lover's smile, I understand that she is conveying her affection, and I interpret her smile as an invitation to an evening of companionship, wine, and laughter. Her smile offers me a glimpse into her intentions and emotions. This is a phenomenological interpretation. An alternative, scientistic interpretation of my lover's smile might focus on the ways innate biological predispositions trigger the synaptic functions that transmit signals between neurons in her brain: These signals pass down from her central nervous system to her facial muscle cells, causing the cells to contract, pulling aside the corners of her mouth, and thereby revealing her teeth.

Both interpretations of the smile, phenomenological and scientistic, are correct, but in different ways. Values and feelings color phenomenological interpretations, with a focus on the intentionality of individuals in their exercise of moral agency. Phenomenology deals with the social environment of our daily, lived experience. In contrast, the scientistic interpretation looks at the biological structures and causal regularities that underpin reality. It is disinterested in the intentionality of my lover's smile, other than as a manifestation of her genetic inheritance of biological mating rituals, and it tends toward a naïve reductionism.

The objectivity of a phenomenological interpretation of a smile is as secure as the objectivity of the scientistic interpretation. The two understandings are both rational, but in different ways. They co-exist without conflict: My grasp of the social reality of the smile does not contradict the laws of biology. Nonetheless, phenomenological interpretation is irreducible to scientistic understanding – the full meaning of a smile cannot be captured solely by biological explanations. The phenomenological world is one of intention and individuality; the world of science is one of measurement and calculation. My lover is more than just a biological machine, and she will likely be disappointed if I view her as merely a bundle of neurons, electrical impulses, and cell tissue.

Applying these concepts to internal auditing, I shall argue in this book that a balance between phenomenology and social science is needed to understand fully how internal auditing serves the public interest. I shall also argue that modern internal auditing has drifted too far into a naïve scientism, and has therefore become dangerously abstracted from the ebb and flow of the world of daily experience. In other words, excessively scientistic views of internal auditing are neglecting our phenomenological experiences. We have collectively impoverished internal auditing by rejecting the notion that internal auditing is a social reality accessible through phenomenological interpretations. If we continue along the current path of scientism, with its dampening of judgment and creativity, internal auditing will be reduced to the domains of the algorithm and the checklist. The stakes for the future of internal auditing are high.

Glossary

algorithm a pre-defined set of steps or processes to accomplish a defined task
auditing an impartial, evidence-based, judgmental assessment for accountability purposes
data a collection of discrete, quantitative values
epistemology theories of knowledge
expectations gap discrepancies in views of the main purpose of external auditing, especially in relation to the detection of fraud or irregularities: Auditors tend to identify the managers of an audited organization as bearing the primary responsibility for the prevention and detection of fraud, but public opinion has doggedly pinned these responsibilities on auditors
external auditing a branch of auditing that focuses on the accuracy and fair presentation of financial statements
financial auditing a synonym for external auditing
information data that have been structured or analyzed into meaningful patterns
internal auditing a branch of auditing that focuses on procedures, internal controls, and risks in the inner workings of organizations
knowledge "actionable inferences made from information" (Sinnreich and Gilbert, 2024, xiii)
moral agency the state of being held accountable for one's actions
ontology theories of being, existence, and reality
phenomenology theories of reality, with a focus on the meanings of appearance and experience
scientism a dogmatic and damaging application of the methods of natural science to social science
solipsistic (adj.) an extremely egocentric condition, in which only the self has importance (or only the self exists)
trust "a psychological state comprising the intention to accept vulnerability based upon positive expectations of the intentions or behaviour of another" (Rousseau et al., 1998).

Chapter 1

Introduction

Increasingly fragmented patterns of accountability and social trust are in the ascendant. This book explores the implications of these changes for a crucial area of our socio-economic existence – internal auditing. Its primary audience is the community of practicing internal auditors, and its secondary audience includes all those with an interest in institutional governance and accountability, and our collective social well-being. Although the focus is on internal auditing, the discussions will contain themes relevant to other auditing specialties.

Internal auditing faces not only a challenge of adaptability to emerging patterns of accountability and social trust – it is also confronted by broader challenges of reforms required to encourage such adaptability. One might prefer the term "crises" to "challenges" but let us avoid leavening our analysis with hyperbolic language. Nonetheless, the severity of internal auditing's two contemporaneous and interconnected challenges discussed in this book is not to be underestimated. Should the challenges remain unaddressed, they may well develop into profound crises.

Regarding the first challenge of adaptability, internal auditing has failed to keep pace with global trends toward a flattening of traditional, vertical hierarchies of the command-and-control variety, and their replacement with complex patterns of horizontally distributed accountability and social trust. Our trust in traditional institutions and in politicians, business leaders, and the cultural elite is eroding. We are increasingly placing trust in non-hierarchical networks, both digital and human. And where trust has been displaced, flows of accountability adapt accordingly. The emergent patterns of accountability and social trust are so far-reaching that they threaten to leave internal auditing marooned, like a shipwreck, in the detritus of history.

Internal auditing is therefore at a crossroads, both practical and conceptual. The most demanding needs of accountability and social trust increasingly fall into three domains – in the inner workings of organizations; in transitional spaces at organizational boundaries; and in extra-mural activities.

DOI: 10.1201/9781032664880-1

Internal auditing remains fixated on the innards of traditional, bureaucratic structures and is ill-positioned to address the assurance demands arising at both the liminal spaces at the fringes of formal organizational structures and from locations beyond institutional boundaries. The peripheral and external domains are characterized by an absence of clear markers of responsibilities, and by fast, flexible, and disorienting flows of accountability that bear little resemblance to the shape of traditional bureaucracy. Their records of accountability are typically digital rather than tangible, and the significance of their assurance demands defies easy evaluation. Importantly for our analysis in this book, we encounter the new patterns of accountability and social trust where the writ of internal auditing, as well as external auditing, runs weakest.

The versatility of both internal and external auditing is hampered by restraints. The external auditor's opinion on an organization's annual financial statements once satisfied the assurance needs of traditional hierarchies of accountability and social trust, but it is ill-equipped to meet the demands of the emergent, horizontally distributed accountability paradigm. In contrast to external auditing, internal auditing's activities are framed in more elastic terms, and internal auditing therefore offers, on paper at least, a greater scope for adaptation. Yet internal auditing, like external auditing, faces an uncertain future, owing to the need for the types of reform without which the necessary agility and adaptation are unlikely to develop.

At this point, a word of caution is in order. Even amid the newly emerging patterns of horizontally distributed accountability, bureaucratic organizations characterized by command-and-control structures will continue to exist. A demand for external and internal auditors' services will therefore remain, as long as stakeholders continue to be interested in financial statements and in the inner workings of organizations. But the real action on accountability and social trust will increasingly be found elsewhere, on the fringes of organizations and in extra-mural locations. Already, assurance is becoming increasingly piecemeal. We can expect the emergence, in the near future, of innovative, diffuse assurance mechanisms to address the pressing demands of the new patterns of accountability and social trust. Both external and internal auditing therefore face a future of marginalization as they remain shackled to the outdated frameworks of bureaucratic institutions.

Internal auditing faces not only a challenge of adaptability. It also contends with a second challenge arising from its increasing tendency toward algorithmic and mechanistic activities. In particular, the dangers arising from a swelling tide of amoral and pedantic literalism in internal auditing are difficult to overstate. This book advocates for a humane approach to internal auditing founded on creativity, individual judgment, and critical thinking.

In this context, a major theme of this book is a sense of loss. This is the type of loss that seems an inevitable accompaniment to progress. Or, perhaps more accurately, an accompaniment to misplaced notions of progress. Internal auditors today have at their disposal vast pools of data, along with powerful technological tools that mine and arrange the data into auditable information. Technological advances encourage internal auditors to approach well-worn topics in fresh ways and to explore newfangled activities. Only a Luddite would be hostile to technological advances in internal auditing, from data analytics to the use of drones for the purposes of aerial surveillance of dispersed inventory. But internal auditing's technological achievements have come at a high cost – as an addictive substitute for critical thinking. Internal auditors are increasingly gripped by an algorithmic mindset, and they tend to look at technology, not as a means to an end, but as an end in itself. This technologically driven approach has crowded out arduously gained humane aspects of internal auditing.

The relentless, metallic clatter of technological advance does not therefore necessarily imply improvements in understandings of underlying concepts. Our collective faith in data analytics and sampling software has created the seductive but dangerous myth that we are better auditors than our predecessors. We seem unaware that accretions of prowess in data handling and number-crunching often offer little more than illusions of certainty, if not groundless uncertainties. The technology of internal auditing may progress, but the cogency of the concepts and principles of internal auditing remain enduring. Diagnostic acumen, analytical rigor, inferential precision, a healthy skepticism, and a resistance to transient faddism are unchanging prerequisites for good internal auditing, and our progressive internal auditing environment now needs them more than ever.

Modern internal auditing does not lack energy. However misplaced, its enthusiasm is in constant motion, exuding an exaggerated sense of industriousness. But the blustering, frenetic pace of internal auditing today masks an underlying intellectual inertia, a kind of hallucinatory lassitude in which highly agitated activity serves only to endow clockwork routines with decreasing significance. Beneath whirlwinds of risk assessments, data analytics, and trending buzzwords, and beyond the dubious recommendations that often flow from such mechanisms, we see process increasingly triumphant over substance. It is at internal auditing's eerily muted core where the absence of timeless concepts of validity and truth are most keenly felt. A technocratic conformity is descending on internal auditing like a smothering shroud, leaving us with muffled reverberations of futile routines, hollow platitudes, and a steady decline in the public's trust.

Only a fundamental overhaul of internal auditing's self-understanding and methodologies, driven by a tempering of its algorithmic mindset, will open the door to a return to a style of auditing marked by creativity and judgment. Without such an overhaul, internal auditing is unlikely to survive a take-over by automated auditing software and machine-processed artificial intelligence, let alone adapt to the evolving paradigm of accountability and social trust.

Internal auditing's flat-footed response to the winds of change in assurance demands and its self-inflicted surrender to technological conformity have been developing incrementally for at least 30 years. The very slowness of the changes has occluded their visibility. At the time of this writing, in early 2024, both challenges seem to have been poorly understood and left largely unaddressed. Individually, the implications of either challenge for the soul of internal auditing are severe. But their combined menace points to a potentially catastrophic decline in internal auditing's future significance. Scientistic internal auditing is unlikely to possess the creativity and critical thinking needed to satisfactorily address the assurance implications of the shifting distributions of accountability and social trust.

This book's title echoes Allan Bloom's *The Closing of the American Mind* (Bloom, 1987). Bloom (1930–1992), a philosopher and literary critic, lamented in *The Closing* the erosion of his students' critical reasoning capabilities and powers of discernment in matters of truth and knowledge. He attributed the decline of the university of his day to cultural relativism and nihilism. Although the malaise of internal auditing originates from different sources, modern internal auditing is also suffering from a narrowing of its intellectual horizons. Indeed, professional associations for both internal and external auditing have tended to muzzle their members' professional judgment, thereby molding auditing into a mechanistic activity that is increasingly reliant on prescriptive standards, algorithms, and checklists. Auditing's findings are communicated through ever more hackneyed language. In parallel, there has been a growing tendency for modern auditing to ferret tirelessly among the building blocks of information, with its explanatory powers petering out as auditors raise their sights to "big picture" perspectives. Moreover, auditing today appears to be under the spell of a pseudoscientific, quasi-superstitious faith in the power of numbers and a collective obsession with quantification that too often leads to a debilitating distrust of qualitative judgment.

An aside on the scope of this book: I address only in passing issues like perceptions of auditor independence, distinctions between fair presentation and compliance-based reporting, and the "expectations gap" that divides defensive auditors, internal as well as external, from their disappointed stakeholders. Second-order issues of this type are extensively addressed in the existing auditing literature (e.g., Hay et al., 2014; King and de Beer, 2018). The challenges to auditing we shall encounter in this book are deeper and more existential. We shall therefore go far beyond tinkering with internal auditing's surface troubles in our attempts to understand the profound and far-reaching socio-economic transformations that raise serious doubts about internal auditing's future ability to serve adequately the public interest. (Throughout the text, the term "auditing" without additional qualification refers collectively to internal, external, and other specialties of auditing. References to specific types of auditing, like internal or environmental auditing, are made explicit.)

In struggling to understand fully the nature and scope of the transformations in accountability and social trust that surround it, internal auditing is still largely addressing yesterday's concerns. This is not to imply that individual internal auditors are unaware of ongoing, revolutionary shifts in socio-economic and political matters. But the Institute of Internal Auditors (IIA), the primary institutional vehicle for modern internal auditing, has largely misdiagnosed our current transformations in accountability and social trust. Like an archer taking aim at chimerical targets, the IIA has been proposing remedies for misidentified problems. An over-hasty embracing of superficial concepts of progress has left internal auditing at the mercy of scientism and faddism. The IIA's brand of internal auditing is therefore struggling to make sense of the rapidly changing world it purports to explain, and it is falling short of its role as a reliable arbiter of reality.

An inquiry into the causes and potential remedies of internal auditing's current malaise is warranted by the importance of auditing's contributions to civilized living. Internal auditing, along with auditing of many varieties, continues to safeguard our collective interests and encourage accountability and social trust on a vast range of important topics. Notwithstanding its degraded present condition, internal auditing is an activity worth preserving and handing on, in a healthy condition, to future generations.

Nonetheless, in taking a look at the increasingly bleak landscape of modern internal auditing, I raise uncomfortable questions and suggest conceptually daring solutions for how internal auditing might navigate its future. My initial observations may seem pessimistic, but my inquiries have also found grounds for optimism. Although the severity of the obstacles to a re-introduction of a humane dimension into modern internal auditing's mechanistic culture is not to be underestimated, the descent into clockwork routines is not yet an irreversible *fait accompli*. The tenacity of auditing to survive and flourish is evidenced by its long role in social accountability, from the earliest written records to the present day. In particular, internal auditing possesses as yet untapped potentialities of resilience and renewal, as I hope this book shall show. And I have been pleased to identify the seeds of a future renaissance of internal auditing in places we might least have expected to find them, including the usually dismissive accusations of auditing's "ritualization". Internal auditing is therefore not predestined to lag behind current socio-economic developments and thereby lose public confidence. Despite its current predicament, it may succeed in adapting to the ongoing transitions in the patterns of accountability and social trust, but such adaptation is a fragile process that will require subtle nurturing by internal auditing's leaders.

In addition, although internal auditing is fumbling clumsily through present challenges, it still attracts individuals of above-average curiosity and intelligence. Many internal auditing practitioners continue to value qualitative judgment over mechanistic activity. They are fully capable of synthesizing building blocks of evidence into broad, "big picture" patterns, and they resist powerful current tendencies toward rigid orthodoxies of opinionated groupthink. These individuals maintain clusters of excellence that flout the general decline, not unlike the way in which the Irish monasteries kept alive the flames of Western European literacy following the fifth-century collapse of Roman authority.

My optimism for a possible future renewal of internal auditing is chastened only by the poisoning effects of the brash commercial pressures that besiege it. Internal auditing sometimes appears to be more of a trade than a profession, and its practitioners too often conflate commercial imperatives with their professional responsibilities to serve the public interest. There is a danger that the allure of the consultant's billable hour will ride roughshod over internal auditing's professional ethos.

Chapter 2 reviews the seismic redistributions of accountability and social trust currently taking place and assesses the likely adaptability of internal auditing to this new world. Chapters 3 through 5 evaluate some of the possible reasons for internal auditing's drift away from judgment and creativity toward mechanistic, clockwork routines. The structure of our analysis in Chapters 3 through 5 is framed through three conceptual lenses, addressing respectively (1) trust, (2) virtue, and (3) wisdom in internal auditing. Our inquiries shall be wide, ranging from the sociology of the professions to numerology and neuroscience. In broad terms, we shall argue that it is through a return to traditional concepts of professional judgment and virtue that internal auditing may seek to save its soul.

Looking through the first of our conceptual lenses, trust, we shall in Chapter 3 assess the dangers of an erosion of public trust in internal auditing itself. Should internal auditing – a mechanism for assurance, accountability, and social trust – itself become mistrusted, we shall face a severe weakening of the collective social glue that binds us together. We shall approach the topic of trust by means of an assessment of the continuing relevance of the "audit society", first identified by the philosopher of auditing Michael Power (born 1957). Contrary to popular belief, Power's concept of the "audit society" is a nexus of interconnected ideas that goes far beyond notions of an excessive proliferation of auditing. The ongoing surge in the volume of auditing (or over-auditing) is only one part of the "audit society" concept: It is covered by what Power described as the "audit explosion". Even the "audit explosion" itself goes beyond the topic of over-auditing – it addresses the proliferation of diverse forms of auditing, and it explores the descent of auditing into little more than a social palliative. Another dimension of the "audit society" is captured by the "audit implosion", which refers to the shift in auditing's center of gravity from external auditors' opinions on financial statements to the internal auditing of the inner workings of institutions. The "audit implosion" is consistent with our analysis of shifting patterns of accountability and social trust, although we see the outcomes not only in the inner workings of organizations but also equally in peripheral and extra-mural activities beyond immediate organizational control. Other dimensions of the "audit society" concept include the increasing "riskification" of auditing and the dangers of a ritualization of practices.

Our focus in Chapter 4 shall shift to the second of our conceptual lenses: Virtue. The question of virtue will address the role of professional judgment, character, and moral agency in an age of increasingly algorithmic processes. We will explore how the concept of virtue as moral excellence (as understood by Plato and Aristotle) might relate to the ways in which today's professional auditors seek to serve the public good. Of importance to our inquiry is an evaluation of the significance of knowledge and expertise in internal auditing. We will also consider the implications of the increasing commodification of internal auditing and try to assess the harm caused by commercial interests, for whom the billable hour often seems more important than serving the public interest.

Our third and final conceptual lens, wisdom, is covered in Chapter 5, in which we consider the extent to which threats to wisdom in internal auditing derive from neuroscientific evidence of a damaging, collective overuse of the left hemisphere of the brain. This tendency may help to explain the prevailing trend of internal auditors to lose themselves in numbers and miss the "big picture". The work of the neuroscientist and philosopher Iain McGilchrist (born 1953) is especially relevant here. We shall also try to take stock of the modern world's irrational faith in numbers, that sometimes amounts to a form of numerological superstition. And we shall consider if there is still a space left in internal auditing for humanistic tendencies that might safeguard it from falling short of its role as a reliable arbiter of reality. In Chapter 6, we shall float possible solutions to remediate modern auditing's most troubling orientations. Chapter 7 presents our concluding arguments. Appendix A provides an overview of the philosophical approach taken in the book, while Appendix B offers aphoristic wisdom relevant to the book's themes.

The book's arguments address several streams of thought, some of which merge and demerge throughout the text, while others chart their own unique course in a complicated delta of rivers and tributaries. Although I have captured and arranged these eclectic concerns under the broad headings of trust, virtue, wisdom, and trust, the three categories are simply a convenient means of structuring my inquiries. There is some overlapping between the three conceptual headings – for example, modern auditing's over-dependency on quantification emerges from (or is connected to) the "riskification" of auditing (Sections 3.4 and 3.5); overly prescriptive auditing standards (Section 4.2), the "algorithmic society" (Section 5.1) and a quasi-superstitious faith in numbers (Section 5.2). Despite the overlapping nature of these conceptual lenses, they provide a handy structural framework for the presentation and analysis of these topics.

In the following pages, we shall encounter some of the widely circulating concepts that aim to identify and define elements of the changing patterns of accountability and social trust that bear on our arguments. These products of some of the best minds in our modern world include, in alphabetical order: The "algorithmic society", the "audit society", "Black Swan" events, the "digital society" (or "digital age" or "digital world order"), the "great degeneration", the "age of neurotechnology", the "risk society", the "age of small thinking", and "surveillance capitalism". Other terms have arisen to describe the ways in which humanity has been impacted by digitalization and shifting socio-economic matters – we shall rub shoulders with "homo economicus", "homo technologicus", and "homo digitalis". Despite their slogan-like tones, all these concepts encapsulate major sources of anxiety relating to our collective social existence, and my inquiries into internal auditing's challenges take place throughout the book at shifting intersections of them all. I was fleetingly tempted to try to coin a new phrase – perhaps the "piecemeal assurance society" – to label my ideas. But the marketplace for new coinages, especially those employing the term "society", is already over-crowded.

Internal auditing, I argue in this book, faces the two severe challenges of adaptability and reform. The origins of these challenges could not be more different. Changing patterns of accountability and social trust have been imposed on internal auditing, but the repudiation of critical thinking and judgmental wisdom has been largely a self-inflicted wound. A profession whose practitioners increasingly struggle to discern universal principles in particular cases is self-referential and almost solipsistic in character. With this troubling thought in mind, we shall begin our inquiries.

Chapter 2

The marginalization of internal auditing in a post-bureaucratic age

2.1 AUDITING, ACCOUNTABILITY, AND SOCIAL TRUST

Auditing is frequently viewed as a vexatious feature of our socio-economic and political life. It often gives rise to fear and loathing. We may wonder why auditing provokes such negative reactions when its benefits are numerous. An external auditor's opinion on the accuracy and fair presentation of a corporation's financial statements contributes to the integrity of markets. An election auditor's opinion on the reliability of a referendum's results reduces disharmony among political leaders and citizens. An environmental auditor's opinion on the origins and extent of carcinogenic particulate matter in the air we breathe reinforces our trust in science-driven public policy. And a clinical auditor's opinion on surgical safety procedures contributes to our trust in the treatment we receive from physicians. In all these cases, and many more besides, good auditing provides objective and credible assurance on important social, economic, and political matters, thereby bridging gaps arising from asymmetries of power and information.

The antipathy to auditing may have its roots in perceptions of auditors as uncompromising custodians of rectitude, and severe protectors of accuracy. In Shakespeare's minor play *Timon of Athens*, Timon's faithful steward Flavius passionately defends his record of protecting Timon's assets: "If you suspect my husbandry or falsehood / Call me before th'exactest auditors and set me on the proof" (Act 2, Scene 2, 156–157). Shakespeare (c.1564–1616) or his presumed co-author Thomas Middleton (1580–1627) placed the reference to auditors in Flavius' mouth to emphasize the power of his appeal to impartial exactitude. Flavius is, in effect, challenging Timon to put him to the test, and the referees of this test would be the most "exact" auditors. Although Flavius' appeal might be considered a rhetorical flourish, off-stage auditors are portrayed in *Timon of Athens* as the ultimate arbiters of correct estate management, who are competent to determine the integrity of Flavius' actions through their make-or-break opinions. In his play *The Inspector General* of 1836, Nikolai Gogol (1809–1852) also presents an incognito government inspector/auditor as an offstage character whose

DOI: 10.1201/9781032664880-2

impending arrival in a small town is an occasion for near-panic among its corrupt officials. An ambitious buffoon misidentified as the government auditor by the town's crooked bigwigs finds himself at the epicenter of acts of greed and sycophancy. Overall, the play's portrayal of auditing is an unsettling mixture of the chilling and the comical. Portrayals of auditing of this type have contributed over the centuries to a rather ominous, eerie, and disturbing depiction of auditing.

A dislike of auditing may also have arisen from a widespread animosity to bureaucratic, hierarchical organizations, the follies and alienating effects of which were memorably conveyed by Franz Kafka (1883–1924) in *Das Schloß* (*The Castle*) and other writings. Auditors, and internal auditors in particular, are the interpreters *par excellence* of traditional command-and-control accountability, with all the negative ramifications of initiative-stifling inflexibility that such traditions evoke. An interpreter of hierarchical bureaucracies has suggested that

> as well as offering some benefits, hierarchy also brings many problems. Hierarchy has become less acceptable in a world in which key knowledge no longer resides at the apex of organizational or political structures, in which upcoming generations are no longer comfortable with traditional forms of authority, and in which there is growing organized protest against the inequalities of wealth and power associated with hierarchy.
>
> *Child, 2019, 1–2*

The pejorative connotations of bureaucracy have, perhaps, attached themselves to internal auditing.

As we shall explore later in this chapter, the center of gravity of accountability and social trust is shifting on its axis, away from the world of the traditional bureaucratic organization to diffuse networks. Internal auditing's slowness to adapt to new patterns of accountability and social trust and its stubborn insistence on focusing on traditional bureaucratic models of accountability threaten to leave it marginalized as a historical curiosity. But let us not jump ahead of our arguments. For our initial purposes, it is appropriate to recognize (1) the value of internal auditing as the modern inheritor of auditing's proud traditions of delivering impartial, evidence-based assessments for the purposes of accountability and the preservation of social trust and (2) internal auditing's inheritance of ambivalent, or even outrightly hostile, attitudes.

Auditors of all specialties tend to avoid cast-iron guarantees of truth, preferring to offer informed opinions. Their opinions, if reliable, provide powerful and persuasive assurance. Auditing has been described, in general terms, as a means of "securing the accountability of individuals and organisations" in the context of "a duty for one party to perform, to be held accountable for their performance, and to give an account of that performance" (Flint, 1988, 3, 24). Throughout history, diverse forms of auditing have served the public interest by encouraging accountability at individual and institutional levels and, in so doing, they have contributed to aggregated social trust. Auditing therefore has long had a role in maintaining the glue of accountability and social cohesion. Throughout our discussions we shall keep in mind the two levels at which benefits flow from internal auditing – accountability at a local or transactional level, and social trust at an aggregated level.

Internal auditing appears to be an undervalued social mechanism. It is no exaggeration to claim that, by solidifying social trust, it is at the core of healthily functioning markets, institutions, and political processes. Auditing of various types has been one of the motors of civilization, alongside more readily recognizable factors like the division of labor, reliable systems of law, mechanisms for economic exchange, and the collective means of communication. From the dawn of literate civilization in agrarian societies, audit-like practices have been evident:

> According to earliest Mesopotamian records dating back to 3600 BC[E], scribes used to prepare summaries of financial transactions ... Tiny marks, dots, and circles indicated the painstaking comparison of one record with another—marks that have survived the centuries and that auditors still use to tick off their verification of records. Thus were born two control devices still used around the world: division of duties [and] provision for the review of another's work.
>
> *Sawyer and Vinten, 1996, 23*

Commentators have identified auditing practices in the writings of ancient Greece (Costouros, 1978) and ancient India (Olivelle, 2013, 117–119), and from Joseph's administration of Potiphar's estate in *Genesis*, the first book of the Hebrew Bible (Davis, 1981), to the *Talmud* (Fonfeder, Holtzman, and Maccarrone, 2003). Auditing has for millennia promoted confidence in markets and fostered accountability and social trust between rulers and citizens (Smieliauskas et al., 2021, 4–13), and the weight of that tradition today falls to a significant extent on the shoulders of internal auditors.

If claims of an enduring civilizing mission for auditing seem exaggerated, one may reflect on the implications of a counterfactual, audit-less world. Without the safeguards provided by audits, what would restrain the publishing of flattering financial statements, the rigging of political elections, the obfuscation of public finances, and the issuing of deceptive tax demands? In a world devoid of auditing, abuses of power would run rampant. Exhortations to action or belief delivered by politicians, bankers, or civil servants tend to ring hollow in the absence of supporting information that is reliably audited. Manifestations of low social trust like vaccine hesitancy, allegations of rigged elections, and disbelief in the need for environmental protection may be tempered by audits, provided that the audits are accepted as credible by all major competing interests. But we need not extend our imaginations too far into counterfactual worlds. The importance of auditing in terms of assurance over accountability is widely visible in our quotidian lives. And, as we have suggested, auditing's contributions to localized accountability reinforces aggregated social trust.

Confucius (c.551–c.479 BCE) suggested that three essential elements underpin a successful community: Weapons, food, and trust. A society should, if forced by circumstances, first sacrifice its weapons. After that, its food. If the bonds of trust that bind citizens together remain intact, a society has a good chance of surviving war and famine. Therefore, trust is the indispensable element of a sustainable community. Even in a well-armed and well-fed community, the erosion of collective trust inevitably dissolves society and government (*The Analects of Confucius*, quoted in O'Neill, 2002, 3).

The truth of the Confucian insight that social trust is the foundation of our collective well-being has been endorsed in the modern era. Among modern sociologists and philosophers, Adam Seligman (1997, 13) has warned us that "the existence of trust is an essential component of all enduring social relationships", while Piotr Sztompka (1999, 5) has argued that the three basic, interrelated requirements of a moral community are trust, loyalty, and solidarity. In what follows, we shall frequently bracket together accountability and social trust even though they address different concepts: Accountability refers to responsibility in the context of a localized activity or organization, while social trust is our overall faith in the honesty and reliability of the strangers who surround us. However, these concepts are so closely connected that they flow in inter-related patterns through our collective life. Accountability engenders, illuminates, and safeguards social trust, and both accountability and social trust prosper or fall together.

We co-exist in "societies of strangers", in Roger Scruton's memorable description, in which "our lives are subject to massive interference from people whom we do not know; and if we accept this, it is partly because of the regular flow of benefits, which arrive anonymously like the weather" (Scruton, 1997, 1). Scruton's claim that we depend for our collecting well-being on anonymous individuals and faceless institutional representatives was correct. We all rub along together for our mutual benefit.

The size of modern society is an obvious constraint on our ability to have trusting, direct relationships with more than a limited number of people. We therefore trust strangers around us who hold political views, religious affiliations, sexual identities, and sports team loyalties unknown to us. But none of these considerations matters in a high-trust society. Through cooperative behavior among people who know little or nothing of one another, individual differences meld into a consensual whole that encourages public success alongside private flourishing. We therefore share our membership of society with millions of people we do not know (and cannot know, given the vastness of our populations), and with whom we are connected in webs of mutual interest, underwritten by social trust.

The importance of social trust between citizens has been described as "essential for social cohesion, integration and stability, qualities that are especially crucial for modern, large-scale, multi-cultural societies under pressure from rapid social and economic change, mass migration, and ethnic and religious conflict" (Newton et al., 2018, 38). An erosion of social trust dissolves social bonds, atomizes society, and puts the legitimacy and functioning of the state's basic institutions at risk. The effect of a breakdown of social trust leads to a demoralized and cynical citizenry. Under such conditions criminality flourishes, social cohesion unravels, and a general *anomie* takes hold. Political polarization is common in such situations, as citizens withdraw into their own social and informational bubbles, surrounding themselves with people and information they feel comfortable with. To quote Sissela Bok: "Trust is a public good to be protected just as much as the air we breathe and the water we drink. When it is damaged, the continuity of the whole suffers; and when it is destroyed, societies falter and collapse" (Bok, 1978, 28).

In the United States, the reciprocal web of obligations of social trust has traditionally informed the concept of citizenship. To become a citizen is to accept a social commitment to stand with other, unknown members of society, and to maintain bonds of trust that transcend any residual allegiance to ancestral cultures. Although partly eroded by aspects of the present day "culture wars", the collective cooperation of strangers in the United States provides perhaps the world's most striking example of the way in which extended social trust binds different interests together. This largely unspoken yet powerful commitment to social solidarity requires us to take a long term view of social trust and cohesion, and to rise above immediate, selfish appetites for individual and cooperative success.

Levels of social trust vary between nations, and the case of Denmark is instructive. It has been estimated that a large proportion (perhaps up to one quarter) of Denmark's wealth in recent decades has been attributable to that country's exceptionally high levels of social trust. Human capital has been estimated to contribute around 50% to Danish prosperity, physical capital around 25%, and the balance is a consequence of low transaction costs in a high-trust society. Anyone who has visited Denmark will likely, through observation and anecdotal evidence, be convinced of this analysis: The author of this book can vouch for it. The Danes are notable for their appreciation of leisure time; they seem to count few workaholics among their number; their working hours tend to be low by the standards of the English-speaking countries; and economic commitments are often confirmed with a handshake rather than a formal contract. And yet Danish prosperity and social cohesion are strikingly high. Remarkably, it has been reported that social trust (defined as agreement with the statement that "most people can be trusted") rose in Denmark from 47% in 1979 to 79% in 2009 (Sonderskov and Dinesen, 2014). In recent years, as Danish society has become more diverse owing to migration from low-trust countries, it is reported that the overall levels of socio-economic trust may be declining (Dinesen and Sonderskov, 2018, 185). Nonetheless, it is clear that Danish national prosperity has been, at least until very recently, accompanied by high levels of social trust and, consequently, by very low levels of formal surveillance of citizens' activities, compliance routines, legal costs, and of course auditing (Svendsen, 2014).

So far in this chapter, we have established the importance of accountability and social trust in maintaining social cohesion, and we have acknowledged the role of internal auditing in this process. Put succinctly, the significance of social trust to our collective existence explains the rationale for reliable internal auditing. Evidence from China confirms that high levels of social trust lower the demand for auditing, or dampen the extent and rigor of auditing, because high levels of social trust mitigate agency problems and social suspicion (Chen et al., 2018; Kuo et al., 2023). Admittedly, auditing is only one of our social levers to maintain and protect collective trust. Of equal or more importance are the fair treatment of citizens by a reliable and impartial rule of law; a system of political governance that warrants our allegiance; and various cultural (and perhaps spiritual) elements of our existence that foster solidarity. But we underestimate at our peril the role of auditing in cementing social trust.

A few words of clarification are warranted at this point. Sociologists sometimes differentiate between levels of social trust in particularized and generalized senses. For instance, we may trust the dentist who attends to our family's needs while being mistrustful of dentists generally. Or we may admire the politician who represents in parliament the constituency where we live, while harboring a dislike for politicians in general. In this book we shall not make distinctions between particularized and generalized social trust, as such distinctions are not central to our arguments. In addition, some sociologists also distinguish between social trust arising from behavior and social trust arising from *expectations of* behavior (e.g., Bauer and Freitag, 2018, 15) but, again, our purposes in this book do not depend on such fine distinctions.

Let us briefly consider the intriguing conceptual links between social trust and risk. In anticipation of the "risk society" that we shall explore in Chapter 3, trust may be interpreted as a means of "taming risks and countering uncertainties" (Sztompka, 1999, 40). When we open a box of breakfast cereal and pour it for our children, we trust that the cereal is fit for consumption and uncontaminated by dangerous ingredients. The expiration date on the box provides us with some assurance, and we might even nibble a piece of the cereal if in doubt of its freshness, but we tend to trust the cereal's manufacturers and retailers, and the governmental systems of safety standards and surveillance that have overseen its production and distribution. In such ways, we place trust in the contingent actions of countless strangers in our daily lives. To mistrust everything would lead to a paralysis of activity.

We may now return to our original question: Why is auditing so often perceived as a vexatious feature of our socio-economic and political life? And why does it frequently provoke fear and loathing? We have already mentioned the damaging effects of auditing's close conceptual links to much-maligned bureaucratic activities. Another reason for the public's ambivalence toward auditing may derive from asymmetric media reporting of auditing's successes and failures. Blunders and criminality are more likely than successes to be publicized and remembered, especially for external auditing. Quiet, efficient, and productive auditing that encourages accountability and bolsters social trust "will not usually yield public acclaim" (Power, 1997, 27). In contrast, an auditing scandal is likely to generate febrile media attention and high profile denunciations. However, this explanation, though helpful, does not take us very far. Other professions are subjected to similar media pressures. A crooked lawyer will garner far more publicity than a thousand legal practitioners unobtrusively and faithfully fulfilling their professional duties.

We should therefore dig deeper into the possible reasons for auditing attracting such a degree of opprobrium. Our argument in this book is that one of the leading specialties of modern auditing – internal auditing – is failing to meet the demands of two contemporaneous challenges. The primary challenge is internal auditing's failure to respond adequately to ongoing, paradigmatic shifts in accountability and social trust: Traditional, command-and-control, vertical hierarchies are flattening, and are being recast into horizontally distributed patterns. Internal auditing has yet to catch up with these momentous changes, and remains fixated on traditional, bureaucratic structures. A secondary challenge for internal auditing has arisen from its prevailing tendencies toward a rigid, algorithmic, checklist mindset that suppresses practitioners' creativity and critical thinking. The second challenge narrows the intellectual and moral horizons of internal auditing. Both challenges have been building for at least 30 years and their combined effect is to hamper internal auditing's ability to fully serve the public interest. The risks of reputational damage to internal auditing, should these challenges remain unaddressed, are significant. We shall explore these challenges in more detail in the rest of this chapter.

The redistributions of accountability may have originated from the "Fourth Industrial Revolution", a term popularized by Klaus Schwab (born 1938) of the World Economic Forum (Schwab, 2016). According to Schwab's interpretation of history, the First Industrial Revolution took place from approximately the middle of the eighteenth to the middle of the nineteenth centuries, as scattered, manual production methods were concentrated in factories using machines powered by steam and water. This period saw the peak of violent, anti-machine activity by the Luddite movement in England. The Second Industrial Revolution lasted from approximately 1870 to the start of World War One in 1914, and it saw an increase in the technological sophistication of production machinery powered by electricity. The start of the Third Industrial Revolution is usually dated to the 1960s, and it was marked by the digitalization of vast swathes of modern life through computerized telecommunications and information systems, including the internet. The Fourth Industrial Revolution grew out of the Third, with a surge in the sophistication of digital technologies, allied to a wide technological innovation and related biological and medical developments. (Some talk of a Fifth Industrial Revolution dating from the 2020s but let us stay with the four-fold structure.)

Schwab talks of a radical combination of the digital, physical, and biological worlds in the Fourth Industrial Revolution: "technology and digitalization will revolutionize everything, making the overused and often ill-used adage 'this time it's different' apt. Simply put, major technological innovations are on the brink of fueling momentous change throughout the world" (Schwab, 2016, 6). If our arguments in this book and those of Schwab are both correct, then the radical redistributions of patterns of accountability and social trust are part of the world-changing impact of the Fourth Industrial Revolution, driven by a combination of digitalization and synthetic biology, and promising equal measures of liberation and risk.

Schwab's analysis sets the scene for our analysis. The two challenges we have identified for modern internal auditing threaten our social well-being. The slowness with which they have been recognized, if indeed they have been adequately recognized at all, only heighten their dangers. Their potential consequences are so serious that we should be highly concerned for the preservation of accountability and social trust in our collective future. In the rest of this chapter we shall look deeper into the nature and implications of internal auditing's two main challenges. Before that, however, we shall discuss the changing patterns of accountability and social trust.

2.2 INSTITUTIONAL DECAY AND THE EROSION OF SOCIAL TRUST

We are living, in many parts of the world, through a period of decay in traditional patterns of social trust. Our faith in politicians, business leaders, and journalists (and the organizations they represent) is eroding with every passing year. We are surrounded by the multiplying symptoms of this decay. Public indebtedness, economic stagnation, grotesque inequalities of wealth, and the growth of crime and anti-social behavior blight not only the industrialized (or post-industrial) countries – they are evident across much of the globe. We are witnessing the unravelling of many of our foundational socio-economic and political institutions.

What lies behind the degradation of our traditional institutions? Why are so many organizations and their representatives failing to deliver safety, wealth, and justice for all? Does institutional collapse provoke declining levels of social trust, or is it the other way round? Or is it a mutual dance of death, a downward spiral as institutional decay and social mistrust grip each other in a macabre embrace? The reasons for the collapse of institutions and the related erosion of traditional patterns of social trust are disputed, but it worth glancing at the nature of this era-defining transformation, as it is central to our arguments in this book.

Niall Ferguson (born 1964), perhaps our greatest living economic historian, has identified in *The Great Degeneration: How Institutions Decay and Economies Die* (Ferguson, 2012) four interrelated areas in which our institutions (meaning the socio-economic and political frameworks in which we collectively either flourish or fail) have decayed. These areas are (1) politics, (2) the economy, (3) the law, and (4) civic society. Ferguson summarizes the troubles in these four areas as follows: (1) In politics, public debt "has become a way for the older generation to live at the expense of the young and the unborn"; (2) for the economy, regulation "has become dysfunctional to the point of increasing the fragility of the system"; (3) in the law, lawyers, "who can be revolutionaries in a dynamic society, become parasites in a stationary one"; and (4) our civil society "withers into a mere no man's land between corporate interests and big government" (Ferguson, 2012, 151). Although Ferguson's analysis focuses on the post-industrialized world, his conceptual model has worldwide relevance.

Ferguson's arguments are intriguing. On the first of his four issues, politics, the public debt problem can now be solved only with painful therapy, including any or a combination of the following – default, inflation, and impoverishment. In the year in which this book was first drafted, 2023, the United Kingdom's public debt surpassed the country's Gross Domestic Product for the first time since 1961, while the public debt of the United States surpassed 33 trillion dollars, equivalent to around one hundred thousand dollars per individual citizen. In addition to such headline numbers, both nations faced additional, unfunded liabilities covering social security and retirement costs for their citizens, adding significantly to the size of the encroaching fiscal cliff. Estimates of the proportion of the citizens of both nations living paycheck to paycheck were as high as 60%, with one-third of British and US citizens having not a penny in savings. The specter of mass impoverishment is presently hovering over both nations.

On the second topic, the debilitating red tape of modern regulation, Ferguson fears we may be too often deploying "quack remedies to mere symptoms" (Ferguson, 2012, 20): We shall later explore, in Section 3.2, to what extent the current "audit explosion" might be an instance of a

Fergusonian quack remedy. The Heritage Foundation's 2023 Index of Economic Freedom placed the United States at 25th place globally in terms of the lightness of red tape, only slightly ahead of the United Kingdom at 28th, and far behind Singapore, Switzerland, Ireland, Taiwan, and New Zealand (the top five countries). On the third issue, the law, Ferguson depicts a transformation of the rule of law into the rule of lawyers, with costly litigation favoring the wealthy. Finally, in terms of civil society, we are experiencing increasingly polarized social attitudes, with high levels of mutual suspicion and low levels of social trust, leading to class-based conflict and a dissolving of social cohesion.

Looking in more detail at Ferguson's fourth issue, civil society, the connections between a robust civil society and strong bonds of social trust are obvious, and a striking aspect of the global erosion of social trust has been a ruinous breakdown of the consensus between rich and poor. The end of such a consensus is never a good sign: Massive disparities of wealth and power threaten a destruction of social trust and evoke the catastrophe of an end to the consensual political order. Let us take the example of the "conflict of the orders" in ancient Rome to illustrate what is at stake. In the first two centuries of the classical Roman Republic (approximately 500 to 300 BCE), plebeian citizens asserted their rights in a struggle for a share of Rome's growing prosperity, pitting themselves against the elite, patrician citizens. Plebeians, tired of seeing the results of their toil lining patrician pockets, undertook a series of protests and revolts, and this resulted in an abolition of (or, perhaps better, a significant reduction in) the plebeians' second class status (Beard, 2015, 110–117). After the plebeian victory, Rome's increasing success and prosperity was undoubtedly underwritten by the stability of the Roman "social pact".

Turning to the present era, social discontent has been expressed in recent years across the political spectrum, and around the world. The Occupy Movement and its offshoots that started in late 2011 targeted corporate greed and inequalities in income. Its slogan "We are the 99%" (Child, 2019, 114) was aimed at the top 1% of wealth owners. From its base in Zuccotti Park, New York, the Occupy Movement spread to other cities in the United States and beyond. The author remembers walking past the massed ranks of the Occupy Movement's tents in McPherson Square in Washington D.C. in late 2011 and early 2012. The colorful, exuberant tent village resembled a large, coiled dragon, ready to burst into revolutionary fervor. Yet the Occupy Movement was soon to fizzle out, but not without changing the wider political discourse.

Although the Occupy Movement was a left-leaning populist phenomenon, the preponderance of social protest in recent years has not come from the left, but from the right of the political spectrum. Reactionary populism has, in Daniel Cohen's words, "replaced leftism as the voice of protest" (Cohen, 2018, 1). Various forms of reactionary populism have arisen throughout the world: Beyond the inevitable local variations, they are united by anti-establishment sentiments, patriotism (or nationalism), social conservatism, and economic protectionism. This international trend has encompassed the outcome of the Brexit referendum in the United Kingdom, and the political successes of Donald Trump in the United States, Giorgia Meloni in Italy, the Le Pen family and Eric Zemmour in France, Geert Wilders in the Netherlands, Viktor Orbán in Hungary, Narendra Modi in India, Jair Bolsonaro in Brazil, and Javier Milei in Argentina. Interpretations of reactionary populist movements are highly contested, but we cannot gloss too quickly over them because they are closely linked to the shifting patterns of social trust central to the book's themes. In the following pages, we shall focus on the example of United Kingdom, as it is central to Niall Ferguson's arguments of institutional decline, but we shall also draw international parallels.

Ferguson identifies England as the nation in which institutions first evolved that favored the development of an open society characterized by the rule of impartial law, property rights, and decentralized, non-oppressive political governance. This is no maverick interpretation: His views are easily reconciled with those of Francis Fukuyama (born 1952) that it was in England that "the three components of a modern political order" first fell into place, with "a strong and capable state, the state's subordination to a rule of law and government accountability to all citizens" (Fukuyama, 2011, 7). If Ferguson and Fukuyama are correct, the successful evolution of England's institutions, in particular during the crucial period from Magna Carta (1215) to the Glorious Revolution (1688), provided the foundation for the world's first modern, open society. With his customary stinging yet charming Scottish irony, Ferguson refers to England's current institutional degeneration as an "Inglorious Revolution", a kind of "Glorious Revolution" in reverse, in which the socio-economic and political achievements of a millennium are unravelling (Ferguson, 2012, 32–36).

It might seem unfair to shine the spotlight so intensely on England. Institutional distress and the erosion of social trust are evident far beyond the white cliffs of Dover. It nonetheless seems both fitting and ironic that England, which led the way in Ferguson's model of the development of robust institutions that promote social trust, is among the nations which today provide the starkest evidence of advanced institutional deterioration and dissolving social cohesion. England was ahead of the pack in its institutional development between the twelfth and seventeen centuries. England today is again at the head of the pack, but this time the movement is in the opposite direction, with an unprecedented pace of institutional dereliction and the dissolution of social trust. England seems to have been an experimental, almost prototype-like model for both the rise of modern institutions and their fall. The evidence for England's institutional rot is not difficult to find, from policing to public health to education to road maintenance services. We shall restrict ourselves to providing only a handful of instances: The decline is arguably so rapid that any description is likely to be quickly outdated.

Matthew Goodwin, in his *Values, Voice and Virtue: The New British Politics* (Goodwin, 2023), documents the gradual evaporation of social trust in the publicly funded, national broadcaster, The British Broadcasting Corporation (BBC): "While in 2003 81 percent of the British people said they 'trusted BBC News journalists to tell the truth' ... this figure has collapsed to 60 per cent in 2010 and a record low of 44% in 2019" (Goodwin, 2023, 125–126). Goodwin also reports that, in 2023, more than one-half of the British population considered that none of the established political parties represented their "priorities and values" (Goodwin, 2023, xiii). This political distrust reflects increasingly acute social discrepancies, with life expectancy eight years lower in much of the north of England than in the wealthier suburbs of London (Goodwin, 2023, 43). And an opinion poll relevant to British reactionary populism revealed that, on the eve of the Brexit referendum, "only 26% of the British low-income expressed trust in government, compared to 54% of the high net worth population" (Newton et al., 2018, 50).

The British trend of declining social trust is echoed in the United States, where there is evidence that the younger generations exhibit far less social trust than their predecessors. This trend has been succinctly summarized as follows: "Trusters are dying off, and distrusters are taking over" (Hawley, 2012, 41). It has also been alleged that, mirroring the British pattern, American populism has been driven by "a deep wellspring of discontent among a section of the electorate [who] disdain the power and condescension of American educational, cultural, and economic elites" (Berman and Fox, 2023, 2).

How far may social trust deteriorate? Zbigniew Brzeziński (1928–1981), National Security Advisor to United States President Jimmy Carter, provided, in the later stages of the Cold War, a striking analogy of the difference between a society divided by mistrust and one held together by strong social cohesion. With Poland in the final years of its unpopular Communist government in mind, Brzeziński used the analogy of the difference between a house and a home: A house is a hard edifice of bricks and mortar, merely a shelter and a place to stay, while a home is a place of shared loyalties and attachments, an intimate place in which one truly "feels at home" (cited in Sztompka, 1999, 10). The Polish revolt against its mistrusted, condescending, Soviet-allied elites of the 1980s took various forms of civil disobedience, from participation in the trade union *Solidarność* (Solidarity) under the leadership of Lech Wałęsa (born 1943) to defiant support for the Catholic Church. The Polish elites used all the levers of state power, legal and illegal, to suppress blue collar dissent, but they were swept away by the broader democratization of eastern Europe at the end of the Cold War. Some British populists claim that modern England increasingly resembles a house more than a home, its decaying socio-economic and political trust increasingly resembling the case of Poland in the final years of the Cold War. If that is the case, we can only hope that wise individuals like Wałęsa will emerge to resolve the country's crisis.

If the decay in social trust seems beyond dispute, there are legitimate differences of opinion over the causes of this tendency in the United Kingdom, the United States, and elsewhere. A more comprehensive exploration of these arguments is beyond the scope and purpose of this book: We shall do no more than provide an outline of the debate. And we shall avoid taking sides, as our aim is not to explain the causes of changes in accountability and social trust, but simply to describe them and to assess their impact on internal auditing.

Is the blue collar revolt an expression of "xenophobic, nihilistic passions" (Cohen, 2018, 69)? Does it represent a reversion to dangerous, outdated hatreds and prejudice, founded on a hatred of the "other"? Opponents of such views argue that patriotism is a manifestation of "humane localism" (Mitchell and Peters, 2018), a legitimate love of local community that has its roots in our deepest civilizational origins. These roots of the love of home are preserved in global epics and mythology – examples include the return after years of exile and war of Odysseus to Ithaca in Homer's *Odyssey*, and of Rama to Ayodhya in India's *Ramayana*. But the role of patriotism or nationalism remains strongly disputed. In terms of class conflict, a commonly encountered narrative attributes the consolidation of power of a new elite caste, the professional–managerial class (PMC), to the root of the problem. The PMC, it is alleged, rose to the height of socio-economic and political power in the aftermath of the 2008 financial crisis (e.g., Liu, 2021). According to this view, the wealthy elites responsible for the crisis were bailed out at a cost to the living standards of the working and lower middle classes, thereby provoking the ongoing blue collar revolt. Portrayals of a narcissistic, virtue-signaling, cosmopolitan, and authoritarian PMC leaving the working class to rot in neglect and poverty may or may not be a caricature. The PMC has been extensively criticized and lampooned, as far back as the turn of the millennium in David Brook's portrayal of "bourgeois bohemians" (Brooks, 2000), and the English philosopher John Gray has argued that "mass movements are often reactions against the hubris of radical elites" (Gray, 2023, 135).

However accurate or false such explanations of the causes of eroding social trust may be, it is indisputable that gaps in wealth and social polarization have increased in recent years. Many believe that the economically vulnerable have been the victims of corporate avarice, a search for ever-cheaper labor, and an ever-narrowing scope for social mobility. Blue collar workers face an increasingly precarious economic existence as the structures of the welfare state weaken and employment is increasingly switching to the uncertainties of the gig economy.

To many, however, the dichotomy between liberal cosmopolitanism and xenophobic nationalism is too simplistic an explanation for the complicated social developments currently taking place. One observation is probably beyond dispute, and acceptable to all sides of the debate: Social trust "is hard earned and easily dissipated" (O'Neill, 2002, 6–7). And the very existence of social mistrust gives rise to irrationality. Returning to our historian, Niall Ferguson, we would do well to heed his warning: "there is a tendency throughout history, at times of acute social stress, for religious or quasi-religious ideological impulses to impede rational responses" (Ferguson, 2021, 15). In the following chapters, we shall meet irrational trends in internal auditing, from a quasi-religious faith in the value of risk control models (Section 3.4) to an unwarranted, almost superstitious trust in numbers (Section 5.2).

The accelerating decline in blue collar consent to be governed by the new elites has led to a worldwide flight to political extremes. This in turn has led to the undermining of the legitimacy of institutions in many societies, perhaps amounting to one of history's world-altering social "earthquakes". The English poet Matthew Arnold (1822–1888) evoked a retreating tide of religious faith in the nineteenth century, accompanied by a "melancholy, long, withdrawing roar" (*Dover Beach*, 1867); the present collapse of collective trust in our institutions seems also to be accompanied by a melancholy and perhaps dangerous roar. But our account of the erosion of social trust is incomplete. In Section 2.3, we shall consider the ways in which social trust has not simply disappeared along with the decay of our institutions, but has been redistributed in novel, complex patterns. And these new patterns are giving rise to challenging demands on internal auditing.

2.3 REDISTRIBUTIONS OF ACCOUNTABILITY AND SOCIAL TRUST

Our account of the erosion of social trust in the United Kingdom and elsewhere does not end with a portrayal of societies in distress, disfigured by decaying institutions and class conflict. Social trust has not entirely disappeared – its remnants are undergoing a redistribution into new patterns. A complex and rather fragile nexus of trust relationships is emerging in new locations. Therefore, before we turn to the implications for internal auditing of the ongoing transformations of accountability and social trust, we should acknowledge the fact that we face a displacement, rather than an elimination, of the trust-based glue that binds society together. More precisely, accountability and social trust are increasingly experiencing a displacement from the hierarchical patterns typical of traditional command-and-control organizations, toward a horizontal distribution among non-hierarchical networks, both digital and human. This fundamental shift of the axis of social trust has therefore been from bureaucratic, vertical institutions to more widely distributed and networked arrangements. With the deconstruction of traditional, bureaucratic organizations into scattered constellations of fragmented flows of activity and accountability, and with "such things as subsidiarization, spin-offs, franchising, and formal alliances as well as varied affiliation arrangements, new patterns of interrelatedness are now ubiquitous" (Ackroyd, 2005, 449).

Rachel Botsman provides the best overall presentation currently available of the newly emerging patterns of social trust, in her book *Who Can You Trust?: How Technology Brought Us Together and Why It Might Drive Us Apart* (Botsman, 2017). Botsman identifies three historical periods of variations in social trust. In the first phase, the small, close-knit communities we inhabited were bonded tightly by shared values and face-to-face trust. In the second phase, the rise of institutional trust accompanied the development of large-scale industrial societies. We have discussed, in Section 2.2, how the patterns of trust of the second stage are currently unravelling. The third and current stage, in our post-industrial era of digitalization, is marked by new patterns of vast, diffuse, horizontal redistributions of trust (Botsman, 2017, 7). Botsman's analysis is compelling: The current shift to the third phase of social trust is genuinely paradigmatic, in the sense of being a rare, major, episodic transformation (Kuhn, 1962).

The current, momentous shifts in accountability and social trust have many implications. In the traditional organization, delegations of authority run downward through hierarchies, while in the opposite direction chains of accountability run upward. John Child has argued that the functional principle underlying hierarchical organizations is that "different levels of authority and responsibility should be distributed among an organized collection of people according to the importance or complexity of the decisions which have to be made, and the capacity of different individuals to make them" (Child, 2019, 2). Even with such clearly defined flows of authority and accountability, individuals often seek to evade responsibility for their behavior by claiming that accountability is distributed collectively along chains of command. A corporation's board of directors might decide on an unethical policy, such as adopting bribery to win contracts or shifting its manufacturing operations to sweatshops, with the aim of keeping knowledge of these practices out of the public eye. Should such a policy come to the public's attention, resulting in reputational damage and even criminal charges, the corporate decision-makers might try to sacrifice those employees lower down the chain of command, by claiming that the policy was hatched and implemented by misguided, junior employees. However, owing to the simplicity of the chains of command under bureaucratic conditions, it is not always easy for high-level decision-makers to conceal or deflect their accountability.

If command-and-control arrangements can on occasion give rise to difficulties in assessing accountability, then how much more complicated it is to discern accountability in complex, horizontally diffused networks. In Rachel Botsman's words: "Trust that used to flow upwards to referees and regulators, to authorities and experts, to watchdogs and gatekeepers, is now flowing horizontally, in some instances to our fellow human beings and, in other cases, to programs and bots" (Botsman, 2017, 8). As we have seen, bureaucratic organizations rely on authority and coercion to make things happen, while networked, diffuse relationships tend to be fragmented and heavily reliant on complex patterns of trust. Diffuse patterns of accountability therefore imply heightened risks: In depersonalized networks, the danger is that if everyone is accountable then nobody is accountable.

Digital applications used by online auctioneers, dating agencies, and gig employers have brought individuals into close proximity to one another in a vast array of atomized interactions, and they have increased the velocity of decision-making. We rent our houses to people we do not know, for a day or two at a time; we sell and purchase household items through global, online auction sites, relying on the trust of strangers we will never meet in person; we would never contemplate hitchhiking but, without hesitation, we share car rides with strangers chosen through a Smartphone application; we fret over food hygiene and organic ingredients, yet we place our faith in processed meals delivered through polluted streets by anonymous scooter riders; we suspect that professional networking social media sites are riddled with liars who embellish and falsify their CVs, yet we still engage in online networking, thereby placing our reputations at risk; we contribute to crowdfunding appeals without reliable guarantees of how our donations will be spent; we are cautious about our personal safety on the streets, but we choose to date strangers after a handful of social media photograph swipes; we adore our pet dogs yet we entrust their custody to dog walkers hired with a click of a mouse; and despite our insistence on humane capitalism we somehow persuade ourselves that the impossibly inexpensive clothes we purchase online are not manufactured in sweatshops.

The COVID-19 pandemic also revealed the difficulties of flows of accountability in matters that reach beyond the boundaries of traditional organizations. Apart from the heroic actions of frontline health workers in hospitals and clinics, the pandemic illuminated the inabilities of traditional bureaucratic structures to satisfactorily protect the public good. Authoritarianism and civil disobedience clashed in public arenas, and the failure of established institutional structures to govern conflicting interests inflamed partisan politics. The emerging, complex, and difficult-to-disentangle patterns of accountability transformed the public health crisis of the pandemic into a catastrophe of damaged social trust.

All these activities suggest that we are exposing ourselves to very high levels of risk as we navigate through the new paradigm of diffuse accountability and fragmented social trust. In terms of information on economic and political matters, top-down information flows from large media outlets struggle to compete with dispersed information flows. Instead of encountering an enriched quality of knowledge, we find massive amounts of digitalized hot air circulating on the internet. Instead of open, democratic networks dedicated to free speech, we find online information to be riddled with authoritarian censorship, politicized echo chambers, and self-contained bubbles of partisan interpretation. And, we have been warned, "[d]igital snake oil isn't always easy to spot" (Sinnreich and Gilbert, 2024, 132). Revenue derived from web traffic levels incentivizes the providers of digital information to supply what consumers wish to hear, thereby reinforcing socio-economic and political attitudes. Algorithmically organized internet search engines guide us to certain web sites and occlude alternative voices. Conspiracies and cranks flourish in such conditions, as does superficiality, misinformation, and disinformation. In this context, cybersecurity breaches may have disastrous compromises. The hacking in 2015 of Ashley Madison, an extramarital dating website for self-professed cheaters, led to the leaking of large numbers of individuals' information around the world. It is reported that the leaking of this information led to an unknown number of blackmail and bribery cases, ruined lives, and suicides (Sinnreich and Gilbert, 2024, 60).

Shoshana Zuboff describes the era we have entered as one of "surveillance capitalism". She characterizes the surveillance society as a "darkening of the digital dream": It is not merely a question of powerful forces in the digital world monitoring our online activity, and gathering and trading our behavioral patterns, but also a manipulative monetizing and shaping of our behavior (Zuboff, 2019, 7–9). The implications of the surveillance capitalism concept are highly troubling. In Zuboff's words:

> Surveillance capitalism operates through unprecedented asymmetries in knowledge and the power that accrues to knowledge. Surveillance capitalism knows everything *about us*, whereas their operations are designed to be unknowable to us. They accumulate vast domains of new knowledge *from us*, but not *for us*.

She suggests that surveillance capitalism is "a rogue force driven by novel economic imperatives that disregard social norms and nullify the elemental rights associated with individual autonomy that are essential to the very possibility of a democratic society" (Zuboff, 2019, 11, emphasis in original). Zuboff's concerns are increasingly shared by many commentators on the tracing of our digital activities: In Sinnreich and Gilbert's words,

> the data traces we leave in our wake as we go about our daily lives can – and likely will – be recorded, archived, analyzed, combined, and cross-referenced with other data and used to generate new forms of knowledge without our awareness or consent.
>
> *Sinnreich and Gilbert, 2024, xi*

As Botsman has argued, "institutional trust, taken on faith, kept in the hands of a few and operating behind closed doors, wasn't designed for the digital age" (Botsman, 2017, 5). And if Zuboff's troubling vision of the harvesting and misuse of data is correct, human experience is becoming little more than an exploitable source of profit. The extent of digitalization in our lives today offers efficiencies, certainly, but it also evokes the chilling prospect of a crushing abuse of power. At best, patterns of accountability and social trust are becoming increasingly fragmented and opaque. Fragmentation in a post-bureaucratic world (i.e., after a shift away from command-and-control organizations) is often characterized by "adhocracy" and "projectocracy", and it leads to piecemeal activity, piecemeal accountability and, inevitably, piecemeal assurance.

Not all the melting away or shifting of institutional boundaries can be explained by digitalization. Significant changes are happening in patterns of work and leisure, allied to but not entirely dependent on digitalization. Some of these changes derive from shifting work patterns: "employees, who previously identified with their employer as part of a conventional organization structure, are increasingly identifying with guild-type professional associations ... a sense of belonging or collective is achieved by grassroots organizing along occupational rather than employer lines" (Vine, 2021, 60). Other commentators envision a broader set of changes, encompassing leisure as well as work arrangements:

> current socio-cultural and technological changes [are] converg[ing] to the re-drawing of the prevailing boundaries of the private and public world, work from leisure, family and community. Under these conditions, the very forms by which individuals have traditionally been tied to social institutions are bound to change. New forms of individual involvement in organizations (e.g. flexible and temporary employment) develop to accommodate the shifts in social institutions, values and lifestyles ... At the same time information and communication technologies become an important agent of organizational and occupational change. The precise ways, though, by which organization forms are connected to these developments remain a contested terrain.
>
> *Kallinikos, 2004, 15*

It is therefore likely that the ongoing shifts in patterns of accountability cannot be attributed exclusively to digitalization.

To summarize this section, accountability and trust are more fluid than in the past, and they are giving rise to additional insecurities. The digitalization of modern life has combined with social changes to assist the reorientation of social trust from bureaucratic to diffuse patterns. The models of future distributions of accountability are not the army, the civil service, the church, the industrial corporation, or similar bureaucratic structures. Instead, future models will increasingly resemble short-term projects; shifting supply chains; unstable markets, and the gig economy. Regarding the latter, the bureaucratic job-for-life is giving way to precarious "transient workforce" patterns (Heckscher and Donnellon, 1994, 8), implying both greater flexibility and greater uncertainties. Horizontally distributed, networked accountability is to be found in liminal spaces at the boundaries of organizations, as well as in extramural places where civic duties might be unclear, where people (and institutions) come and go, where the writ of the policy and procedures manual runs weakest, and often where current mechanisms of internal audit and assurance fade away. In the following section, we shall review the implications for internal auditing of our new era of social trust.

2.4 INTERNAL AUDITING'S PRIMARY CHALLENGE: MARGINALIZATION

So far in this chapter, we have reviewed the centrality of reliable internal auditing to both accountability in individual organizations and aggregated social trust (Section 2.1), and we have described the ongoing, paradigmatic shifts in patterns of accountability and social trust, away from traditional, command-and-control hierarchies toward high-risk, horizontally distributed patterns (Sections 2.2 and 2.3). We have also touched on the possible dangers of authoritarianism through digitalized surveillance in the new environment (Section 2.3).

We now turn to the implications for internal auditing of the momentous splintering and redistribution of flows of accountability and aggregated trust. A first, vital point to keep in mind is the continuation, amid all the current socio-economic and political changes, of traditional, hierarchical bureaucracies. Notwithstanding our loss of trust in politicians and their institutional frameworks, in business leaders and their corporations, and in the media's institutions, many of us still work in organizations of the traditional command-and-control type. Reports of the death of bureaucratic structures as vehicles for collective endeavors are therefore premature. In the words of Amitai Etzioni (1929–2023):

> We are born in organizations, educated by organizations, and most of us spend much of our lives working for organizations. We spend much of our leisure time paying, playing and praying in organizations. Most of us will die in organizations, and when the time comes for burial, the largest organization of them all – the state – must grant official permission.
>
> *cited by Vine, 2021, 99–100*

The continuing existence of traditional, hierarchical institutions suggests that vertically distributed accountability will remain an enduring feature of institutional life, although with reduced importance. The growth of horizontally distributed accountability and the dangers of surveillance capitalism suggest that the most pressing risks of accountability and social trust are increasingly to be found along and beyond organizational boundaries, at the fringes of formal institutional structures as well as in extra-mural locations. It is increasingly recognized that institutional governance

> is not restricted to the board of directors. Rather, governance … spills out beyond the boundaries of the board, or even of the corporation. This involves shifting the locus of governance from internal preoccupations to a more sprawling set of … institutions.
>
> *Spicer and Banerjee, 2016, 408*

The most acute questions of accountability and social trust are therefore increasingly located in fluid, fast-moving, semi-occluded, and networked activities. As the importance of bureaucratic structures declines, accountability is in the process of transference to the grassroots of social, economic, and political life, where the traditional dichotomies of principal/agent relationships are barely discernible. The new patterns of accountability are taking slightly anarchic forms and are not always readily amenable to traditional internal auditing practices. (Enterprise Risk Management, as we shall see in Sections 3.4 and 3.5, may be deployed to identify and assess the gravity of extra-mural threats. But our primary concern is not with risk identification and mitigation, but with matters of assurance, accountability, and social trust.)

Some internal auditors may, understandably, turn toward nostalgia for the simpler world of traditional, command-and-control organizations, in which accountability patterns are reassuringly clear. The post-bureaucratic world is complex and often troubling: "the opposite of hierarchy (in the form of post-bureaucracy) is routinely more frustrating and alienating than hierarchy itself" (Vine, 2021, 63). With the surge of risks in extra-mural accountability, no sole auditor or assurance provider is currently in a position to provide assurance on the vast range of topics of interest to modern stakeholders. In the words of Mervyn King and Linda de Beer:

> Larger entities now generally have internal risk and compliance functions, an internal audit function, stronger corporate governance schemes and, in many instances, internal assurance providers on matters such as valuations (an actuary or in-house valuer in financial services); safety, health and environmental officials and in-house auditors in mining and manufacturing; as well as many similar roles depending on the nature of the business of the entity.
>
> *King and de Beer, 2018, 66*

Mervyn King has a long history of tapping into the deep processes at work in auditing and assurance and, in these cited comments, he and his co-author point to a problem at the root of the challenge facing internal auditors and all providers of assurance – the increasingly diffuse distribution of patterns of accountability and social trust have generated a diffuse and piecemeal distribution of demands for assurance.

It is unsurprising that solutions to the emerging demands on or beyond organizational boundaries that transcend traditional auditing and assurance frameworks are slow in coming and piecemeal in nature. The world of accountability and social trust has shifted dramatically on its axis, but internal auditors are still largely focused on the traditional hierarchical patterns of yesteryear. Internal auditing practices evolved from within the old, bureaucratic structures with vertical lines of accountability, overseen by boards of directors, and are struggling to adapt to the chaotic horizontal redistributions of accountability and social trust. New forms of assurance are required: We are on the threshold of a new age of fragmented accountability and piecemeal assurance.

The specialties of auditing and assurance face various challenges in the new accountability dispensation. As long as the traditional organization subsists, external auditing will be in demand, with its focus on the annual opinion on the fair presentation and accuracy of financial statements. However, as horizontally distributed networks increasingly become the main pattern of socio-economic activity, the external audit faces a future of managed decline. Keeping a watchful eye on financial statements will continue, but its relative importance in the overall picture of accountability and social trust will decrease. The new patterns of accountability and social trust demand contemporaneous, flexible, innovative, and forward-looking assurance mechanisms. In contrast, the auditing of financial statements is historically oriented, narrowly focused on accounting, and its strengths are its handling of tangible assets and financial capital, to the neglect of intangible assets and other forms of capital (including human, intellectual, and social capital).

Incapable of wriggling free from its tight connection to financial statements, external auditing will therefore continue to struggle to offer comprehensive insight and meaningful foresight. Some elements of financial statements and external auditing do offer glimpses of the future, but only weakly. Going concern evaluations, assessments of contingent liabilities, discussions of risks that might or might not crystallize in the future, assessments of the reasonableness of forward-looking comments in ancillary reports outside the core financial statements – all these offer limited insights into the future, but they cannot compete with contemporaneous assurance mechanisms in delivering current and future insights. External auditing will therefore continue as a niche form of assurance, providing assessments of the types of accountability that are transmitted through financial statements. Meanwhile, at the aggregated level of social trust, the real action is already moving elsewhere, to the plethora of piecemeal assurance mechanisms that are emerging to address the demands of the new paradigm of social trust and accountability.

We predict a continuance of a rump of external auditing for traditional organizational structures, but some commentators are already predicting the disappearance of the external auditing profession. King and de Beer, for example, advise that "the real threat of the [external auditing] profession facing extinction, in some form, should not be under estimated" (King and de Beer, 2018, 97). They argue that the annual opinion on financial statements does not provide assurance on

> the viability of the business, strength of internal controls, quality of corporate governance practices in the entity, the competence of the board or management or, most pertinently, the non-occurrence or non-detection and disclosure of fraud and non-compliance with laws or regulations.
>
> *2018, 28*

Indeed, the external audit has little, if anything, to say about the modern, diffuse patterns of accountability.

Before leaving external auditing to evaluate the impact of redistributed patterns of accountability on internal auditing, we may glance at one way in which the external auditing profession might reinvent itself through possible future changes in the substance of financial reporting. Should the requirement for annual financial statements, the *raison d'être* of external auditing, either disappear or be significantly modified, the mission of the external auditing profession will be recast. For example, Baruch Lev and Feng Gu, in *The End of Accounting: and the Path Forward for Investors and Managers*, argue that the traditional assets and historical transactions given prominence by financial statements are not necessarily the best guide to investors of future performance. In particular, financial statements do not capture value-enhancing intangible assets and "strategic resources" that possess the traits of being valuable, rare, and difficult to imitate (Lev and Gu, 2016, 120–121). They propose instead the use of a range of non-accounting information for the investing public. Should the substance of financial statements be modified to provide a range of forward-looking considerations, the substance of external auditing would also change accordingly. Such a change in the foreseeable future is not inconceivable. At the time of this writing, the *Integrated Reporting Framework* of the International Financial Reporting Standards Foundation aims to integrate into traditional financial statements more creative sustainability measures. Already, many endorse the so-called "triple bottom line" of sustainability in profit, people, and the planet in "integrated" reporting.

These types of development may revolutionize corporate financial reporting and revitalize the external auditor's role, or they may alternatively consolidate various auditing specialties in a fragmented, piecemeal assurance environment. As King and de Beer warn us, integrated reporting

> has resulted in a whole new regime of combined assurance, where the external auditor's work forms but one piece in a puzzle of assurance services by internal and external assurance providers, in order to support the integrity of the information in the integrated report. It is currently virtually impossible for an auditor to provide a single opinion on an integrated report, not only from a cost perspective but also as auditing standards do not accommodate such a diverse assignment.
>
> *King and de Beer, 2018, 46*

Notwithstanding our pessimistic predictions for the future of external auditing, the large audit firms are tenacious defenders of their commercial interests. Within the framework of their remit, and pending any revolution in financial statements, we can expect them to try to boost their involvement in parallel types of assurance. The emerging topic of "extinction accounting" is one such potential area of interest, but it is unclear that external auditors are best placed to audit "species loss and habitat destruction" (Maroun and Atkins, 2018). The tight connection between external auditing and financial statements will therefore probably continue to hamper the ability of external auditors to respond to the emerging patterns of flexible, piecemeal assurance. Nonetheless, the large firms are likely to expand their suite of advisory services and ancillary assurance services beyond the traditional external audit. Writing in 2018, King and de Beer tell us that only 40% of the Big Four's fee income is derived from assurance services, but they do not state if this is a global or country-specific figure (King and de Beer, 2018, 430).

Internal auditing is the specialty of auditing with the greatest potential to meet the demands of the new paradigm of widely diffused accountability. The knowledge basis of internal auditing is more flexible than that of external auditing, and this elasticity should allow internal auditing readily to identify and implement new types of assurance mechanism. As we shall see in Chapter 3, internal auditing has already demonstrated its versatility by its creative adaptation to shifting assurance demands in the inner workings of organizations.

Despite the potentialities inherent within internal auditing, its flat-footed response to the changing demands of assurance suggests that it is struggling to understand fully the nature and scope of the radical, ongoing transformations that surround it, let alone adapt to them. The revised *Global Internal Audit Standards* (GIAS) of the Institute of Internal Auditors (IIA), published in January 2024, are dominated by traditional perspectives of accountability: They give prominence to bureaucratic, command-and-control structures under the unitary control of boards of directors, and make no reference to the emerging assurance demands on and beyond formal organizational boundaries (and beyond the scope of influence of boards of directors). Like their cousins in external auditing, internal auditors are still largely addressing yesterday's concerns, focusing on old-fashioned institutional arrangements, rather than on the growing demands for extra-mural accountability. Shifting patterns of accountability and social trust are giving rise to assurance demands in three organizational areas – in the inner workings of organizations; in intermediary, transitional spaces on organizational boundaries; and in extra-mural activities. This book reviews the likelihood of internal auditing unshackling itself from the first area to satisfactorily address the other two areas, for which innovative assurance mechanisms are steadily incubating.

In particular, the identity and purpose of the IIAs' approach to internal auditing seems, therefore, to be intertwined with bureaucratic concepts to such a degree that it is extremely difficult for internal auditors to tear themselves away from the command-and-control structures from which they emerged and over which they act, like benevolent watchdogs, as prudent eyes and ears. These orientations toward traditional hierarchies are so profound that, for all the expansions of accountability into new domains, internal auditing's destiny appears to rest in bureaucratic institutions.

In comparison with its external auditing counterparts, the IIA is a young, upstart professional association. It was founded in 1941 and, as we shall see in Section 4.2, its knowledge base is rather slippery and elusive to define. The following citation is taken from a popular IIA publication at the turn of the millennium, and it summarizes the dominant trend of thought at that time in terms of internal auditing's development: Internal auditing, we were told,

> has passed through two dominant paradigms and is poised on the edge of a third. The first internal auditing paradigm focused on observing and counting; ... [later] a new concept of the system of internal control ... changed the internal audit paradigm from a focus on *reperformance* to a focus on *controls* ... A third paradigm for internal auditing is emerging, based on auditing the business process through a focus on risk.
>
> *McNamee and Selim, 1998, 6, emphasis in original*

These comments were accurate up to a point, but they overestimated the significance of risk. With hindsight, we can now see that, in the third paradigm of internal auditing, a heightened consideration of risk was merely one aspect of more profound changes in patterns of social trust and accountability. As we shall see in Sections 3.4 and 3.5, the "riskification" of auditing was simply a part of a wider trend that Michael Power attributed to the nature and impact of the "audit society".

The internal auditing profession has been far from inert in recent years. It has not been shy of embracing change: Buffeted by the winds of its changing environment, it has developed a passion for innovation, modernization, and relevance (e.g., Lenz and Hoos, 2023). But an appetite for change does not guarantee the identification of the right kinds of change. The IIA has yet to grasp the kinds of emerging accountability demands we have discussed in this chapter, which both originate from and manifest themselves powerfully in peripheral and extra-mural spaces. Its curricula and written standards seem ill-designed for internal auditing to stake out the ownership of assurance responsibilities in the emergent areas. For example, boards of directors in bureaucratic organizations, so prominent in the IIA's 2024 *Global Internal Audit Standards*, are no longer the fulcrum around which the new patterns of assurance revolve.

On the other hand, although it frequently takes a misguided direction, the IIA possesses a kind of adolescent energy, and this may give rise to hopes for internal auditing to deliver its full potential in the future. We have seen how, with the continuing erosion of vertical hierarchies of accountability and social trust, and their replacement by new patterns of widely distributed trust, external auditing has been largely marooned on the shore of auditing history. In contrast, internal auditing possesses attributes fit for the new era – a flexible (albeit poorly defined) knowledge base and a contemporaneous approach to assurance – that suggest a potential for adaptability to the accountability demands of our advanced digital age.

As we conclude Section 2.4, let us pull together our thoughts on the struggles internal auditing will face to adapt to emerging patterns of accountability and social trust. The conservatism of internal auditing's bureaucratic heritage is the biggest obstacle to change. The IIA's official and semi-official rhetoric of innovation and improvement do not appear to encompass an appetite for (or, perhaps, an adequate understanding of) the redistributions of the demands of modern accountability and social trust. Internal auditing therefore has little to say on the topics of peripheral and extra-mural accountability: It remains wedded to traditional, organizational pyramid structures. Just as the pyramids of Egypt and Mexico symbolize solidity and stand as testimony to longevity, the institutional pyramid, with its bureaucratically administered, vertical, command-and-control structures may offer a kind of existential consolation to those anxious at the pace and implications of the increasing fragmentation of accountability. One awaits with interest the future direction of the IIA's focus of interests – will it remain tethered to a rather cramped, bureaucratic mentality, or will it rejuvenate itself through a conceptual overhaul?

2.5 AUDITING'S SECONDARY CHALLENGE: THE CLOSING OF THE AUDITOR'S MIND?

We have suggested that modern internal auditing is at a crossroads, practically and conceptually. It remains largely focused on traditional institutions with hierarchical command-and-control structures, and it has yet to embrace the ongoing, profound changes in the patterns of horizontally distributed accountability and social trust among complex digital and human networks. A radical overhaul of internal auditing is necessary to creatively address the new patterns of post-bureaucratic accountability, and to break away from an excessive focus on the vertically structured organization. In this section, we shall consider aspects of internal auditing that appear to dampen its prospects of adaptability.

Although internal auditing has a history of resilience and versatility, in recent decades it has tended to inculcate in its practitioners an algorithmic, checklist mindset that hampers creativity and critical thinking. As we shall see in Section 4.2, the IIA's prescriptive professional standards have encouraged conformity and discouraged judgment, thereby narrowing intellectual horizons and running the risk of closing down practitioners' inventiveness and moral agency. At the present time, the intellectual agility needed to respond to radical redistributions of accountability is in short supply.

Related aspects of internal auditing's malaise include a growing tendency to focus on the building blocks of information, to the detriment of handling "big picture" perspectives. This excessive concentration on details has been reinforced by a resurgence in a pseudoscientific, quasi-superstitious faith in the power of numbers. The consequence of these trends is an ever-deepening distrust of qualitative judgment.

Internal auditing's shift away from its humanistic elements toward clockwork routines implies a dilution of major aspects of professionalism. A tendency of de-personalization has closely accompanied internal auditing's technological progress: Modern internal auditing has embraced areas of technical excellence in the use of data analytics and powerful, automated information-sorting tools, but it is doubtful that the diagnostic abilities, analytical skills, skepticism, and logical acumen of today's internal auditors exceeds those of previous generations. Preserving the soul of internal auditing should be consistent with technological innovation: However radically the technology of internal auditing may change and progress, the cogency of the discipline's concepts and principles are enduring. But internal auditing's sacrifices to the imperatives of technological efficiency have resulted in serious damage to the judgment and creativity of its practitioners.

Without a remediation of these problems, internal auditing is unlikely to possess the wherewithal to satisfactorily address the primary challenge of adapting to new demands of accountability. Moreover, it is doubtful that algorithmic and non-humanistic methods of internal auditing will survive a take-over by machine processing and Artificial Intelligence. The logic of such a trend is unassailable: If humanistic judgment and creativity are vanishing from modern internal auditing, it makes more sense to deploy efficient automated auditing software than to employ individuals with algorithmic mindsets. The possible reasons for, and the consequences of, internal auditing's retreat from judgment to prescriptive, algorithmic, and checklist-based attitudes shall occupy most of the rest of this book.

2.6 EMERGING MECHANISMS OF POST-BUREAUCRATIC ASSURANCE

Owing to the limited perspectives of organizational accountability provided by both internal and external auditing, a plethora of assurance mechanisms has already arisen in recent decades. These new instruments are characterized by contemporaneous activities and narrowly defined expertise. Examples include clinical auditing in healthcare facilities, election auditing in political processes, royalty auditing for intellectual property rights, and environmental auditing in the fight for the sustainability of the natural world. The narrow focus of these specialties, in responding to the demands of accountability beyond the remit of traditional internal and external auditing, is a symptom of a trend toward the fragmentation of auditing and assurance. Reflecting the breakdown of older, simpler patterns of accountability in command-and-control organizations, assurance mechanisms are becoming increasingly piecemeal. Already, as we have suggested in Section 2.4, in the context of integrated reporting and the "triple bottom line", groups of auditors and assurance providers are working in parallel, dealing with separate subsections of the elements of a broad spectrum of assurance demanded by stakeholders.

At this point one may ask: Can the audit committee pull together these various strands of assurance? Unfortunately, audit committees are at risk from limitations similar to those experienced by the providers of specialized auditing and assurance activities – an irrational faith in numbers that leads to an overreliance on quantification; a mechanistic rather than judgmental approach to auditing and assurance; and a struggle to apprehend the big picture perspectives that arise from the building blocks of information. A consolidation of the findings of piecemeal auditing and assurance serves little value if the information is simply aggregated and paraphrased by those with low levels of interpretative expertise. A sophisticated level of expertise is required to interpret the agglomeration of piecemeal information, and to identify duplications and gaps in consolidated assurance. It takes a rare, visionary understanding to apply concepts like surveillance capitalism to institutional settings and to identify and remedy the problems of semi-occluded pockets of peripheral and extra-mural accountability. An audit committee is therefore unlikely to provide the solution to the challenge of shifting patterns of accountability. Audit committees have the benefit of a bird's eye view of accountability and assurance, but they tend to gather existing activities in the oversight of oversight, rather than explore innovative interpretations.

Fresh concepts of assurance are needed to pull together the findings of piecemeal assurance. We should be moving toward a different type of dialogue that includes a broader spectrum of stakeholders and embraces traditional assurance while simultaneously transcending it. As accountability increasingly repositions itself on and beyond organizational boundaries, alternative instruments to the assurance- and risk-focused audit committee are called for. We may therefore expect the emergence of fresh approaches that promote a pluralistic civic dialogue over the typical audit committee's narrow focus on assurance and audit testing. Traits of the fresh approaches may include more conversation and less auditing. Less bureaucracy and more creativity. Less distance and more interaction. Less compliance and more creativity. Where necessary, the new instruments that will replace the audit committee should consider alternatives to auditing when the public interest demands higher levels of social trust. That, needless to say, would be the topic for another book.

Beyond the audit committee, novel and as yet undefined assurance mechanisms will emerge to address the paradigm shift in accountability and social trust from command-and-control organizations to more widely diffuse, horizontally arranged patterns. The outlines of these new mechanisms are still under formation. Perhaps the audit and assurance methods applied currently to supply chains, franchise outlets, and outsourcing and consortium arrangements, might provide prototypes of extra-mural instruments of assurance. Or perhaps the emerging mechanisms will take on the characteristics of the diffuse, horizontal networks over which they will seek to provide assurance: Informal, temporary, flexible, fast-moving, assurance instruments that mirror the contingencies of the gig economy. Alternatively, public sector mechanisms might arise, or even supranational assurance instruments, perhaps linked to the United Nations or other international organizations.

Chapter 3

Social trust and the audit society

3.1 PUBLIC DISQUIET, THE CRITICAL ACCOUNTING MOVEMENT, AND THE ORIGINS OF THE AUDIT SOCIETY

In Chapter 2, we reviewed the implications for internal auditing of shifting patterns in the distribution of accountability and social trust. We now turn our attention to the trustworthiness of internal auditing. The credibility of internal auditing as a mechanism that promotes accountability and social trust is fragile – it is vulnerable to our collective distrust, the very fault for which internal auditing purports to be the remedy. The outlook for social, economic, and political accountability under such circumstances is concerning. We shall approach this topic through the lenses of Michael Power's concept of the audit society, perhaps the most remarkable and far-reaching attempt to make sense of the social purposes of modern auditing. Although now somewhat dated, and despite its focus on external rather than internal auditing, Power's original articulation of the audit society was prescient, adumbrating many of the problems facing internal auditing today.

Michael Power (born 1957), a professor of accounting at the London School of Economics and Political Science, developed the notion of the audit society in the late twentieth century to address the increasingly pervasive and often damaging influence of auditing and audit-like activities. Contrary to popular notions, the audit society concept goes far beyond merely a troubling increase in the volume of auditing: It is a complex and many-sided concept that grapples with qualitative factors like auditing's role as a social palliative; its increasing emphasis on the inner workings of organizations (in contrast to external governance documents like financial statements); its impact on shaping organizational behavior; and its complex interactions with the analysis and "management" of institutional risk.

Power's writings on the audit society include two small but powerful books published in 1994 by Demos, a politically non-partisan British think tank – *The Audit Explosion* (Power, 1994a) and *The Risk Management of Everything: Rethinking the Politics of Uncertainty* (Power, 1994b).

DOI: 10.1201/9781032664880-3

Power later provided more extensive treatments of the broad themes of audit and risk in two monographs published by Oxford University Press – *The Audit Society: Rituals of Verification* (Power, 1997) and *Organized Uncertainty: Designing a World of Risk Management* (Power, 2007). Already, in these four titles, we can discern parallel yet inter-related tracks in Power's thought: Auditing and risk. In addition, Power has set out his thoughts on these topics in scholarly articles that continue to appear to the present day. For example, he has conveyed his thoughts on the audit society in an era of digitalization in *Afterword: Audit Society 2.0?* (Power, 2022a).

Power's writings on auditing are among the most informative and elegant on the subject. His doctoral training in philosophy at Cambridge University provided him with the ability to provide startling theoretical and practical insights into the role of auditing in institutional governance. As two commentators have noted: "It is, perhaps, difficult to recapture fully the buzz that *The Audit Society* engendered on its publication" (Bottausci and Robson, 2023). However, as the history of his publications shows, auditing is far from the sole (or even the most important) stream of Power's interests. Indeed, he is probably more widely known today for his work on risk than for his writing on auditing. However, both topics are deeply connected in his work, and an appreciation of either topic is best informed by an appreciation of both.

The allure of Power's work arises not only from the polished magnificence of his prose and his writing's almost inexhaustible theoretical richness, but also from its predictive accuracy and ongoing real-world validity. Power's core messages belong to a small collection of enduring writings on auditing that hold our attention across the decades: Examples include Mautz and Sharaf's work on the postulates of auditing (Mautz and Sharaf, 1961), Wolnizer's *Auditing as Independent Authentication* (Wolnizer, 1987), and Flint's *Philosophy and Principles of Auditing* (Flint, 1988). Discussions of auditing tend to be rapidly perishable owing to auditing's socially evolving nature but, like the aforementioned books, Power's writings possess a long shelf life. When reading his pages, one feels as though Power has pressed his ear closely to the beating heart of what is meaningful in auditing. And the issues he first brought to our attention in the 1990s are still working their way through our socio-economic structures, albeit in new patterns.

Before looking in detail into the audit society, let us first put the origins of Power's critique in context. In the late twentieth century, and through the turn of the millennium, the external auditing profession was severely damaged by the large audit firms' greedy obsession with the billable hour. Cut-throat competition frequently took precedence over professional responsibilities to the public interest. The large audit firms' thirst for revenue led, among other things, to the tolerance of questionable, "creative accounting" techniques that flattered corporate results (Whittington, 1995, 1), and the phenomenon of "lowballing". The latter refers to the offering of low audit fees to undercut competitors, often at a loss to the supplying firm, in the hope of attaining a counterbalancing profit from the sale of lucrative non-audit services. For the participants in such shenanigans, the audit became merely "a loss-leader commodity ... to secure new clients" (Sharma, 2014, 67). The excessive commercialization of external auditing resulted in a minefield of conflicts of interest, impaired objectivity, and tarnished reputations.

The debasement of external auditing culminated, following a decade of disreputable rascality, in the collapse in 2002 of the once-respected audit firm Arthur Andersen, in the aftermath of an infamous accounting fraud at one of its major clients, Enron Corporation. An even larger fraud was subsequently uncovered at another Arthur Andersen client, WorldCom, after the Enron debacle (Giroux, 2017, II:136.) Ironically, given the circumstances of its demise, Arthur Andersen had long stood out among the large audit firms for its principled stance on the correctness of accounting methodology, even at the risk of losing clients (Spacek, 1989). By 2002, however, Arthur Andersen had become a rotten apple in the external auditing profession, although it was just one bad apple in a generally poor crop from a mismanaged orchard. Reports of the shredding by Arthur Andersen staffers of thousands of audit documents in the immediate aftermath of Enron's bankruptcy shocked public opinion. Although the Supreme Court later overturned the firm's conviction for "obstruction of justice", the reputational damage was irreparable (Mazzucato and Collington, 2023, 64). The external auditing profession became a laughing stock: In relation to inspections of weapons of mass destruction prior to the second Gulf War of 2003, the president of the United States at the time is reported to have made the following quip: "The good news is that [Saddam Hussein is] willing to have his nuclear, biological, and chemical weapons counted. The bad news is he wants Arthur Andersen to do it" (quoted by Fox, 2003, 294).

We should always bear in mind the asymmetrical relationship between auditor failure and auditor success. The quiet successes arising from the unobtrusive performance of external audits "will not usually yield public acclaim" (Power, 1997, 27). Audit-phobic outbreaks of indignation over perceptions or allegations of external auditors' poor performance – in relation to India's Satyam Computer Services in 2008/2009 (de Swaan, 2020, 9 and 143) and the United Kingdom's Carillion plc, liquidated in 2018 – are therefore unlikely to be matched by outbreaks of fevered praise for external auditors' quiet successes. Blunders are more likely than successes to come to the media's attention. Nonetheless, the Arthur Andersen scandal was authentically shocking, and a symbol of the consequences of unbridled greed in a once-reputable profession.

The immediate reactions to the Arthur Andersen debacle in the United States included the *Sarbanes-Oxley Act* (SOX) of 2002, with its stringent requirements for corporate records and reporting, and its creation of the

Public Company Accounting Oversight Board (PCAOB). Many other countries have followed a similar legislative and regulatory path, notably Japan's 2006 *Financial Instruments and Exchange Act* ("J-SOX") and China's 2008 *Basic Standard for Enterprise Internal Control* ("CHINA-SOX"). These regulatory-based reforms have restored the professional ethos of external auditing to a large degree. Nonetheless, despite the calming effects of regulation and the order restored to the external auditing profession in the post-SOX years, external auditing itself has arguably never fully recovered from the turbulent years that led to the catastrophe of 2002. We have seen a reorientation of the center of gravity of auditing, away from the external auditor's opinion on annual financial statements to a plethora of assurance mechanisms (including internal auditing) operating within the inner spaces of organizations. Today, as we suggested in Section 2.4, the redistribution of patterns of accountability and social trust have left external auditing facing, at best, a future of increasing marginalization.

The years in which Power developed his concept of the audit society were therefore characterized by a growing public disquiet over rampant misconduct in external auditing. To gain a flavor of the events surrounding the frauds at Arthur Andersen's clients, one may consult the shocking insider, eyewitness accounts by Schwartz and Watkins (2003) for Enron and Cooper (2008) for WorldCom. The decline of public trust in corporate reporting and external auditing had nonetheless set in long before Arthur Andersen's spectacular demise in 2002, and Power elaborated his critique of auditing from the early 1990s, amid the darkening public mood.

In parallel with public unease over the deteriorating performance and ethical standards of external auditing in the late twentieth century, another source of criticism was gathering momentum – the university-based critical accounting movement, which has been a fiercely implacable critic of the external auditing profession. Through an active, at times aggressive, literature in both academic and public domains, including its landmark journal *Critical Perspectives on Accounting* (first published in 1990), the movement has provided a relentless condemnation of official discourses of corporate reporting and external auditing.

Critical Theory, of which the critical accounting movement is a branch, has developed into a broad school of intersectional thought, inheriting the traditions of the Frankfurt School and other strands of leftist theory, from the environmentalist movement to the portrayals of disciplinary social constructs of knowledge and power set out by Michel Foucault (1926–1984). The Frankfurt School arose from the Institute for Social Research (founded in 1923 in Frankfurt, Germany). Described as the "first Marxist think tank" (Bronner, 2017, 7), the Institute and the movement it produced were born in the tumultuous years of the Weimar Republic (1918–1933), between the horrors of World War One and the horrors of the National Socialists. Weimar Germany survived the economic distress, diplomatic squabbling, and political instability of its earliest years, and achieved a kind of deceptive exuberance in the second half of the 1920s (the "Golden Twenties"), a rare liberal eye at the center of the gathering storm of Europe's violent political ideologies.

In the year of the Institute's founding, 1923, hyperinflation destroyed Germany's currency, and in Bavaria a small, aggressively anti-Marxist and anti-Semitic political party – the National Socialist German Workers' Party, known by its German acronym NSDAP – attempted a failed coup. Largely dismissed at the time as the act of a tiny, fringe, paramilitary movement of little significance, it would take only a decade before the National Socialists achieved total political control over Germany. The strongly Marxist-influenced Institute relocated to the United States in 1934 and returned to Frankfurt in the aftermath of the Second World War. Beyond the vicissitudes of the Institute's history, however, the impact of the broader movement of Critical Theory has been significant in the wider academic community and, increasingly, in the public sphere.

The interests of Critical Theory have evolved during its century-long existence (Rush, 2004, passim), but there has been a broad continuity in its challenges to what it considers to be alienating and oppressive social arrangements inherent in the socio-economic practices of an exploitative mass culture. In this spirit, the critical accounting movement has always aimed to be emancipatory: It has sought not merely to describe the world but to transform it, to imbue it with a fierce impetus for reform, and to dismantle inequitable power structures. It has been suggested that "the objective of critical accounting research is to contribute to the process of creating a better society", entailing "the active pursuit of radical social change" (Roslender, 2018, 12). Critical accounting seeks to gives space to the previously suppressed voices of both historical and current victims of social power.

The Critical Theorists have not been without their critics. Some of their opponents have accused them of peddling destructive, utopian, or authoritarian ideologies. The English philosopher Roger Scruton (1944–2020) described the influence of radical progressive movements in negative terms:

> The liberation advocated by left-wing movements today does not mean simply freedom from political oppression or the right to go about one's business undisturbed. It means emancipation from the 'structures': from the institutions, customs and conventions that shaped the 'bourgeois' order, and which established a shared system of norms and values at the heart of Western society ... Much of their literature is devoted to deconstructing such institutions as the family, the school, the law and the nation state through which the inheritance of Western civilization has been passed down to us.
>
> *Scruton, 2015, 6*

Another English philosopher, John Gray (born 1948), building on the observations of Eric Voegelin (1901–1985), has characterized both Marxist movements and their free market opponents as militant political religions promising heaven on earth, their participants acting as secular millenarians gripped by apocalyptic desires to remake the world and sweep away human imperfections: "Marxism and the cult of the free market are only the latest in a succession of Enlightenment faiths, in which the Christian promise of universal salvation reappears as a political project of universal emancipation" (Gray, 2004, 2). In relation to what he refers to as the "woke movement", Gray has written that it expresses the nihilism of "an antinomian intelligentsia, which professes to instruct society by deconstructing its institutions and values" (Gray, 2023, 71). He has described the movement's purpose as careerist: "Woke is a career as much as a cult. By advertising their virtue, redundant graduates hope to gain a foothold on the crumbling ladder that leads to safety as one of society's guardians" (Gray, 2023, 114).

The arguments in favor of and against Critical Theory are fascinating, but are beyond the scope of this book. For our purposes, participants in the critical accounting movement might be identified as modern Socratic debunkers, challenging the social prejudices of our day and proposing radical remedies. One may describe the approach of the critical accountants through the analogy of cartography: The Critical Theorists do not merely challenge the maps of official discourse, but prefer to deconstruct such maps, and to redraw fresh interpretative maps that deploy radically novel approaches. Where official discourses identify frameworks of civic order, the critical accountants tend to perceive structures of exploitative power. And the critical accountants' rejection *in toto* of official auditing discourses has made the movement one of the most vehement and compelling challengers of orthodoxies in auditing. Treating with a skepticism bordering on disdain the official narratives of auditing's contributions to the public good, the critical accountants had been skewering the pretensions and reputation of external auditors before Power's work on the audit society.

Some critical accountants have downplayed direct political activism for a more detached role of influencing attitudes toward socio-economic and political issues. In the United Kingdom, in contrast, Professor Prem Sikka (born 1951) has long been associated with activism, especially in his collaborations with political ally Austin Mitchell (1934–2021), a polymath member of the British parliament with a background in academia, journalism, and broadcasting. The combination of Sikka's academic critiques and Mitchell's high profile communicative reach resulted in some of the critical accounting movement's most devastating attacks on the external auditing profession.

Sikka and his allies have tended to view auditing as an unstable, socially constructed activity in permanent flux:

> The social practice of 'audit' does not have a single unambiguous meaning but rather, numerous competing meanings that exist side by side ... This is not to say that 'audit' is meaningless, but rather that its meaning is contingent and negotiable: its fixing within relations of power is precarious and subject to redefinition.
>
> *Sikka et al., 1998, 303–304*

In the 1990s, in their mission to "unfreeze and challenge conventional discourses and practices" (Sikka and Willmott, 1997, 161), the critical accountants described the large external auditing firms as "pre-occupied with fees and client appeasement" (Cousins et al., 1998, 9), and even as "emperors of darkness" (Dunn and Sikka, 1999, 4). At the time of this writing, Sikka continues to criticize official auditing narratives from his position as a life peer in the British House of Lords.

Although the concept of the audit society emerged from the co-occurrence of public disquiet and academic hostility in relation to the external auditing profession in the late twentieth century, it is important to differentiate Power's thought from that of the critical accounting movement. Without doubt, Power's writings share some concerns with critical accounting: He acknowledges the implications of auditing for socio-economic power relations, and his intellectual debt to Foucault is evident from his characterization of an alleged "disciplinary" role of auditing in making its objects observable, calculable, and therefore amenable to control. The Foucauldian inheritance is solidly in the broad critical accounting tradition: For example, Mihret and Grant (2017, 700) have attempted to reverse the mainstream neglect of "the complex social context in which internal auditing is deployed as a technology for exercising power". Also, as its name suggests, the audit society envisions auditing more as a social construct than as a scientific practice. In Power's words, "auditability cannot be defined; it is negotiated" (Power, 1997, 81). Notably, he has questioned the objectivity and stability of auditing's knowledge base, writing of auditing's "essentially elusive epistemological character" (Power, 1997, 11) and highlighting a circularity in definitions of auditor expertise: "there is no robust conception of 'good' auditing independent either of auditor judgments or of the system of knowledge in which those judgments are embedded and against which particular audits could be judged" (Power, 1997, 29). He has also treated with suspicion many of the claims made in the official discourses of the professional auditing associations.

Despite these affinities with the critical accounting literature, Power's critique emerges from a more neutral political background. In contrast to the exhortatory, transformative political tone of the critical accounting movement, it is impossible to ascertain Power's personal political opinions from his written output. Power's impartiality has been of crucial importance in terms of the effectiveness and credibility of the audit society concept: He did not elaborate and sharpen his critique as part of a radical political agenda, but rather as an even-handed observer of social trends.

Power's distance from the critical accounting movement was demonstrated in his reaction to a multi-authored Fabian Society discussion paper, to which Sikka and Mitchell contributed, that denounced the large external audit firms as "accessories to casino capitalism" (Mitchell et al., 1991, 3). Power joined a group of accounting and auditing academics who pushed back against the Fabian Society paper, accusing it of "anecdote instead of analysis, assertion instead of arguments" (Shaw et al., 1992, 275). Power, as one of the co-authors of the pushback paper, placed himself at arm's length from the critical accounting movement, or at least from the Sikka-Mitchell brand of critical accounting.

In developing our theories in this book, we owe a significant debt to Power's path-breaking work. Power has provided the giant's shoulders on which we have been standing. In approaching the audit society, it is worth emphasizing two matters of prudence. First, from the 1990s, the audit society concept has been modified and developed, by Power and others: It is a far from static concept. Second, as we mentioned earlier, Power's audit society concept opens the door to a significant degree of complexity. It is a capacious concept that accommodates several main strands of argument. The popular understanding that the audit society refers to an unwelcome quantitative expansion of damaging auditing is only partially true, as the concept encompasses parallel considerations.

In what follows, and at a risk of some simplification, the present author has extracted from Power's writings on the audit society four themes that strike him as being most pertinent to the arguments in this book: (1) Section 3.2 reviews the audit "explosion", a quantitative expansion of auditing that seems often to serve as a social palliative, generating empty or false assurance in the facing of declining socio-economic trust; (2) Section 3.3 looks at the "audit implosion", the internalization of organizational regulatory, compliance, and auditing activities around the turn of the millennium, and the transformative impact of auditing in making its objects auditable, with the consequential dangers of distortion of institutional objectives and incentives; (3) Sections 3.4 and 3.5 address the "riskification" of auditing; and (4) Section 3.6 discusses the implications of ritualism in auditing.

Through these conceptual lenses we can perceive threats to the public's trust in internal auditing. These threats include the generation of empty or false assurance to the detriment of facing up to genuine risks; audit-driven distortions of institutional objectives and incentives, with a costly displacement of emphasis onto second-order activities; and, at worst, a possible degeneration of internal auditing into a meaningless ritualism. We also find, however, sources of hope for a future renaissance of internal auditing in the very ritualism that presently seems so damaging.

3.2 THE "AUDIT EXPLOSION" AND THE GENERATION OF FALSE ASSURANCE

The notion of an "explosion" of auditing is the most widely known aspect of the audit society. It evokes a damaging proliferation of auditing and audit-like activities that consumes an inordinate amount of time and energy. The term "explosion" embraces not merely increases in the volume of existing categories of auditing, but also the emergence of new auditing specialties. In Power's words: "In addition to financial audits, there are now environmental audits, value for money audits, management audits, forensic audits, data audits, intellectual property audits, medical audits, teaching audits, technology audits, stress audits, democracy audits, and many others besides" (Power, 1994b, 1). His critique of auditing goes beyond external auditing to a range of emerging auditing and assurance mechanisms.

Power attributed the rise of over-auditing to three factors: "the 'new public management'; increased demands for accountability and transparency; [and] the rise of quality assurance models of organizational control" (Power, 2000b, 111). The first of these factors, the "new public management", is a theory (or ideology) popular in the United Kingdom and some other English-speaking countries from the 1980s: It envisions a style of administering public sector organizations through private sector principles, with an emphasis on cost cutting, value for money, and the promotion of efficiency. The "new public management" approach stops short of privatization but it claims to inject into public sector organizations efficiency, cost-consciousness, and a competitive mindset, the idealized traits of private organizations. One element of the "cultural logic" (Prasad, 2015, 108) of new public management is an emphasis on auditing and other systems of verification.

The second factor identified by Power as being behind the explosion of auditing is the pressure for institutional accountability through performance measurement. Power's assessment of this drive for accountability is that it has involved a questionable shift of focus from performance to review, and from professional activity to supposedly impartial oversight: "the spread of audits constitutes a major shift in power: from the public to the professional, and from teachers, engineers and managers to overseers" (Power, 1994a, 47). He perceives the audit society as "a symptom of the times, coincidentally a fin de siècle, in which a gulf has opened up between poorly rewarded 'doing' and highly rewarded 'observing'" (Power, 1997, 147). The transaction costs and opportunity costs of this displacement of energy and focus are incalculable, yet undeniably significant: Sometimes Power comes close to portraying auditing as parasitical on society. The third factor affecting auditing has been, according to Power, quality assurance models of organizational control, typified by a checklist-based, bureaucratic mindset.

We shall examine two implications for modern internal auditing of the "audit explosion" of recent decades. We shall review its significance for accountability and social trust in general, and its implications for the trustworthiness of internal auditing. First, although Power acknowledges that assurances given by auditors have the potential to enhance the orderly conduct of human affairs, he warns that increasing layers of burdensome and overlapping systems of assurance (and pseudo-assurance) mirror a declining public trust in our institutions. The explosion of auditing

> can be understood as a label for a loss of confidence in the central steering institutions of society, particularly politics. So it may be that a loss of faith in intellectual, political and economic leadership has led to the creation of industries of checking which satisfy a demand for signals of order.
>
> *Power, 2000b, 188*

This aspect of Power's critique is consistent with our suggestion (in Chapter 2) of a dramatic erosion of social trust in recent years, marked by a reorientation from traditional, bureaucratic institutions to horizontally distributed networks (Sections 2.2 and 2.3).

Turning to the public's trust in internal auditing, Power's linking of the audit explosion to declining socio-economic and political trust is connected to his concern at auditing's increasing role as a social palliative that delivers a false impression of an orderly society. Auditing is rarely if ever undertaken for amusement or frivolity – it is a costly, time-consuming activity that arises strictly from demands for intermediary assurance on accountability between two (or more) parties. In short, people turn to auditing as a response to an inadequate sense of trust. That patterns of diminishing social trust entail over-auditing is therefore highly plausible. Tom Lee described the financial audit as "the principal means by which accountability is attempted when trust in relationships disappears" (Lee, 1998, 219). If Lee was right, it should be no surprise that the erosion of traditional patterns of social trust we discussed in Chapter 2 has been accompanied by an explosion of auditing and assurance, in both quantity and variety. At the same time, auditing's role as social palliative is likely to reduce its trustworthiness.

At this point, it is worthwhile delving a little deeper into the concept of trustworthiness in the context of internal auditing. An internal auditor's trustworthiness derives from reliability in meeting commitments. And reliability, in turn, may be analyzed into the two elements of competence and good intentions. We cannot double check most expert judgments, and we therefore have little option in day-to-day life other than to trust the levels of competency and good intentions of experts like internal auditors. The public's trust in internal auditors is therefore founded on expectations of demonstrable competence and good intentions. As we suggested in Section

3.1, the quiet, unobtrusive successes of auditing are likely to go unnoticed. Instead, auditing's blunders and misjudgments are more likely to come to the public's attention. As a consequence, if internal auditors appear to betray trust in their competence and good intentions, public trust will inevitably evaporate. These concerns suggest that we should not neglect the stated intentionality of internal auditors, as "[p]art of being trustworthy is trying to avoid commitments you know you cannot fulfil" (Hawley, 2012, 65).

Intentionality, discussed further in the philosophical appendix to this book (Appendix A), is central to an understanding of internal auditing's relations to the surrounding world, and it explains why the kinds of trustworthiness we attribute to individuals or organizations cannot be extended to inanimate objects. Your trust in your car not to break down on the way to an important meeting, or the trust you place in your chair not to collapse beneath your weight, are of a different kind to the trustworthiness you attribute to internal auditors, or to internal auditing as an institutional practice. The trustworthiness of inanimate objects lacks the intentionality and moral dimensions of inter-personal trust.

Tom Lee argued that "[b]y attempting to alleviate human anxiety created by uncertainty surrounding specific phenomena, verification or auditing acts as a stabilizing factor in the management of human behavior" (Lee, 1993, 20). The audit explosion suggests that the ongoing proliferation of over-auditing has failed to satisfy the widening sense of social distrust in our traditional institutions. Instead of providing much-needed trust in our institutions (and their leaders), audit reports too often provide little more than hollow signals of order that act as a distraction, numbing us to reality while feeding a false sense of reassurance and security. Auditing in general, and internal auditing in particular, have therefore largely failed to provide the public's craving for reassurance. Despite its ostensible purpose as an accountability mechanism, auditing has failed to bolster traditional patterns of trust. In Power's words: "The dystopian vision of a world of fully compliant organizations heading over the cliff into oblivion is not too far-fetched" (Power, 2023). Yet, ironically, as public trust in the external auditing mechanism of opinions on annual financial statements declines, an "audit implosion" has tended to boost the standing of internal auditing, as we shall explore in Section 3.3.

3.3 THE "AUDIT IMPLOSION", THE INNER WORKINGS OF ORGANIZATIONS, AND THE EMERGENCE OF PIECEMEAL ASSURANCE

We suggested in Section 3.2 that the audit society is often narrowly associated with just one of its manifestations – the audit explosion. If that were the case, public perceptions of the trustworthiness of auditing and therefore of auditing's contributions to aggregated social trust would be disheartening. But the capaciousness of the audit society concept captures a far broader range of considerations. In this section, we shall review Power's notion of an audit implosion that has occurred in tandem with the audit explosion. While auditing and other assurance mechanisms have been exploding in volume, the center of gravity of assurance activities has been relocating (or, in Power's idiom, imploding) into hitherto unexplored regulatory spaces inside organizations. The audit implosion has entailed "competitive transformations of elements of auditing practice to service a more explicitly regularized inner space of organizations" (Power, 2000a, 22). Through a provocative and at first sight contradictory explosion/implosion dichotomy, Power has depicted quantitative increases in the volume of auditing alongside significant qualitative shifts in the increasing internalization of regulatory, compliance, and auditing activities in the inner workings of organizations.

In contrast to the erosion of socio-economic trust implied by the audit explosion, the audit implosion has entailed the emergence of alternative trust mechanisms. With the gradual seeping away of the significance of the external auditor's opinion on annual financial statements, stakeholders have been increasingly trusting the type of auditing that takes place within institutional domains. This of course reflects the rise to prominence of internal auditing, alongside other forms of assurance. The internalization of assurance mechanisms "suggests the necessity of trust between strangers remote from each other in space and time who must rely on the representations of the other" (Power, 2007, 39). Internalized auditing and assurance can therefore be perceived as a kind of moral technology that promotes social trust, and the same might also be said of the internal controls that are subjected to these assurance activities. In Power's words, internal control "is now much more than a collection of control routines and tests – it sets the ethical 'tone' of the organization, and is the formal manifestation of trustworthiness" (Power, 2007, 49).

If this account is correct, the center of gravity of accountability in institutional governance shifted around the turn of the millennium from external perspectives of organizations to their inner workings. From the 1990s, corporate governance codes like the British Cadbury Report (1992) and the series of South African King Reports on Corporate Governance (from 1994) have emphasized the importance of ongoing assurance on the reliability of internal controls. In the United States, Section 404 of the sharp-toothed Sarbanes-Oxley Act of 2002 raised stakeholder interest in internal controls to new levels. Gradually, inexorably, the gaze of stakeholders has shifted away from the financial auditor's opinion on annual financial statements toward auditable spaces within organizations. (Moreover, as discussed in Sections 3.4 and 3.5, an increasing emphasis on the "riskification" of auditing and internal controls has embedded risk frameworks inside organizations, thereby creating new internal auditing demands.)

Although the external auditor's opinion on annual financial statements has loosened its centrality to institutional governance, it has nonetheless retained a residual importance for stakeholder confidence. A modified external auditor's opinion can have a shattering effect on an organization's credibility, but the overall significance of the periodic opinion on financial statements has been eclipsed by demands for contemporaneous internal auditing. The internal auditor is no longer the "poor cousin" of the financial auditor. Instead, she has moved to the forefront of institutional governance. This trend has gone a small part of the way to meeting Power's hope, expressed at the end of his small think tank book, *The Audit Explosion* (Power, 1994a, 49), as follows:

> we need to reposition audit as a local and facilitative practice, rather than one that is remote and disciplinary, so as to enable rather than inhibit public dialogue ... This will require a broad shift in control philosophy: from long distance, low trust, quantitative, disciplinary and ex-post forms of verification by private experts to local, high trust, qualitative, enabling, real time forms of dialogue with peers. In this way we may eventually be in a position to devote more resources to creating quality rather than just to policing it.

Auditing has become more localized and closer to "real time" assurance today, with the shift of emphasis from external auditing to internal auditing. And "ex-post forms of verification" have been mitigated by the trend of "riskified" auditors looking forward to risk prevention. But Power's hopes for the future of auditing as a constructive social dialogue have not yet been achieved: Internal auditing remains damagingly quantitative, painfully low in trust, and stubbornly driven by claims to professional expertise rather than by inter-peer dialogue. All these areas have seen not only little improvement since the turn of the millennium, but rather a consolidation of undesirable traits. The demoralizing and dispiriting impacts of the audit society continue to be a wound on the civic order.

Nonetheless, the shift of emphasis from external to internal auditing is still in progress and has yet to be fully worked out. The Institute of Internal Auditors (IIA) has provided clarity to this volatile auditing space through its Three Lines Model (first published in 2013), a concept based on military (or sporting) analogies that envisions concentric layers of risk management activities and risk-mitigating internal controls within organizations. Management is responsible for the first and second lines. The first line relates to the operation of day-to-day internal controls, and the second to monitoring and compliance. Internal auditors provide the third line of assurance. Put differently, the first, managerial line owns risks; the second, managerial line oversees risks; and the third line of internal auditors advises on risks. In 2020, the IIA dropped reference to the term "lines of defense", to discourage an unduly risk averse focus. Subsequently, although the word "assurance" has often substituted for "defense", the phrase "three lines of defense" has remained in currency. (Some commentators have added additional lines for external auditing, regulation, and other forms of assurance.)

The Three Lines Model differentiates managerial responsibilities from internal auditing. Organizational managers design, maintain, and monitor systems of risk management and internal control, and internal auditors provide opinions on the effectiveness and efficiency of these systems. Organizations seek to coordinate the three lines to encourage a comprehensive coverage of risks, while eliminating duplications and overlaps in coverage. The model's delineation of responsibilities provides a framework for ongoing conversations on matters like whether the second or third lines should take primary responsibility for the documentation of internal controls for Sarbanes-Oxley Section 404 purposes. Various actors – including internal auditors, quality systems engineers, and compliance specialists – continue to jostle to achieve pre-eminence within these competitive and lucrative professional spaces, rubbing shoulders as they seek ever-firmer footholds in their quest for power and wealth. Rittenberg and Covaleski (2001) provide a compelling overview of the competition between in-house and external providers of internal audit services at the turn of the millennium.

The process of internalizing auditing within organizations may already have reached its high tide mark. As we saw in Section 2.5, new forms of contemporaneous assurance have been emerging to meet fresh demands for accountability at and beyond organizational borders. Therefore, in addition to the struggle for competitive advantages among assurance providers within organizations, we should also bear in mind the ongoing emergence of new, competitive forms of peripheral and extra-mural assurance.

If the foregoing analysis is correct, the notion of an audit implosion offers a partial corrective to the troubling implications of the audit explosion. It suggests a potential means of rehabilitating public trust in institutions, by constructing new bridges of trust between stakeholders and various organizational players. However, with new forms of assurance already emerging to meet the demands for accountability at or beyond organizational borders, the audit implosion already has an outdated feel.

Turning now to the topic of the ways in which the institutional internalization of auditing might shape as well as reflect the matters it addresses, internal auditing has a transformative impact by making its objects auditable (Power, 2003), and this transformative impact may distort institutional objectives and incentives. Organizations have increasingly shifted to meet the demands of auditors, to make themselves more "structured to conform to the need to be monitored" (Power, 1994a, 8). Auditing often "in highly reductive ways ... shape(s) organizations to be receptive to, and aligned with, auditing and evaluation processes" (Power, 2022a, 4).

In boiling down complex realities into quantifiable measurements, internal auditing may distort institutional objectives and create perverse incentives. We may see "acute problems for anxious managers, who, much like their former Soviet counterparts, will need considerable creativity to manage auditable performance favorably in the face of objective decline" (Power, 2000b, 115). Moreover, the internalization of auditing in organizations has tended to drift in the direction of a focus on second-order rather than primary activities. The result is that organizations are wasting time by responding to simple-minded and sometimes distorting performance measures unrelated to their core activities.

The "emergence of quality assurance from an industrial production context ... require[s] that organisations and their sub-units establish objectives, design performance measures to reflect those objectives, monitor actual performance and then feed the results of this monitoring back for management attention" (Power, 2000b, 115). Quality auditing focuses not solely on the integrity and accuracy of the verification and reporting of performance measures – it assesses the integrity of the quality system loop as a whole. This focus becomes a kind of "control of control", with a focus on second-order rather than primary activities. For example, external auditors place reliance not only on the outputs of internal auditors, in terms of their findings and recommendations – they also place reliance on the integrity of the internal audit process. This is, quite simply, the auditing of auditing. Process become paramount as primary activities fade into the background.

On a more positive note, and contrary to the implications of the audit explosion, the audit implosion suggests that trust is being handed over to organization themselves. Although there is potential unfinished business for internal auditing in the growth of accountability demands on and beyond organizational boundaries, the internalization of assurance through internal auditing has increased social trust in institutions.

3.4 THE "RISKIFICATION" OF AUDITING: THE HISTORICAL BACKGROUND

Power's critique of Enterprise Risk Management (ERM) is as sharp and troubling as his critique of auditing. ERM refers to any attempt to undertake an all-encompassing, holistic, integrated, and strategic approach to identifying and "managing", through elimination, mitigation, transfer, or acceptance, the perceived threats to (and their potential impact on) an institution's achievement of its objectives. Power has described ERM as "suggestive of a bird's eye view of organizational life", and as a discourse existing "at the interface between regulators, finance specialists, insurers, and accountants" (Power, 2007, 67 and 68). (Of course, he might well have added internal auditors to this list of key players within the panoptic purview of risk-based institutional governance.)

Before we consider Power's contributions to understandings of risk in the context of auditing and wider institutional governance, we may allow ourselves a short digression to consider the development of the concept of organizational risk, and how it relates to trust. If we accept Rachel Botsman's definition of trust as a "confident relationship with the unknown" (Botsman, 2017, 2), we may ponder how to access knowledge of the unknown. Navigating the knowledge gap between what is known and what is unknown is difficult, and in some cases impossible. Risk, therefore, is inherently mysterious because of an epistemic or knowledge gap. Quite simply, "what the future state of the world will be is always principally unknown, precisely because it does not yet exist" (Sztompka, 1999, 19). This existential truth has always haunted the human imagination. For many, the notion of not being able to assess, let alone control, future risks is an affront. Yet the faith placed in ERM models sometimes resembles a superstitious belief, contributing as much to the taming of risk and uncertainty in an organization as the nailing of a talismanic horseshoe to an organization's front door. Indeed, even advocates of ERM concede that much of what passes for ERM is "no better than 'astrology'" (Hubbard, 2020, xiv).

Modern institutional risk management did not emerge from a vacuum. It is the latest manifestation of trends over the past two centuries in the ways institutions have understood and come to terms with risk and the unknown. For example, the British physician John Snow (1813–1858), a pioneer of risk assessment, researched medical hygiene in nineteenth century London. He is best remembered today for his mapping of London's "Broad Street cholera outbreak" of 1854. He found a concentration of cholera cases around a public water pump and, although he could not yet fully explain the reason for the water pump's connection to the cholera outbreak (as the cholera bacterium had yet to be discovered and its water-borne nature had yet to be understood), he persuaded the local authorities to remove the pump. The cholera outbreak subsequently eased off. At the time cholera was largely assumed to be transmitted as an airborne disease, but Dr. Snow's evidence highlighted the pump and its water as a contamination risk (a good example of evidence-based risk assessment), and the pump's removal was a major contribution to public health (a good example of risk management).

Dr. Snow's work illustrated that risk management need not involve a complete understanding of the issues at stake in order to be at least partially effective. On the basis of his evidence, Dr. Snow intuited that water quality was linked to cholera outbreaks, and he went on to amass comparative data for different water pumps. Decisive proof of his suspicions lay in the future: It was only in the late 1860s that the risks of cholera and other diseases arising from poor water quality were properly understood, from which point the population of London was advised to boil potentially contaminated water. Today we remember Dr. Snow as one of the founders of scientific epidemiology (Hempel, 2007). We might also remember his work as a precursor of modern, evidence-driven risk management.

In the early twentieth century, American economist Frank Knight (1995–1972) stressed the need to differentiate between risk and uncertainty in a way that still carries influence. He portrayed risk as measurable, and therefore amenable to quantification and attempts to assess and act on it. In contrast, uncertainty was not measurable and it therefore demanded qualitative responses, thereby problematizing attempts to assess it (Knight, 1921). This differentiation between risk and uncertainty is still widely considered to be valid: "when one speaks of uncertainty one refers to situations in which the individual knows the outcomes of … choice[s] but not the probabilities involved" (Maldonato and Dell'Orco, 2011, 45), and it has become part of mainstream ERM discourse (Hopkin and Thompson, 2022, 15). There is, therefore, an acknowledged realm of uncertainty beyond calculable risk. But even within the categories of risks subjected to probability calculations, we should be prudent – the abstraction or reduction into numbers of complex future contingencies may be misleading. Knight considered all one-off decisions to be made under conditions of uncertainty, while only large numbers of similar decisions could be subjected with validity to probabilistic inference.

Moving closer to the present day, a series of catastrophes punctuated the late twentieth century, and these events appeared to have encouraged the formalization of ERM. The deadly horrors of the Union Carbide gas poisoning in Bhopal, India in 1984; the Chernobyl nuclear disaster in Ukraine in 1986; the Piper Alpha oil platform explosion in 1988; and the Heysel and Hillsborough football stadium disasters in 1985 and 1989 all had in common the realization that human error, procedural shortfalls, negligence, and outright mismanagement had caused or contributed to the disasters. In other words, the disasters should all have been preventable, had the relevant risks been assessed and addressed.

Moving into the early twenty-first century, a series of Islamist terrorist attacks around the world (including the United States in 2001; Bali in 2002; Beslan, Russia in 2004; London in 2005; and Mumbai in 2008) contributed to demands for more effective actions by governments to protect their citizens. Following these events of mass murder, the instability caused by the financial crisis of 2008, arising from the collapse of markets for collateralized debt obligations, of which half of the collateral was based on unsafe mortgages in the United States, almost led to a collapse of the international financial system. Again, it seemed to many, these events might have been preventable, had they been subjected to careful risk assessment and appropriate planning. Dr. Snow's evidence-driven risk assessment hovered over these catastrophes like a counterfactual specter of what might have been done to prevent or minimize them.

Stimulated in part by these disasters, and by notions of a "risk society" that we shall discuss below, ERM arose and solidified its position as a central plank of organizational governance. The rise of ERM in turn created new demands on, and expectations of, auditors. Sector-specific risk management initiatives took place – for example, the Basel Committee on Banking Supervision issued a series of accords on banking regulations, starting in 1988, with recommendations on minimum capital requirements. More broadly, ERM became the touchstone of a new approach to organizational governance, in both the private and public sectors. In 2004, the Committee of Sponsoring Organizations of the Treadway Commission (COSO) issued a rather limp but influential document, *Enterprise Risk Management – Integrated Framework*, to complement its already well-established *Internal Control – Integrated Framework* (that had been published in 1992 and was later updated in 2013). In 2017, COSO updated its 2004 guidance in its document *Enterprise Risk Management – Integrating with Strategy and Performance*. Another influential source of guidance has been the ISO 31000 family of risk management standards of the International Organization for Standardization, first published in 2009 and revised in 2018. New narratives of good governance were increasingly conveyed through the language of risk.

A frequently encountered justification for ERM is that, in today's high-risk society, we face hazards more acute and more fast-moving than in the past. An internal auditing text of 2024 claims that "[s]ince the first edition of this book was published in early 2021, the world has experienced one of the most consistently disruptive periods in its history" (Chambers and Pérez, 2024, xii), and they adopt the term permacrisis (i.e., permanent crisis), a commonly encountered buzzword that indicates a world lurching from crisis to crisis. It is undeniable that risks are no longer easily localized and containable: For example, in our globalized world of mass international transport, viruses (literal and metaphoric) are transmitted quickly and dangerously. In our digitalized era, risks may crystallize and spread through a handful of mouse clicks. This perspective of increasing risks may be correct, but we should prudently assess such claims through historical lenses. Is the severity of today's risks really far worse than in the past? The ahistorical tendencies of the modern internal auditor are a hindrance to understanding our present challenges: In the words of economic historian Niall Ferguson: "Never in our lifetimes, it seems, has there been greater uncertainty about the future – and greater ignorance of the past" (Ferguson, 2021, 1). To correct this weakness, let us glance back to 1923, 100 years prior to the first drafting of Chapter 3 of this book.

In 1923, the world was still coming to terms with the devastation caused by the international Spanish Influenza pandemic of 1918 to 1921, which infected a third of the world's population and killed probably more than 50 million people worldwide. (The term Spanish Influenza is misleading, as it is now thought that the disease originated in a military facility in the United States.) Overstretched public health systems in 1923 were still struggling globally to cope with the aftermath of the pandemic. Meanwhile, in politics, in a world still recovering from the carnage of World War One and from the upheavals of the Russian revolution, political extremism and violence were flourishing. In the previous year, 1922, the Fascist Party of Benito Mussolini (1883–1945) had seized power in Italy following his Blackshirts' March on Rome. Mussolini's successful power grab inspired far-right groups across Europe. As we mentioned in Section 3.1, in southern Germany in 1923, a small, unsuccessful *coup d'état* by an upstart political grouping made the news, but at the time few realized the extent of the threat to the future world posed by the fledgling National Socialists led by Adolf Hitler (1889–1945).

In addition, economic risks were alarming in 1923. The storm clouds of the Great Depression that would hit the global economy from 1929 were already gathering, and hyperinflation was rampant in Germany. An exchange rate in 1923 of more than a trillion between one unit of the German currency and the US dollar indicated that the former was effectively worthless. Newspapers published photographs of German citizens pushing wheelbarrow-loads of their debased currency to purchase a loaf of bread. The French government, seeking to enforce German reparation payments relating to World War One, sent its troops to occupy the Ruhr Valley, among the most heavily industrialized areas of Germany. The economic chaos of 1923 and the subsequent years was a major factor behind Hitler's rise to political power in 1933, with all the horrible consequences of World War Two to follow. Both contemporaneous and retrospective "risk assessments" of the interconnected politico-economic risks of 1923 would arguably identify risks far greater than the claims of proponents of today's-world-has-never-been-riskier arguments. In the words of the Austrian writer Stefan Zweig (1881–1942): "I have a pretty thorough knowledge of history, but never, to my recollection, has it produced such madness in such gigantic proportions [as in 1923]" (cited in Ullrich, 2023, ix).

One might object that 1923 is an unfair comparison, in that it was an exceptionally dangerous time in the world's history. Let us then glance back a mere 50 years, to 1973. In that year, the Cold War between the Soviet bloc and the United States and its allies was at its peak, with the threat of mutual nuclear destruction hanging over the world, and with superpower proxy wars unfolding in Africa and elsewhere. President Richard Nixon was promoting in 1973 the Paris Peace Accords that were to put a halt to the United States' combat involvement in the long-running Vietnam War. But, as Nixon sought peace in South East Asia, he was engulfed by the political earthquake of the Watergate Scandal, resulting in his 1974 resignation from office. To the time of this writing, Nixon has been the only US President to resign from office, a reflection of the magnitude of the 1973 political crisis. In economics, the Organization of Petroleum Exporting Countries (OPEC) retaliated against the industrialized Western countries over their support for Israel in its victory in the 1973 Arab-Israeli (or Yom Kippur) war. The resulting "first oil shock" (the second oil shock was to occur in 1979, following the Iranian Revolution) saw a deliberate restriction of oil supplies, driving the price of oil damagingly high for the global economy to handle. The consequence was economic devastation throughout the major industrialized economies, nowhere more so than in the United Kingdom. The British oil-induced recession would last officially until 1975, but the oil shock rocked an already weak economy and the effects reverberated for many years. The problem of "stagflation", a combination of a sagging economy and high inflation, lasted even beyond the 1979 election of Margaret Thatcher (1925–2013) as British Prime Minister. In the aftermath of the oil shock, the actions taken by the British government were unprecedented in peacetime, including a three-day working week (effective from January 1974), in which commercial organizations were provided with only three days' supply of weekly electricity. The slide of the enfeebled British currency was halted only by an emergency loan from the International Monetary Fund (IMF) in 1976. In addition, the United Kingdom faced in 1973 escalating civil unrest and terrorism originating from sectarian conflict in Northern Ireland.

One might still protest that 1973, like 1923, was an unusually "risky" year. Let us then go back 150 years, to 1873. In that year, the events known to history as the "Panic of 1873" saw severe economic turmoil across Europe and North America. The effects of economic recession lasted for several years, perhaps two decades in the British case, where it was called the Long Depression. In the United States, where more than 100 banks failed as a consequence of the 1873 panic, the events were known as the "Great Depression" until the economic collapse of 1929 eclipsed them and stole that title. Around the world, trends toward protectionism and high tariffs resulted from the 1873 panic. Meanwhile, with the post-Civil War Reconstruction era in the United States coming to an end, several states (including Florida, Kentucky, Tennessee, and West Virginia) passed "Jim Crow" laws in 1873 to mandate racial segregation in public establishments and in civic life generally. These events were part of a traumatic socio-political history of racial oppression whose consequences are still felt today.

This brief historical excursus shows, perhaps, that today's world is not necessarily inherently more risky nor more hazard-filled than in the past. Only our ahistorical attitudes deceive us into thinking so. Too many internal auditors and ERM specialists, unmoored from history, deceive themselves into a narrow conception of risk as a newly relevant phenomenon, thereby undermining the intellectual legitimacy of ERM. The modern world only *seems* more volatile, chaotic, and unpredictable than in the past. In the words of Onora O'Neill:

> Those who saw their children die of tuberculosis in the nineteenth century, those who could do nothing to avert swarming locusts or galloping infectious disease, and those who struggled with sporadic fuel shortages and fuel poverty through history might be astonished to discover that anyone thinks that ours rather than theirs is a risk society.
>
> *O'Neill, 2002, 16*

Ahistorical perspectives may explain, at least in part, why ERM activities often express a certain naivety and, at worst, a mild collective paranoia. They may also suggest why carefully constructed ERM models often fall apart when ambushed by realities (like the COVID-19 pandemic) they fail to predict. Nonetheless, it is true that modern communications are unparalleled in history in terms of facilitating the rapid spread of information and risk. Perhaps only the *velocity* (rather than the nature) of risk has been the most significant risk-related change in the modern era.

3.5 THE "RISKIFICATION" OF AUDITING AND THE AUDIT SOCIETY

We now turn to assess Power's contributions in this area. The concept of the audit society places a significant emphasis on the "riskification" of auditing, alongside the "riskification" of one of auditing's main objects – internal controls. As in other areas, Power was prescient: He anticipated the trend of organizing uncertainty "in auditable form" (Power, 2007, 165). It is now taken for granted that internal auditing is closely intertwined with risk. In the words of a prominent internal audit practitioner: "I am often asked for the one piece of advice I would give to someone new to the internal audit profession. The answer has been the same for almost two decades: follow the risks" (Chambers and Pérez, 2024, 1).

Power connected the notion of the "risk society" developed by German sociologist Ulrich Beck (1944–2015) to both the audit society and ERM. Beck conceived of the risk society as a post-industrial, reflexive modernization that imposes decisions on society's participants, both collectively and individually: "The axial principle of industrial society is the distribution of goods, while that of the risk society is the distribution of 'bads' or dangers. Further, industrial society is structured through social classes while the risk society is individualized" (Beck, 1992, 3). Beck's original German work, translated into English as the *Risk Society*, was published in 1986, in the same year as the Chernobyl disaster. The popularity of his analysis was connected to the alarm unleashed in Europe by the environmental catastrophe in Ukraine. But the impact of Beck's analysis has been wider and deeper than the influence of Chernobyl might suggest: He presented a strong case that the dispersion of risks today is less constrained and less structured than in the past, and their consequences are potentially more far-reaching.

Risks, he argued, "can no longer be limited in time – as future generations are affected. Their spatial consequences are equally not amenable to limitation – as they cross national boundaries" (Beck, 1992, 2). In the risk society, individuals struggle to insulate themselves from the hazards that surround them. In addition, Beck also drew attention to the importance of knowledge in confronting risks, and he warned that both the awareness and understanding of risks are often distorted by media bias.

Owing to Power's dual interests in risk and auditing, Beck's concept of the risk society overlapped with, and provided a background to, the development of the audit society. Power was undoubtedly prescient in terms of risk: It is no exaggeration to assert that risk has become a root phenomenon of modern internal auditing. Risk and internal auditing seem irrevocably intertwined. In particular, internal auditing's relations with ERM are crucial to the auditable inner spaces of organizations that, in the audit implosion (Section 3.3), are increasingly both a setting and a justification for internal auditing. Scherz (2022, 3–4) identifies two main uses of probabilistic risk predictions – in decision making, and in the rationality of policy development. "Riskified" internal auditing and ERM have elements of both uses, aiming to provide guidance for future action as well as promoting policy interventions to address future uncertainties.

In Power's work the parallelism of auditing and risk is reflected in similar assessments of both activities. As might be expected, Power does not uncritically accept the claims made by the advocates of ERM. To the extent that auditing frequently appears to be a social palliative that provides hollow comfort certificates and empty assurance, tending toward "a cosmetic response which hides real risk" (Power, 1997, 123), he perceives that ERM, in parallel, might often have a palliative effect, contributing little or nothing to the authentic reduction of organizational risk and uncertainty. Faced by decision fatigue, or general anxiety, we tend to run impetuously to the sanctuary of ERM, there to create illusions of mastery over risk and uncertainty through spurious notions of quantifiable risk mitigation. While ostensibly symbolizing good governance, ERM often seeks to dispel real or imaginary threats via pseudo-scientific approaches of limited value.

At its worst, ERM acts as an insubstantial, ghostly place-holder for creative thinking. Or it resembles a talisman – an object of faith wielded to ward off criticism. ERM discourses of rationality and objectivity explain away, rather than explain, institutional vulnerabilities. The pseudo-scientific attitudes to risks in many modern organizations resemble the fears of a superstitious character in an Isaac Bashevis Singer (1903–1991) short story: Hurrying past dark and spooky woodlands on the bleak winter plains near Warsaw, a credulous individual fears the ghouls, goblins, and dybbuks hidden among the gnarled trees, waiting to curse or kill unwary passers-by. Singer's character is unable to confront the risks posed by the woodland spirits – he can only pass by, hoping to remain unscathed.

Power has suggested that ERM, like internal auditing, often possesses the faults for which it purports to be a remedy. In capturing the anxieties and aspirations of the senior officials of an organization, ERM has little more to offer than "rational myths of controllability" (Power, 2007, 185). Modern organizational attempts to come to terms with risk are therefore frequently often a "bureaucratic defence against anxiety or disorder" (Power, 2007, 97). To counter the defensive tone of much ERM discourse, the "riskification" of internal controls and especially the ERM process is often cast as an opportunity to add value to organizations as much as to mitigate risks. However, despite the rhetoric of risk-originated opportunities, ERM has remained essentially defensive. Power explains these tendencies in terms of the existence of "a functional and political need to maintain myths of control and manageability, because this is what various interested constituencies and stakeholders seem to demand" (Power, 1994b, 10). We accept risk-based internal auditing and ERM not necessarily for their alleged truths, but for the illusory power they confer on those who promote them. But a risk model that claims to totally conquer uncertainty is an illusion. Or a deceit.

Power may be correct in suggesting that ERM is essentially defensive, driven above all by a wish to minimize reputation risks. "Reputation, reputation, reputation! Oh, I have lost my reputation! I have lost the immortal part of myself, and what remains is bestial" (*Othello,* Act 2, scene 3). The words Shakespeare placed in Cassio's mouth have echoed down the centuries as a heartfelt cry for those who feel shame and disgrace. The preservation of a good reputation is fundamental to the human condition, and reputations are highly vulnerable to danger. In Colin Mayer's words, "reputations take years to establish and seconds to destroy" (Mayer, 2018, 154). In modern organizational life, the exposure of senior officials to legal liability goes hand in hand with their reputations, and ERM is often seen as a protective shield against such dangers.

Overall, ERM (and related risk-based auditing practices) are often over-simplistic and disconnected from reality in their unattainable desire for certainty and control. Agglomerations or combinations of small risks may lead to major risks, but our risk models may fail to capture the creeping dangers of risk accumulation. Our self-deception arises from not recognizing that ERM's over-tidy models detract from the real uncertainties facing organizations. For example, a Black Swan event (i.e., a random event with catastrophic impact) can upset many a carefully crafted risk model. The coiner of the term Black Swan event has suggested that the problem goes beyond the event itself to cover our "blindness" to it, and has described a risk model that excludes the possibility of a Black Swan event as having "no better predictive value for assessing the total risks than astrology" (Taleb, 2010, xxviii and xxiii). The analogy of astrology reappears frequently in our discussions of risk and ERM.

An unforeseen Black Swan event therefore typically smashes to smithereens a tidy risk model. For example, "the bell curve ignores large deviations, cannot handle them, yet makes us confident that we have tamed uncertainty" (Taleb, 2010, xxix). Major risks to institutions are perhaps governed more by power laws and Poisson distributions than by normal (or indeed any traditional) probability distributions. The Black Swan event, as a bewildering, unforeseen catastrophe, is completely random. Meanwhile, In contrast, the political commentator Thomas Friedman (born 1953) has coined the term "Black Elephant", a combination of the Black Swan and the phrase "elephant in the room", to designate a major problem of which everyone is aware but which nonetheless remains unaddressed (cited in Giroux, 2017, II:177). And, continuing with the animal metaphors, Michele Wucker's term "Gray Rhino" designates a "dangerous, obvious, and highly probable event" (Wucker, 2016, 8). All these metaphors point to weaknesses in typical ERM models.

ERM is not only frequently disconnected from the surrounding reality, but also from the structures of our mind. It has been suggested that

> the difficulty in deciding and facing up to uncertainty is not only linked to the inadequacy of the architecture of our minds but also to an 'external' model of uncertainty which does not correspond to the way in which our mind naturally functions.
>
> *Maldonato and Dell'Orco, 2011, 92*

In addition, as other perceptive commentators have noted, risk deals not only with facts, but also with values: risk analysis entails "claims about facts (what might happen) and claims about value (what might matter)" (Fischhoff and Kadvany, 2011,1). Facts and values are inseparable but are often not treated as such in the cold analysis of ERM practices. In particular, as Paul Scherz has suggested, humans are now "treated as the objects of probabilistic analytics that use the same mathematical tools deployed to describe physical objects like gas molecules ... people [are] envisioned as predictable objects through the lens of natural science" (Scherz, 2022, 84). Ferguson (2012, 9) suggests five categories of "malpractice" in relation to disaster management and, perhaps by extension, to ERM: "1. Failure to learn from history. 2. Failure of imagination. 3. Tendency to fight the last war or crisis. 4. Threat underestimation. 5. Procrastination, or waiting for a certainty that never arrives".

Power's critique does not mean that ERM cannot be implemented in a manner that is helpful to an organization. He has acknowledged some advantages of ERM: It pulls together considerations of risk and uncertainty, processes and internal controls, strategy, and auditing. ERM therefore demolishes internal organizational barriers through a "de-balkanization" effect (Power, 2007, 98). ERM is in a unique position to pull together the connections between various topics. When done effectively, the "riskification" of strategy, performance, internal controls, and the auditing process has the advantage of focusing the attention of an organization's senior management on potential adverse events and conditions, and encouraging value-focused decision-making. Too often, ERM focuses excessively on dangers rather than on embracing uncertainty as one element among many in decision-making for the achievement of organizational objectives. In Paul Scherz's words, "risk assessment can be an extremely valuable tool when it is understood as an aid for counsel rather than as a calculation that dictates decisions" (Scherz, 2022, 102).

A successful ERM program is likely to use a range of risk indicators to record, measure and analyze outcomes for the topics it addresses. For example, Fischhoff and Kadvany (2011, 33–36) recommend for environmental risk assessments a suite of indicators, to mitigate the dangers of over-simplification that tend to arise from applying single measures to complex systems. Thus: "water quality at a treated sewage outfall might be measured by dissolved oxygen available to aquatic life, peak water temperature, dissolved and suspended solids, alkalinity (pH), and pesticide residues ... [with] observations over finer timescales ... and areas". This suite of indicators should promote a synthesis of risk information, rather than isolated building blocks of risk analysis. Such a synthesis of evidence is only possible if modern risk assessment methodologies deploy disciplined methods of critical reasoning. In addition, organizational risk appetites are likely to be multi-faceted, with multiple attitudes to risk within an organization, instead of a single number, nor even a number at all for more qualitative risks (Mungaray, 2017). For instance, administrative or back office functions are likely to have different risk appetites than operational, profit-seeking front offices: The cautious assurance of the former probably sits uneasily with the operational embracing of risks.

A composite assessment of a range of risks, assessed qualitatively as well as quantitatively, is therefore likely to be central to a successful ERM program. Other traits of a successful ERM program are likely to be a nuanced, imaginative, non-dogmatic approach, founded on dialogue, focused on managing the effects of uncertainty on the organization's main objectives (both COSO and the ISO 31000 standards emphasize the impact of uncertainty on objectives), and informed by (but not a hostage to) internal auditing. In Power's words: "There is a need to design soft control systems capable of addressing uncomfortable uncertainties at the limits of manageability which are not hostages to logics of auditability" (Power, 2007, 201).

Too often, however, the practices of modern risk assessment are harmful, not helpful, to organizations. Approaches to ERM convey an unwarranted belief in the predictability of events, as though Laplace's infamous "demon" has returned from the mists of time to haunt and deceive the modern era. Pierre-Simon Laplace (1749–1827), the genius polymath who first developed the methods of inductive reasoning that would later underpin the Bayesian interpretation of probability, posited a powerful intelligence (dubbed a "demon" by later commentators and critics, but not by Laplace himself) that was capable of predicting all past and future possibilities. Laplace's arguments in favor of a strict causal determinism suggested that, with complete knowledge of the laws of nature and the state of the universe, every detail of the future is predictable. Laplace placed in the Western mind not only the notion of the existence of a strictly objective knowledge, but also the notion of the precise predictability of everything. Laplacean causal determinism has been disproved (by quantum mechanics, for example), but its predictive aspirations continue to hold a strong fascination for many. The discourses surrounding risk assessment often, in their naivete, invoke Laplace's notions of understanding through deterministic routines, rather than the interpretative engagement for enhanced decision-making that we should be seeking. In other words, we have yet to exorcise Laplace's discredited "demon" of determinism.

In summary, ERM, like internal auditing, relies on and provides symbols of control, order, and stability. ERM and the riskification of internal auditing and internal control attempt to inspire confidence in organizations by masking the fact that many uncertainties are beyond our control. Put differently, ERM doesn't necessarily improve the "management" of uncertainty – instead, it sends a signal that an organization that uses ERM is a well-ordered institution that deploys its resources to rational ends. How we approach risk reveals a lot about ourselves: Risks "provide windows into how societies express and define themselves" (Fischhoff and Kadvany, 2011, 1). The explosion of auditing that started from the 1980s, and the spread of modern organizational risk theory from the 1990s, have combined with ambiguous results. Internal auditing has absorbed risk considerations in a rather uneasy manner. For Power, the interweaving of the audit society and the "risk society" leads to an uncomfortable situation in which auditing and ERM both tend to fall short of delivering what they promise. Their roles, both jointly and separately, appear to serve more as a social palliative through a deceptive sense of certitude, rather than to provide accountability and effective risk mitigation. In his words: Auditing is situated "at the boundary between the older traditional control structures of industrial society and the demands of a society which is increasingly conscious of its production of risks" (Power, 1994a, 6). This implies that internal auditing's focus on ERM and on the encouragement of organizational infrastructures to quantify risk and performance might sit badly with the vestiges of internal auditing's compliance orientations, left over from its heritage in traditional, command-and-control structures.

ERM fits more comfortably in organizations whose activities are readily quantifiable – in financial services, and insurance. We should therefore resist an unwarranted faith in the tools of risk assessment and ensure they do not become an end in themselves rather than a means to an end. An imaginative approach to risk "would need to be decoupled from an industry of managerial and auditor certifications, and auditor certification of these certificates, which are the very antithesis of an intelligent, honest and experimental politics of uncertainty at the organizational level" (Power, 2007, 201).

Just as the volume of internal audits perhaps provides an impression of comfort amid chaos, the integration of risk and internal auditing seems to convey a message that risks are *controllable* through internal auditing. Perhaps we still need the modestly conceived but effective approach to risk of Dr. Snow.

3.6 AUDITING AS RITUAL

In what appears to be an overarching concern in the audit society, Power has warned of the dangers of auditing becoming not a means to an end (providing assurance on accountability in the context of information and power asymmetries) but rather a hollow end in itself. In spreading its palliative effect through society, auditing may slide into a self-referential activity of limited practical utility. As Power puts it: "The audit society ... endangers itself because it invests too heavily in shallow rituals of verification" (Power, 1997, 123). The subtitle *Rituals of Verification* of Power's *The Audit Society* suggests the centrality of ritualism to Power's arguments.

Power is right to inform us that the audit as "an organizational ritual, a dramaturgical performance" (Power, 1997, 147) is not entirely meaningless, owing to its palliative purpose. It has "the character of a certain kind of organizational script whose dramaturgical essence is the production of comfort" (Power, 1997, 123). As Power has implied, we might legitimately expect more from auditing in delivering a practical contribution to social trust. Applying Power's ideas to internal auditing, a ritualistic internal audit conjures images of an activity of limited value and ambition, with unimaginative, dull results. A ritualistic internal audit might therefore create no more than an impression of orderliness and serve simply to produce empty assurance. Philosophers, psychologists, sociologists, theologians, and animal behaviorists have all acknowledged the importance of ritual in collective life. And our preliminary questions should include how to view ritualism in internal auditing. Is ritualization creative or conservative? Valuable or worthless? Power and others (e.g., Pentland, 1993) seem to discern little of value in ritualistic auditing, beyond its function as a palliative social mechanism. Such an analysis, if correct, points to a collective self-deception, and to a misallocation of social resources. Like Lewis Carroll's Cheshire Cat that gradually disappeared until nothing was left but its grin, will internal auditing fade away, leaving behind only the melancholy fragments of empty, worthless rituals? Or is a ritual a valuable means of integrating individuals into social and organizational realities?

The notion of a ritual serving to dissipate anxiety rather than to solve underlying problems is not new. It is widely recognized that illusions of problem solving provide comfort to a ritual's participants and observers, and this may extend to a sense of social belonging. In his 1930s novel *Brave New World* Aldous Huxley describes the effects of a ritual on one of his characters: "Hers was the calm ecstasy of achieved consummation, the peace, not of mere vacant satiety and nothingness, but of balanced life, of energies at rest and in equilibrium" (Huxley, 1932, 86). As Huxley suggests, rituals can create a sense of balance that serves communal purposes. (In the context of *Brave New World*, the rulers of an authoritarian society seek to pacify any possible dissent from their machine-like system of reproducing humans.)

Power's portrayal of the ritualized futility of modern auditing through the use of a dramaturgical metaphor echoes on occasion throughout the internal auditing literature (e.g., Gustafsson Nordin, 2023). It also reflects the characterization of the United Nations' General Assembly by the Irish intellectual and former United Nations staffer Conor Cruise O'Brien (1917–2008). O'Brien envisioned the importance of the diplomatic and political ritualism of the General Assembly as residing less in its ability to reach practical decisions than in its function as a quasi-theatrical, institutional setting in which frustrations are vented and dissipated, achieving a kind of dramaturgical catharsis. In O'Brien's words, the United Nations is the setting "of verbal nationalist contending, of ritual confrontations and ritual retreats, of dramatic supplications and sanctified concessions, [that] represent ... our best hope of reducing danger in recurring crises" (O'Brien and Topolski, 1968). In this case, ritualism is perceived as having value in terms of informal conflict resolution or, at a minimum, as a safety valve to release anger.

Building on the sociological and mythological analyses of Emile Durkheim (1858–1917) and Mircea Eliade (1907–1986), some of most insightful writings on ritualism focus on spiritual and transcendental aspects. Rituals can be used by participants to aim for larger or higher sources of meaning. Ritualized prayer is an obvious example, from the Eucharistic rituals of Christianity to the various forms of Hindu *puja* (worship). By analogy, internal auditing rituals, through their repetitive nature, might remove us from the here and now, and project us briefly into higher, timeless, transcendent realms of truth in which we fleetingly glimpse perfection. In such ritualistic moments, we go beyond the squalor and desecration of the temporal order. While internal auditing ritualism might serve such lofty goals, it strikes us as highly unlikely, to say the least, that individuals would seek transcendent enlightenment through internal auditing rather than through existing, established spiritual channels.

There is also hint of magic in many rituals: Perhaps, like conjurations lifted from *grimoires* (medieval spell books), the utterances in internal auditing rituals operate at an aspirational, non-scientific level, to falsely reassure or provide comfort in alleviating our social anxieties. If this line of thought is correct, the tendencies toward ritualism in internal auditing may be deemed unhealthy, insofar as they are essentially escapist, and detached from socio-economic reality, as Power has warned us.

Alternatively, rituals may be considered not so much magical as purificatory. Many religious rituals – like fasting and symbolic washing with water – aim to cleanse adherents of their spiritual impurities. The ritualism of internal auditing might, therefore, symbolize a purging of impurities from our social and economic lives. The participants in a ritualistic internal audit may seek the achievement of a collective purity through the elimination of socio-economic transgressions. If this were true, the rituals of internal auditing would seek to overcome a fear of desecration by providing symbolic opportunities for the purging of corruption, falsehood, error, crime, and greed, and to safeguard what is sacred. However, just as we found implausible the notion of individuals seeking transcendent insight through internal auditing rituals, this interpretation appears to grant an unwarranted spiritual significance to internal auditing rituals.

We may conclude that, although internal auditing's ritualism may be allegorized as a practice saturated with spiritual significance, such notions are at best suggestive rather than conclusive. To many, such suggestions might seem palpably absurd. For internal auditing, more convincing analogies are likely to be found in down-to-earth collective rituals. Some rituals seem to arise from our genetic endowment. We tend to dismiss analogies between human and animal rituals, as we generally prefer to insist on a profound differentiation between humans and animals. We are, however, part of the natural order, and we probably share with animals a bio-sociological inheritance of somatic rituals as a response to social life. The figure-eight pattern of the honeybee's "waggle dance" communicates to other members of the hive the location of useful resources like flowers and water. The honeybee's ritualized dance therefore serves a functional purpose. Of course, the waggle dance of a honeybee is genetically imprinted, and it is not really a dance at all, as it lacks the creativity, intentionality, and choice in human dancing. But it is difficult to dismiss entirely the overall comparison.

Let us push our consideration of the biological aspects of ritualism a little further. There are intriguing parallels between the pre-combat rituals of some animals with the ritualized pre-fight violence between (often drunken) young men. With humans, the pre-combat engagement often starts with initial eye contact, leading to hard stares, aggressive words, and snarls. Taut faces, wide-armed posturing to augment one's size, and circling, stalking movements precede the antagonists' invasion of the other's space, to engage in chest- or forehead-bumping (Miller, 2008, 42). These ritualized gestures resemble the behavior of combative cats, with their belligerent eye contact; intimidatory wailing and spitting; aggressively arched backs to appear larger than normal; slow-motion circling movements; and fierce displays of teeth and claws. And here we can identify an interesting commonality in the ritualized, pre-combative contest displayed by young men and cats: The ritual is often sufficient to encourage one of the parties to back down unscathed, saving bloodshed. One of the parties slinks away with hurt pride and perhaps a territorial loss, but without wounds. These rituals have a functional role in diffusing actual combat and, reflecting O'Brien's observations, they therefore serve as a ceremonial negotiation to seek conflict resolution and to restore peace. (Sometimes, of course, a genuine fight follows such behavior.)

Our example of recurring patterns of pre-combative formalities suggests that ritualism is as important for quotidian social life as it is for aiming at the heavens. Some rituals might serve esoteric purposes, while others have a functionalist role in our day-to-day lives, from reducing conflict to strengthening social bonds. For internal auditing, therefore, we might most profitably explore ritualism as a socializing tool in the context of down-to-earth, daily existence.

In our daily lives, rituals serve to inculcate values and to establish and maintain collective frameworks of meaning (Rappaport, 1999). Rituals have been described as "public, emotionally salient, formalized behavioural practices, bringing actors together and communicating shared social means" (Islam, 2016, 542). There are instances in which the meanings of rituals are not immediately obvious. For example, it has been suggested that the marching drills performed extensively in military institutions serve little practice purpose for combat. Their value resides instead in their role of creating bonds of cohesion and solidarity among soldiers (Xygalatas, 2022, 99). Sigmund Freud (1856–1939) suggested that "when members of a group perform a repetitive act together, the individual becomes part of a larger, synchronized whole, at least for that moment" (cited in Davis-Floyd and Laughlin, xii). In the case of internal auditing, ritualism perhaps fosters a similar sense of solidarity for internal auditors, and reinforces the cohesion of that community. The internal auditing community consists, for the most part, of those who share a belief in the value of internal auditing, and a voluntary participation in ritualism implies consent with the beliefs symbolized in the ritual.

Internal auditing rituals thereby inculcate beliefs in the distinctions authorized both explicitly and implicitly by internal auditing's social purposes, namely the differences between corruption and honesty, and falsehood and truth. Additionally, by patterning behavior into predictable channels to outside eyes, they also through "impression management" send a broader message of social cohesion between internal auditors and the wider society (Pentland, 1993, 608 and Smieliauskas et al., 2021, 29).

Impression management operates on observers through visibly predictable ways of dressing, behaving, and communication.

If this line of argumentation is correct, we may conclude that rituals not only synchronize the actions of their participants – they also penetrate the participants' collective cognitive processes. Rituals may thereby serve community cohesion and the cementing of social bonds by the transmission of shared values. In other words, internal auditing rituals provide didactic as well as social functions. The didactic element instructs internal auditors on the values of their activities and supplies models for behavior. Rituals thereby encourage the flourishing of internal auditing principles and actions, perhaps in a more authentic manner than is achieved through the formal, committee-created, written standards of professional associations.

If we accept that a ritual is a "patterned, repetitive, and symbolic enactment of cultural (or individual) beliefs and values" (Davis-Floyd and Laughlin, 2022, 6), we may endow a positive significance to internal auditing rituals. Internal auditing, however debased and formulaic in its current prevailing practices, contains in its quotidian rituals the roots of a potential renewal. Rituals preserve and transmit internal auditing's values in our increasingly value-neutral, postmodern world, and these values seem to resonate deeply with the ritual's participants, perhaps below the threshold of consciousness.

Pulling together our thoughts, Power appears to be on to something when he writes of the ritualization of auditing. He is also on to something in perceiving that ritualized auditing acts as a socio-economic palliative and a collective surrender to illusions. Such illusory practices perform a social function through a shared alleviation of anxiety. And ritualism tends to be self-reinforcing: A ritual gains its significance through cycles of repetition. Rituals impose discipline on, and provide solace and consolation to, both participants and observers. We therefore have no hesitation in agreeing with Power that the main task of ritualism is to console us amid our current socio-economic chaos. Nonetheless, while recognizing this consolatory effect of ritualism, we can say more about the possible interpretations of internal auditing rituals. Rituals arise and persist because they satisfy deep-seated fears, values, and aspirations. Rituals are rich in ambiguity, and although a ritual can be understood in many ways – as action, celebration, performance, embodied intelligence, negotiation, symbolism, and as a means of transmitting knowledge – they tend to re-enchant the world and, at least symbolically, to reconcile competing interests and judgments. The rituals of internal auditing are perhaps a mechanism that confirms the adherence of internal auditors to values of truth and honesty. Those who engage in ritualistic audits do not merely minister a form of deceptive comfort to those in socio-economic distress – they are preserving and transmitting an enduring vision of internal auditing aligned with safeguards against crime, error, and corruption.

Internal auditing rituals therefore offer more than we might expect from Power's depiction of a mechanistic, hollow sham. They promise channels for cultivating both continuity and change within defined communities of internal auditors (and among those in contact with internal auditing). They keep our cultural memory of internal auditing alive for future generations. As one scholar of ritual has claimed: "Ritual is serious business; it is not mere performance, not mere play" (Stephenson, 2015, 88). Ritualism may be perceived as an interactive social activity, consisting of an unending unfolding of reciprocal gestures and meaning: "Rituals transcend us in three senses: they outlive us; we are socialized into them rather than creating them ourselves; they regulate our behaviour" (Whitehouse, 2021, 10). The public rituals of internal auditing create a special space of privacy without imprisonment. in which to connect to other internal auditors – dead, living, and as yet unborn.

The aspiration to perfection of ritualized internal auditing may be an antidote to the haphazardness of life. This remedy may also act as a refuge during the unsettling paradigmatic shifts in accountability and social trust that we suggested (in Chapter 2) are currently taking place. The repetitive and formulaic rituals of internal auditing contain clues as to the core "meaning" of internal auditing, a path of knowledge available only to those perceptive individuals who can interpret, even implicitly, the rituals' significance. The rituals of internal auditing bestow a kind of artful intimacy on its practitioners, refining aspects of psychology and personality in addition to technical knowledge. Rituals therefore might have the capacity to repurpose internal auditing to meet the emerging assurance demands of fragmented and redistributed flows of accountability. In short, they contain the seeds of a possible future renewal of internal auditing.

3.7 WIDER STILL AND WIDER: NEW DIRECTIONS FOR THE AUDIT SOCIETY

The auditing literature is not generally noted for its engaging tone, but Power has conquered new heights of both substance and style in communicating his concept of the audit society. Through refined and elegant books and articles he has articulated a critique of auditing that, in the current author's view, has never been satisfactorily refuted. Power's writing, with its many-layered complexity and its unique combination of philosophical insight and hard-hitting argumentation, is a pleasure to experience. But it is far more than an aesthetic experience – his arguments on auditing have captured the imagination of many auditors and its influence in the academic community is extensive (e.g., Bebbington and Larrinaga, 2024; Bottausci and Robson, 2023; Jeacle and Carter, 2022).

Power's analysis of auditing was prescient. The notion of the audit explosion foresaw the unremitting proliferation of auditing and audit-like activities of limited value. Three decades later, the flood of over-auditing has swollen to gargantuan proportions. Similarly, Power's concept of the internalizing of auditing and related accountability mechanisms within the inner spaces of organizations, in the audit implosion, has been borne out by events: It is a process, not without both problems and promise, that is still unfurling. Internal auditing has been a notable beneficiary of this trend. And Power's expectations of a continuing riskification of auditing and wider institutional governance have been correct.

Our institutions, in the audit society, have been subjected to a swollen tide of internal auditing and other assurance mechanisms, involving a vast investment of time and resources, the opportunity costs of which are impossible to calculate. Riskified internal auditing (and its cousin, ERM) are often little more than palliative responses to our present and future anxieties. It may be argued that auditing in general, and internal auditing in particular, act more to obscure accountability than to improve it. The Dutch architect-philosopher Rem Koolhaas (born 1943) has suggested that a "new trinity is at work ... liberty, equality, and fraternity have been replaced in the 21st century by *comfort, security*, and sustainability" (cited in Scherz, 2022, 60, emphasis added). By generating a tsunami of empty comfort certificates, against a backdrop of failing institutions and socio-economic chaos, internal auditing's role as a soothing social medicine doesn't cure anything, but rather diverts attention away from dangerous socio-economic pathologies. We are increasingly reacting to the fickleness of fortune by searching for consolation in riskified internal auditing and the hollow assurance it generates. This can hardly amount to a satisfactory role for internal auditing in promoting social trust. Moreover, as internal auditing's palliative effects satisfy the hunger for comfort and security identified by Koolhaas, internal auditing is forfeiting characteristics of enduring importance, as we explore throughout this book. Internal auditing's ossified ways of thinking may turn it into a curiosity, an outdated oddity like a steampunk movie with quaint images of a bygone era.

If our bloated auditing and assurance regimes genuinely improved organizational performance or civic society more widely, then our toleration of them might be justified. But, at the time of the writing of this book, and to the consternation of internal auditors and the public alike, economic instability abounds, the pollution of our environment worsens, crime continues to rise, educational standards continue to fall, and public finances are stretched to breaking point in the United Kingdom, the United States, and elsewhere. The onus is on the defenders of our assurance regimes to explain the positive contributions of internal auditing and other assurance mechanisms. It seems legitimate to respond to our socio-economic chaos and widespread institutional decline by questioning the ability of current arrangements to safeguard accountability and social trust.

We therefore accept Power's broad analysis, and its application to internal auditing's current malaise. We also suggest ways in which the audit society is already developing in new directions. Above all, for our purposes, we suggested in Chapter 2 that internal auditing is likely to face a future of marginalization. To the extent that traditional, bureaucratic systems of accountability will persist, internal auditing (and, for that matter, external auditing) will continue to provide the preeminent methods of assurance in such environments. However, in wider terms, the real action for accountability and social trust will be elsewhere, distributed in horizontal patterns across digital and human networks. The overarching framework of accountability and social trust is shifting dramatically on its axis, and internal auditing is struggling to adapt to this paradigmatic change. The center of gravity of organizational governance imploded in the early twenty-first century, as Power foresaw, in the sense of shifting inside organizations, and now the center of gravity of accountability and social trust is on the move again – this time toward peripheral and extra-mural spaces. Internal auditing's entrenchment in the inner workings of organizations leaves it ill-placed to address the growing assurance demands on and beyond organizational boundaries. (Perhaps the very name "internal auditing' might act as an impediment to the growing need for internal auditors to reorient their attention to the edges and outer spaces of their organizations, as it suggests an unyielding, inward-looking focus.)

Although Power's concept of the audit society has influenced many, it also caused a backlash from less visionary auditors and academics. In 2000, in his essay *The audit society – second thoughts*? (Power, 2000b), Power expressed "second thoughts" about the audit society, downplaying some of the radicalism of his earlier arguments. For the "audit explosion" specifically, he assessed it in the following terms: "though successful in the sense of striking a chord in public policy discussions, [it] posed more questions than it answered" (Power, 2000a, 2). This leaves us to ponder why we seem still to be struggling fully to articulate the relevant questions, let alone provide the answers.

Power also agreed in his "second thoughts" paper with some of his critics that more empirical evidence was warranted to substantiate the audit society. He even went so far as to claim that the greatest value of the audit society concept rested not so much in itself, but in its use as a springboard for ideas. One is reminded of the self-description of Plato's Socrates (in *Theaetetus*), not as the possessor of truth and wisdom, but rather as an intellectual "midwife" assisting others to produce (or "give birth to") truth and wisdom. I suspect that Power, like Socrates, was perhaps conceding too much ground to his critics: The audit society concept still contains more value than simply an ability to stimulate further reflection and research. In addition, Power appears to have underestimated the depth and duration of the "audit explosion", assessing 30 years ago that it was "likely to be a passing phase" (Power, 1994a, 41). On the contrary, the proliferation of auditing and verification activities throughout civic life has continued relentlessly to the present day. The audit society remains relevant to our understandings of the social impact of auditing. In particular, as Power foresaw, the erosion of social trust in our institutions has extended to auditing itself. As we have suggested in Chapter 2, internal auditing has struggled to keep up with the ongoing paradigm shifts in flows of accountability and social trust. We appear to be losing faith in one of the principal mechanisms that provides the assurance needed for social trust – internal auditing itself.

It is not in the nature of a philosopher like Power to rest content with his conceptual achievements. In recent years he has revisited the original audit society and proposed revisions to the concept. In an essay titled "Afterword: Audit Society 2.0?" he has written of a new era for the audit society, driven by developments in digitalization, and in which there is a blurring of the boundaries between accounting, security, and surveillance (Power, 2022a). In this essay, and in "Theorizing the economy of traces" (Power, 2022b) he also considers the implications of Zuboff's "surveillance capitalism" (see Section 2.3). The profile and purposes of auditing might be undergoing change:

> consumers and the public are very far from being digitally empowered to hold organizations to account. Rather, each of their online traces is a source of valuable data or 'digital exhaust', which is captured for both economic gain and enhanced social control.
>
> *Power, 2022a, 5*

And he proposes "the analysis of [digital] traces and traceability as a basis for reframing the audit society agenda" (Power, 2022b, 2).

Arising from Power's work, we have identified a source of optimism for a future escape for internal auditing from what ostensibly might appear to be a symptom of its death-knell. The ritualization of auditing suggests *prima facie* a hollow activity of limited practical value, and even a deceptive outcome of false assurance that acts as a socio-economic palliative. However, ritualism can also be understood as a social practice that preserves, nurtures, and transmits enduring values across time and space. If ritualism successfully protects and nurturing the essential truths of internal auditing, it might contain the seeds of internal auditing's future renewal.

Power's brilliance cut pathways through the murky conceptual undergrowth of auditing, and we still walk today along these pathways. The theory of emerging, piecemeal assurance in response to patterns of peripheral and extra-mural accountability that we have developed in this book owes an immense debt to Power's work on the audit society.

Chapter 4

The erosion of professional virtue in internal auditing

4.1 PROFESSIONAL EXPERTISE AND THE PUBLIC GOOD

The division of labor in complex social settings necessarily requires us to turn to professional expertise. From food safety to the reliability of financial statements, and from environmental pollution to engineering principles in bridge construction, we as individuals lack the time and knowledge to arrive at reliable judgments. We therefore place our trust in the expert knowledge of individuals organized into the collective associations of the modern professions.

Some sociologists (e.g., Burns et al., 1994, 87–92) identify two broad paths to defining a profession – an "intimidation" model and a "shopping list" model. The former involves an assessment of the extent of a would-be profession's menacing power arising from the cruciality of its services and the possession of a sublime, threatening mystique. The intimidatory model does not appear to be closely relevant to internal auditing. It is perhaps more suited to professions whose services possess a make-or-break or life-or-death cruciality that might form the basis of threats: Examples are an external auditor bullying a recalcitrant client with threats of issuing a modified audit opinion, and a physician's use of frightening-sound jargon to browbeat a patient into submitting to a course of treatment. Internal auditing does not normally possess a heightened cruciality comparable to such instances. The "shopping list" model, consisting of the application to a would-be professional association of items in lists of typical traits of a profession seems a more suitable approach for internal auditing.

Sociologists (e.g., Kultgen, 1988, 60) have identified as many as 20 traits of a profession. We shall consider some of these traits in this chapter, but we shall argue that only two traits are necessary for professionalism – expertise and a commitment to the public interest. The remaining traits are of secondary importance. As Andrew Chambers put it, nearly half a century ago in the context of internal auditing, "autonomous expertise and the service ideal are perhaps the most distinctive attributes of a profession" (Chambers,

DOI: 10.1201/9781032664880-4

1980, 273). For our purposes, therefore, and at the cost of some simplification, we may affirm that the co-existence of expertise and altruism provides the necessary (though perhaps not sufficient) basis for a professional activity like internal auditing.

The concept of professional expertise usually implies that the expertise derives from a largely abstract body of knowledge and the possessor of the abstract knowledge is capable of applying that knowledge in practice. The importance of applying expertise tends to be reinforced by the requirements of professional organizations for extensive education and certification processes (and continuing development) that explicitly blend theoretical knowledge and practical experience.

Another important characteristic of professional knowledge is the assumption that a profession's knowledge is hard-earned. It is therefore common for the knowledge base of a profession to be perceived as "*exceptional* expertise" (e.g., Saks, 2021, 2, emphasis added). As the ancient Greek physician Hippocrates (approximately 460–370 BCE) suggested, "life is short, but the acquisition of knowledge takes a long time" (an aphorism generally known to English speakers through its Latin translation, *vīta brevis, ars longa*). It is not everyday knowledge that a profession deals with, but rather a type of esoteric knowledge acquired only by lengthy and arduous study and practice.

Another characteristic of professional knowledge is that it is cumulative: It is not merely a matter of mastering a defined body of knowledge at a fixed point in time, but rather of mastering a foundation of expertise upon which further experience and study accumulates. Lifelong, steady accretions of knowledge acquisition tend to be encouraged: The professional associations of auditing typically required their members annually to confirm (and if necessary provide confirmatory evidence) that they have kept up to date with developments in the field.

In terms of professional expertise in auditing, the authority of an auditor's work and opinions is presumed to derive from a mastery of a formal body of auditing knowledge. This mastery carries powerful social signals of professionalism. Flint has suggested that the

> auditor's opinion must carry authority if it is to have a special utility: if it did not carry sufficient unquestioned authority, it would add little to the unaudited information already available ... there must be confidence in the technical competence, reliability and integrity of the auditors.
>
> *Flint, 1988, 45–46*

Flint highlights here not only reliable technical competence, but also integrity. The notion of integrity points to the second necessary trait of a profession – a commitment to serve the public interest. A profession (or would-be profession) with serious deficiencies in either expertise or altruism would fall short of the mark of an authentic profession in the public's eyes, and undermine "the sanction of the community" (Chambers, 1980, 273).

The co-existence of the two foundational characteristics of expertise and altruism is therefore crucial to professionalism. Altruistic intentions are insufficient without expertise. For example, we should surely give short shrift to the generosity of an individual offering *pro bono* dental services if he discloses that he has had no formal dental training. However public-spirited such an uncredentialled individual might be, it would be foolish to let him loose on our teeth. Similarly, to trust our legal affairs to a sincerely magnanimous individual who has never studied law would be the height of absurdity. A well-intentioned fool's altruistic commitment to the public good must be backed up by expertise. Such a fool does not therefore fit the description of an authentic professional in the sense we understand in this book.

In like manner, we may acknowledge the athleticism and window-breaking skills of a cat burglar, the technological proficiency of a hacker, or even the rigorous attention to detail of a banknote counterfeiter. But, in all such instances, we withhold our approval: The professional criminal's expertise is undermined by the absence of an ethos of public service. Instead, professional criminals are motivated by greed and self-enrichment. Professional expertise therefore must be backed by a commitment to the public good. A professional criminal does not therefore fit the description of an authentic professional in the sense we understand in this book.

Secondary traits of professions include tendencies toward legally sanctioned monopolistic control over their markets; a high social status; publishing programs both to convey their expertise and to raise public awareness of their expertise; and even a self-deprecating sense of humor. On the latter, as the current author has suggested, "we should take seriously any profession that can laugh at itself" (O'Regan, 2024, xii). We shall discuss some of the secondary traits as we proceed. Yet we may assert with confidence that expertise and a commitment to the public good are the foundational traits of a profession. We shall look a little more deeply into both these traits, and how they relate to modern auditing, in Sections 4.2 and 4.3.

Before we proceed, however, we should address three potential problems in relation to our characterization of the necessary attributes of a profession. The first problem is that any credible, professional individual or institution must possess not only good intentions in relation to both expertise and altruism, but also the capability of simultaneously demonstrating these two characteristics. In other words, it is inadequate merely to declare an aspirational commitment to these principles in written standards or codes of ethics. Professionalism goes hand in hand with practicality. In what follows, we shall constantly keep in view the importance of professional pragmatism. The second problem is that professionals must reliably exhibit, on a continuing basis, their expertise and commitment to the public good. Sporadic evidence is unlikely to convince the public of professional intentions – a demonstrable reliability is crucially important, and we may discern here the outlines of the Aristotelian concept of virtue as cultivated habits that we shall explore further in Section 4.3. The third problem is the well-established critique of alleged hypocrisy in the professions.

The third of our three problems is the most damaging to the claims and credibility of professions. An entrenched narrative in the sociology of professions is the self-interest and greed of professional organizations as they seek to achieve and maintain an elevated socio-economic status. Professions typically operate in competitive fields of activity in permanent flux, and they selfishly seek to dominate the market for their services. Sociological critics (e.g., Abbott, 1988; Macdonald, 1995) portray the professions as erecting barriers to entry through stringent certification requirements and the use of legislation to monopolize control of their activities. Financial auditing tends globally to be undertaken by the members of professional associations like the institutes of Chartered Accountants and Certified Public Accountants, whose monopoly rights are enshrined in law. By encouraging demand for their services, limiting the supply of qualified individuals, and achieving monopolistic control over their markets, it is argued that the professions are rent-seekers (in the general economic sense of the term, meaning those who seek profits above normal levels through rigged markets and manipulations of supply and demand).

Sociological critiques of the auditing profession are profound and compelling. Nonetheless, a preliminary observation is in order. Allegations of professional greed and hypocrisy are points well taken, but a strong counter-argument is that a comfortable standard of living is reconcilable with a dedication to public service. For instance, physicians with specialist expertise often earn very high levels of income, but they have achieved their socio-economic status through years of difficult study and hard work. It can be argued that the physician's lifetime dedication to life-saving or life-enhancing knowledge, and to serving the public interest, warrants her material rewards. Of course, some physicians are lazy and incompetent, and some – like Josef Mengele (1911–1979) and the British general practitioner and mass murderer Harold Shipman (1946–2004) – are evil. But exceptional instances of scoundrels and mass murderers do not invalidate the value of a profession as a whole. The most trenchant denouncer of professional rent-seeking behavior is likely, faced with the prospect of the urgent removal of her appendix, to put aside her reservations over professional greed to be treated by a credentialled physician. The existence of murderous physicians, corrupt lawyers, immoral priests, cowardly soldiers, and incompetent auditors does not therefore undermine the concept of professionalism, provided that such rotten apples remain infrequent and do not constitute a generally bad harvest.

To deploy their expertise in the service of the public good, professionals need to exercise moral agency. Moral agency is an ability to rationally arrive at moral decisions, and to face accountability for those decisions. Professional associations should cultivate a space in which the moral agency of their members can flourish through flexible standards and practices that are sensitive to interpretation, inculcate a sense of personal responsibility, and promote sound judgment. In Section 4.2, we shall cast a critical eye at the nature of knowledge and expertise in modern auditing, but first we shall round off our general discussions of the fundamental attributes of professionalism.

The professions with the greatest antiquity are the "learned professions" of medicine, law, and divinity. This trinity of professions tends also to have a very high social status, except for perhaps the priest in our increasingly secular age. To this trinity of professions some would also add architect (Kultgen, 1988, 5) and the soldier (Uhlmann, 1998, 65), both professions of equally ancient pedigree. The Industrial Revolution witnessed a slew of new trade organizations seeking professional status, from engineers to bankers to auditors, but the true precursors of modern professions were medieval Europe's guilds. The guilds were proto-professions that cultivated expertise for centuries prior to the industrial age.

A digression on the guilds will illuminate some of the central themes of this book. Richard Wagner (1913–1883) gave us the most spectacular and enduring portrayal of the medieval guilds in his opera *Die Meistersinger von Nürnberg*, first performed in 1868. The opera, described by one of today's finest Wagnerian conductors, Christian Thielemann, as "the pivot and central point of Wagner's entire oeuvre" (Thielemann, 2016, 201), portrays a song contest undertaken by a guild of German "Mastersingers" in sixteenth-century Nuremberg, with the historical Hans Sachs (1494–1576), the most famous Mastersinger of his day, as the principal character. The Mastersingers are all experts in other crafts, and they have brought to song composition and performance an inflexible structure of precise rules and parameters. And, following the general tendency of rules and parameters that require years of dedicated training, their craft has fossilized into a pettifogging, nit-picking proceduralism.

In *Die Meistersinger*, Wagner contrasts the bourgeois guild's constrained and formulaic song craft with the more creative, passionate, and beautiful song of Walther von Stolzing, a newly arrived, impoverished aristocrat. Walther's musical expertise derives from traditional sources and an intuitive aesthetic sense, rather than from a guild's rule book (*Am Stillen Herd*). In guild terms, he is a non-conformist and a rule-breaker. A committee of plodding, unimaginative guild members, but not Sachs, resent and deride Walther's song – in truth, they lack the capacity to understand and appreciate the song's beauty, so blinkered are they by their checklist approach to the song-craft rules. Hans Sachs, however, is open to innovation. Rattled by the beauty of Walther's song, his reflections in Act Two on the song's merits, under the perfumed elder tree near his cottage (*Was duftet doch der Flieder*), provide one of the most profound and beautiful literary meditations. Sachs determines to use Walther's innovations to rejuvenate the guild's jealously protected song framework. He alone discerns in Walther's untrammeled creativity the possibility of refreshing the tired path of committee-constrained tradition, thereby opening the door to a new and loftier beauty. (In contrast to Walther, Sach's apprentice David is a future committee-man in the making – an unimaginative dawdler from whom nothing remarkably creative can be expected.)

So what can the modern internal auditor learn from Wagner's Hans Sachs? *Die Meistersinger* explores the tensions between reliable yet rigid structural frameworks and individualistic creativity. The contrasting themes of conformity and individualism, beauty and mediocrity, and conservatism and innovation resonate down to our day. Modern professions with prescriptive, inflexible standards stifle the creativity of their members. The practitioners of such professions are constrained by checklist-ticking and algorithmic processes that suppress their moral agency. Rather than carefully incorporating creative innovations, intransigent professional structures exclude them entirely. Modern internal auditing has been moving in the direction of the Mastersingers' comically stifling rigidities.

In the opera's closing scene, Sachs reveals his philosophy: Walther's creativity has succeeded in rejuvenating the guild, but only by operating in a manner consistent with the traditional mechanism of the Mastersingers' rules. Thus creativity need not be anarchic or destructive. Walther's effervescent spontaneity interweaves harmoniously with traditional structures, simultaneously confirming and improving them. In Sachs' guild, creativity therefore co-exists with a mastery of traditional forms. In relation to the themes of this book, the *Meistersinger* shows us how written rules are not ends in themselves, but rather channels of both stability and creativity. The Institute of Internal Auditors' (IIA's) *Global Internal Audit Standards* (GIAS) should therefore be flexible enough to accommodate change rather than acting to obstruct innovation. As we shall see in Section 4.2, the IIA's prescriptive standards fall short of achieving this balance.

A final word on the resonance of Wagner's opera with our themes. We need not sit through the four to five hours of the opera (depending on the conductor's choice of tempi) to grasp its meaning. For Wagner, music "did the talking" whenever words alone failed to convey his message (Vine, 2021, 2), and the ten-minute overture condenses the themes of the entire drama. The Mastersinger's gloriously grounded theme battles throughout the overture with Walther's strange melodies and harmonies. The two musical opposites alternate in a tense struggle for supremacy. Eventually they start to merge, first interweaving as separately identifiable entities before Wagner deploys the orchestra to fully reconcile them. Guild conformity and individual creativity are unified through the idiosyncratic contrapuntal complexities of Wagner's genius. The overture conveys, far better than words could manage, a thrilling blend of rules and creativity.

Internal auditing faces a more prosaic version of the dilemma Wagner reconciles through his music – how to balance the integrity of frameworks with judgment, creativity, and development. It is a topic we shall explore in more detail in Section 4.2.

4.2 KNOWLEDGE, EXPERTISE, AND INTERNAL AUDIT STANDARDS

Expertise, we have argued, is one of two necessary traits of a profession, the other trait being an altruistic commitment to the public good. We now take a closer look at the types of knowledge that underpin internal auditing, the practical mastery of which comprises the internal auditor's expertise. We also consider the significance and relationship to expertise of written professional standards. The main advantage of professional standards is their encouragement of consistent, uniform activities. They aim for reliable decision-making by individual professionals. However, four disadvantages of professional standards have been identified (in Myddelton, 2004, 96–109): (1) The stifling of professional judgment, (2) the discouragement of competition in ideas, (3) the legitimization of bad practices, and (4) a misleading of the public by unduly raising expectations of the quality of performance. We shall focus on the first of these weaknesses.

The tendency of professional internal auditing standards toward overly prescriptive requirements has narrowed our intellectual horizons. Overly prescriptive standards diminish judgment and petrify individual initiative and critical thinking. The shortcomings of "cookbook" professional rules, in providing only a limited number of "recipes" insufficient to cover every possible combination of circumstances, is widely acknowledged. A balance is needed – a professional framework should guide internal auditors in the exercise of judgment, rather than serve as a pretext for the shedding of moral responsibilities. Professional standards should therefore encourage internal auditors to see the universal principles in particular cases, and thereby to apply abstract principles to concrete examples. The balance to be achieved is between an amoral, method-driven type of knowledge contained in rules-based standards, and moral insight based on tacit customs and creative expertise promoted by principles-based standards.

We shall structure our discussion into three categories of knowledge – we may possess knowledge *of something* (e.g., "her knowledge of the IIA's Standards is thorough"); we may possess knowledge *of how to do something* (e.g., "she knows how to implement the IIA's Standards"); and we may possess knowledge *that something is the way it is* (e.g., "she knows that the inventory most at risk from shrinkage is stored in the overspill warehouse down at the docks") (Lenz and O'Regan, 2024, 19). The first category of knowledge (knowledge *of something*) is theoretical knowledge. Professional standards do not attempt to capture theoretical knowledge. On the contrary, the first category of knowledge is the abstract foundation on which professional standards are constructed. The second category of knowledge (knowledge of *how to do something*) is performative or applied knowledge. The third type of knowledge (knowledge *that something is the way it is*) corresponds to the evaluative expertise that derives from (and transcends) a blending of the first two categories of knowledge. It is in the third category, in the most sophisticated of our three forms of knowledge, that advanced expertise is to be found – this advanced expertise encompasses know-how, the interpretation of evidence, and the formulation of value judgments that underpin professional opinions. We shall argue that written standards are incapable of capturing the expertise that arises from the third category of knowledge, as it is too complex to be distilled into words.

Turning in detail to the first of our three categories of knowledge, the abstract knowledge base of a professional activity, we encounter an immediate problem for internal auditing. Other auditing specialties tend to have far more rigorous, abstract bodies of knowledge than internal auditing possesses. For instance, external auditing is based on double-entry bookkeeping; the accounting equation of assets = liabilities + capital; economic concepts of valuation; and the methods of abstracting accounting information into financial statements. The quality assurance of pharmaceutical products is grounded firmly in medical science. The knowledge base of election auditing is rooted in the mechanics of the political franchise. Royalty auditing is based on the dissemination (e.g., through sales of tangible items or the occurrence of events) of identifiable units of intellectual property. Environmental auditing is constructed on a range of "hard" sciences relevant to the sustainability of the natural world, including chemistry, ecology, oceanography, and zoology. In contrast to the preceding examples, we encounter a significant problem with the fuzzy and slippery knowledge base of the "Common Body of Knowledge" (CBOK) of the IIA.

At the time of this writing, the CBOK constitutes an ongoing project, started in 2015, that has generated a suite of reports mainly summarizing the opinions of practitioners and stakeholders. The CBOK is therefore founded, not on abstract reasoning, but on a consensus of opinions on the desirability of existing practices. To a greater extent than one finds in other specialties of auditing, internal auditing is an overtly social construct, in which a preponderance of opinions matters more than abstract facts. A far-reaching consequence of the CBOK's slippery knowledge base is that the ambiguities of internal auditing convey multiple meanings to different audiences and elicit ambivalent expectations from different stakeholders (Jokipii and Rautiainen, 2024; Roussy and Brivot, 2016). It was therefore to be expected that the levels of transparency in the IIA's exposure draft review for its 2024

GIAS were perhaps unprecedented among current professional bodies. The IIA's CBOK is founded on a body of knowledge that lacks cohesion, and transparency was the main mechanism of balancing opinions in the transformation of the CBOK into written standards.

One is reminded of the old joke of the definition of a camel as a horse designed by a committee. All committee-issued pronouncements require compromise and accommodations of conflicting interests, and all face the challenges of attempting to iron out inconsistencies without taking on unnecessary complexities or embracing logical flaws. Committee-designed camels arise from the attempted appeasement of irreconcilable ideas in the search for consensus. The GIAS exposure draft process focused on dialogue, compromise, and trade-offs, an inevitable consequence of consultations driven less by fact-gathering than by reconciling opinions. Owing to the GIAS's foundation on opinion-based rather than fact-based knowledge, the risks of producing a camel-like horse were greatly magnified.

The current author has suggested that the foundation of internal auditing's knowledge amounts to "a rather insecure and fragmented agglomeration of elements taken from management theory, accounting, information technology, legal topics, bureaucratic proceduralism, fraud awareness, corporate governance mechanisms, and risk assessment, bound together by logical assessments of the evidential material encountered in auditing" (Lenz and O'Regan, 2024, 18). More succinctly, Michael Power described the eclecticism of internal auditing activities as a "ragbag of tasks and routines in search of a unifying role or idea" (Power, 2000a, 18). The insecurity of internal auditing's knowledge base perhaps explains, at least in part, why the curriculum of the IIA's flagship Certified Internal Auditor certification is intellectually undemanding and reluctant to ask much from its students. Despite the many drawbacks arising from the elusive and obscure character of the IIA's knowledge base, the persistence of ambiguous and fuzzy knowledge concepts affords internal auditing a degree of flexibility and creative interpretation. The elasticity of internal auditing knowledge might even stretch to meeting some of today's emerging assurance demands arising from the new patterns of accountability and social trust we reviewed in Chapter 2. The elasticity of the IIA's underlying knowledge base has the potential to accommodate a wide range of opinions. It is not inevitable that the CBOK should result in inflexible, prescriptive standards.

Turning now to our second category of knowledge, performative or applied knowledge, we should acknowledge that this type of knowledge is the most translatable into written standards. However, capturing the complexities of knowledge in written professional standards is no simple task. The challenges facing the IIA in articulating its written standards should not be underestimated. A body of knowledge, like the IIA's CBOK, is an accumulation of concepts or, one might say, an inventory of largely socially constructed concepts. The purpose of the written professional standards is to arrange the CBOK into a formal, logical, coherent structure for practical purposes. By analogy, a pile of bricks does not make a house – it is the builder's arrangement of the bricks in logical and orderly patterns that is needed to construct a house. The primary purpose of the IIA's GIAS was to provide a coherent, logical arrangement of the raw materials of the CBOK's building blocks of knowledge, so as to create a credible, and socially acceptable framework for internal auditing practice.

The GIAS are part of the broader initiative of the "IPPF evolution project" (IIA, 2024a, 6), a revamping of the IIA's *International Professional Practices Framework* (IPPF) that began in 2021. The IIA issued its GIAS in January 2024, granting a year of adaptation and transition before the implementation date of January 2025. The GIAS are to be combined with Topical Requirements and Global Guidance to form an updated IPPF. (The older IPPF included, in addition to the then-in-force *International Standards for the Professional Practice of Internal Auditing*, a statement of the core principles of internal auditing; a definition of internal auditing; and a code of ethics.) Prior to the issuance in 2023 of an exposure draft of the GIAS for public comment, the IIA's IPPF Oversight Council issued a *Framework for Setting Internal Audit Standards in the Public Interest* (IPPF, 2022). This *Framework* cleared the ground for the subsequent work undertaken by the International Internal Audit Standards board (IAASB), the architect of the details of the revised standards, under the guidance of the IIA and the IPPF Oversight Council. Initial consultations on the proposed GIAS involved significant stakeholders, including the European Commission, the World Bank, and the U.S. Public Company Accounting Oversight Board, as well as the leading consulting and advisory firms (in IIA parlance, its "principal partners"). The IIA undertook a survey in 22 languages (IIA, 2024b, 9) in the public consultation of the exposure draft: The survey, and comments transmitted through other sources, resulted in approximately 19,000 comments that required analysis and assessment by the IIA. The levels of transparency in the review process were astonishingly high. Dealing in opinions is a tricky affair: It is little wonder, therefore, that public commentary on an exposure draft of the GIAS led, in 2023, to intensely emotional, idiosyncratic and polemical encounters, especially on social media platforms (Lenz and O'Regan, 2024).

In the words of the IIA's President and Chief Executive Officer at the time of publication of the GIAS, the IIA undertook "more than two years of research, outreach, and fine-tuning" after the realization that "our existing Standards, while robust, were struggling to keep pace with the ever-evolving nature of business and the accelerating pace of change" and, moreover, the changes went "beyond mere adaptation – it necessitated a bold and visionary reimagining of the Standards" (Pugliese, 2024). Major aspects of the changes have included a transition from the older structure of "attribute" and "performance" Standards to the arrangement of 52 of the revised standards arranged under 15 guiding principles, within five domains (although the first domain consists of only a purpose statement and covers no principles or Standards). In its *Report on the Standard-setting and Public Comment Processes for the Global Internal Audit Standards* (IIA, 2024b), the IIA explained how it addressed the comments it received, ranging from the prescriptiveness of some of the IIA's Standards' language to performance measures for internal auditing.

We have suggested that the professional platform for internal auditing expertise in the service of the public good has been hampered in recent years by the failure of the IIA's rules-oriented standards to cultivate the flourishing of their members' moral agency. The IIA has described the GIAS of 2024 as "principles-based", and it is correct that the GIAS grouped 52 standards under 15 principles. However, it seems disingenuous to claim that the 2024 GIAS are principles-based: The GIAS are *arranged by principles* rather than *arranged into principles*, and the principles in the IIA's Standards serve primarily as classificatory headings. The majority of the GIAS's text consists of a bloated inventory of rules and requirements. To this extent, one may argue that the role of principles in the GIAS resembles a layer of appetizing icing covering an otherwise unpalatable cake. Or, to use a different analogy, the GIAS are like old wine poured into new bottles (Lenz and O'Regan, 2024). Or, to return to our camel-as-committee-designed-horse metaphor, the use of principles as classificatory headings resembles the erratic placing of a camel-like hump on a horse's back. The outcome is clumsy and unpersuasive.

Reality is stubbornly indifferent to the prescriptive internal auditing standards, in which process takes precedence over substance. "Despite being widely and commonly criticized, box-ticking approaches persist because they correspond to a particular climate of auditability which pervades risk governance" (Power, 2007, 164). Prescriptive, checklist-based methodologies have serious flaws and their products, boilerplate reports, tend to be far from persuasive and, to many, untrustworthy (if not unreadable). Under such circumstances, individual judgment is downplayed and a collective opinionizing takes over. A socially negotiated group conformity encourages a narrow consensus of views, with a dampening effect on creative judgment. In the words of Dutch auditing theorist Theodore Limpberg Jr. (1879–1961), auditing "ought to be characterised by the application of intellectual effort and expert insight ... rather than by thoughtless reliance on established routine" (quoted in Camfferman and Zeff, 1994, 123–124).

At worst, as the auditor tries to fit reality to prescriptive professional standards, the activity of auditing becomes increasingly "Procrustean", in the sense of blaming reality for not fitting the auditing model. Procrustes, in Greek mythology, was a cruel bandit who forced his guests to fit into an iron bed – he stretched those individuals too short to fit the bed, and chopped off the legs of those who were too tall. In the words of Nassim

Nicholas Taleb, "we humans, facing limits of knowledge, and things we do not observe, the unseen and the unknown, resolve the tension by squeezing life and the world into crisp, commoditized ideas, reductive categories, specific vocabularies, and prepackaged narratives" (Taleb, 2015, xii). We may suspect that Procrustes would be happy with modern internal auditing's attempts to try to force reality into narrowly designated frameworks.

The third of our categories of knowledge is the evaluative expertise that arises from a blending of the first two categories of knowledge. This third category is more than merely the addition of theoretical and performative knowledge – it deals with expertise that is difficult, or perhaps impossible, to capture in written standards. This type of knowledge is too complex to be distilled into words, as it contains deep perplexities that escape easy articulation. The best we can hope for is to state the principles on which this expertise is founded, and leave the application of expertise to the creative judgment of the individual internal auditor.

We have already suggested that the GIAS are problematic, in consisting largely of rules-based requirement that dampen judgment in internal auditing. Auditing rarely involves cast iron guarantees: Auditors apply judgment – founded on knowledge, logic, and diagnostic skills – to both the selection and evaluation of audit evidence, to reach informed opinions. Written standards should provide a framework within which internal auditors can exercise critical thinking processes (including causal and probabilistic inference), assessments of evidential validity, the reconstruction of past events and transactions, and the evaluation of testimony and outside expertise. These processes culminate in an opinion on the coherence and consistency of all the evidence available for an audit. (The wide range of testing and judgment methodologies in auditing allows for occasional mistakes, favoring overall consistency over comprehensive accuracy as a means of reaching an opinion on the totality of the evidence.) A notable characteristic of judgment in auditing is that auditing is usually a time-constrained activity. It has been suggested that "time is of the essence in the collection of audit evidence and the formation of audit judgments" (Mautz and Sharaf, 1961, 95). Auditors tend not to make judgments at a leisurely pace, as they usually work in contexts of limited time in which to make sense of significant volumes of information (Dierynck and Peters, 2022). A cognitively busy auditor is like a circus performer dashing to and fro between spinning plates atop tall rods. Under such stressful conditions, expediency, heuristic thinking, and arbitrary decision-making may overwhelm critical reasoning. (It is here that the importance of the supervision of audit work by more experienced auditors can be appreciated as a corrective control.)

Various types of cognitive bias impact judgment in internal auditing. The dubious heuristic shortcuts commonly encountered include anchoring and adjustment bias, in which interpretations of initial information acts like a heavy metaphorical anchor on the mind, unduly influencing interpretations of subsequent information (Henrizi et al., 2020; Kahneman, 2011, 119–128); availability bias, that favors the interpretations and explanations that come most readily to mind; and recency bias, that places too much reliance on recent memories. These types of cognitive bias pressurize the auditor's rationalism (Chin, 2022), but they can be counterbalanced by careful logical reasoning. Logical reasoning refers to structured argument in the context of problem-solving. Logic is central to auditing: Mautz and Sharaf (1961, 192–193) went so far as to assert that auditing, even financial auditing, "has its primary roots in logic, not in accounting". Ratliff and Reding (2002, 1) suggested that "if there is a single secret of successful auditing, it likely lies in the concept of *persuasive evidence* ... [which in turn is] generally governed by the principles of logic" (emphasis in the original). Logic should therefore underpin an internal auditor's reasoning, so as to eliminate cognitive bias and logical fallacies. In other words, cogent reasoning should cement an auditor's knowledge and expertise. Reasoning is cogent when it is based on inductively strong and deductively valid arguments, supported by unambiguous terms and warranted premises. Here we are not talking of formulaic symbolic logic or the algorithmic logic deployed in information systems programming, but rather of traditional, humane logic (especially inductive logic) condensed into cogent arguments expressed through everyday language (O'Regan, 2024, 172–179). We shall return to the theme of logic in auditing in Section 6.7.

For internal auditors, there is no equivalent of the Hippocratic Oath and its exhortation of what has become the principle of *primum non nocere* ("above all, do no harm"). On the contrary, the technocratically focused and committee-sieved revision of the 2024 internal auditing standards seems to have deferred, rather than answered, the core questions of how to encourage a strong foundation for ethical judgment in internal auditing.

In addition to auditing-specific knowledge and expertise, the auditor should also possess a broader proficiency in historical and cultural knowledge, within which to frame judgment, interpretation, and wisdom. We shall argue that historical and cultural awareness are of immense importance for effective internal auditing. (The author provides, in Appendix A, a more detailed justification of the role of tradition, history, and cultural inheritance in the interpretation of our modern social environment, in a discussion of the philosopher Hans-Georg Gadamer's positive evaluation of the role of such matters in interpreting the world.) Our historical and cultural inheritance provides us with voices from the past that might guide us to a higher level of judgment and understanding. Historical and cultural literacy should not therefore be considered a luxury for internal auditors, but rather a way of equipping ourselves for higher professional achievement.

An example from the author's experience can elucidate what is at stake here. As a relatively junior internal auditor on assignment with a large, mainly anglophone team in Italy, he was surprised to hear from a colleague an intention to recommend a rationalization of an organization's branches throughout the Italian peninsula. The reasoning was as follows: The commercial, engineering-focused organization under audit had a dense network of service branches, often in relatively close proximity to each other. To an auditor more familiar with the vast surface area of the United States, the dense cluster of organizational branches made little sense. He perceived an opportunity for a radical, cost-saving rationalization of branches, consolidating service activities into a small handful of branches throughout the country.

In discussions of the proposed audit finding, it became clear that the auditor had very little or no understanding of the ways in which Italy's historical and cultural inheritance had created the conditions and requirements for the audited organization's dense network of branches. The author explained to his colleague how modern Italy's political unification occurred only in the second half of the nineteenth century, with the culmination of a complex diplomatic, military, and cultural process known as the national "Resurgence" (*Risorgimento*). Owing to its late unification, Italy has not undergone the centuries-long processes of national institution-building and the ironing-out of regional variations experienced by European countries like France and England. As a result, and notwithstanding the strong sense of Italian national cohesion – manifested for example in fanatical support for *gli Azzurri*, Italy's football (soccer) team – regional linguistic and cultural variations remain marked in Italy. The Italians refer to this tendency of local pride as *campanilismo*, a word difficult to translate into English – the often-used term "parochialism" has pejorative connotations of small-mindedness and insularity not necessarily implied in *campanilismo*. The Italian word derives from *il campanile*, the belltower that dominates traditional Italian towns, and it indicates a positive love of one's locality – a "humane localism" (Mitchell and Peters, 2018) – rather than a smalltown backwardness.

The author cannot remember if the draft audit finding was eliminated or toned down. But he remembers his colleague's surprise at the extent to which Italian *campanilismo* explained the audited organization's distribution of its activities. In northern Italy alone, residents of provinces like Piedmont, Lombardy, Liguria, and the Veneto often prefer to deal with service centers staffed by locals who share their dialect and understand the nuances of their regional cultural inheritance. It would be unreasonable to expect from all auditors a profound knowledge of cultural history. Yet the example from an audit in Italy of the importance of *campanilismo* illustrates how an ahistorical auditor may struggle to understand the context of an audit. Data sorting tools, materiality algorithms, and the other scientistic paraphernalia of modern auditing are blind to such matters. The more clockwork auditing becomes, the more philistine it appears to those subjected to audits.

Professional expertise, it should be clear by now, is more than a rote learning of prescriptive standards. The GIAS of 2024 are like a catechism – a doctrinal manual that tolerates no deviation and brooks no dissent. Instead, the processes of understanding and interpretation in internal auditing involve judgment, creativity, and critical thinking. We have argued that modern auditing standards are serving auditing poorly in these respects. We shall proceed, in Section 4.3, to consider the importance of professional virtue, which is dependent on situational and context-driven qualitative judgment as the ultimate foundation of professional wisdom.

4.3 VIRTUOUS INTERNAL AUDITING

Virtue is not a fussy, old fashioned, classical Greek or even Victorian construct. Nor is virtue a Western construct: The ancient literatures of China and India both emphasized the essential role of virtue in governing society. Confucius considered virtue to be the foundation and guiding light of socio-political order, and he compared virtue to "the Pole Star which commands the homage of the multitudes of stars without leaving its place" (*The Analects*, II:1, cited in Child, 2019, 22). The Hindu *Vedas* contain discussions of the importance of virtue and, closer to our time, Rabindranath Tagore (1861–1941) stated that "society is the expression of those moral and spiritual aspirations of man which belong to his higher nature" (cited in Dalton, 1993, 70). There are subtle differences of emphasis, between East and West, in the traditional virtues, but they share a common denominator of aspiring to social and political structures based on non-selfish, altruistic principles and excellences of character. The longevity of virtue ethics in public life therefore warrants our attention. As one commentator has observed: "Virtue ethics has a very long history – longer than any other tradition in moral philosophy" (Russell 203, 1). But let us start our review with a modern instance of how virtue ethics relates to internal auditing.

In December 2023, Pope Francis (born 1936) met representatives of the Holy See's Office of the Auditor General. In the meeting, the Pope drew attention to the importance of three central characteristics of auditing: Independence, attention to international practices, and professionalism. He also encouraged the auditors to administer their audits "with both firmness and merciful discretion" to address the "insidiousness of corruption" (Holy See Press Office, 2023). The Pope's advisory comments in favor of "merciful discretion" led to sneering social media reactions from some in the auditing community. They interpreted the phrase "merciful discretion" as a bullying misuse of spiritual and temporal authority to discourage the auditors from looking too deeply into fraud and corruption in the Vatican City.

The criticisms of the Pope's comments were indicative not merely of misunderstandings of the import of his humanistic message. They pointed to a broader decay in moral judgment in the internal auditing community. Internal auditors of narrow intellectual horizons, who adhere to the gritty literalism of written professional standards and the barren rigors of algorithmic auditing, seem incapable of comprehending the moral significance of judgment and critical thinking. The Pope's mockers misunderstood the phrase "merciful discretion" as both a call for an unwarranted deference to authority and an appeal to cover up corruption, but the message was, on the contrary, a call for a humane approach to auditing. The Pope's advice was a gentle rebuke to internal auditors who suffer from a narrow, scientistic faith in internal auditing's clockwork routines and a mechanical sense of right and wrong. To audit is a moral act: This was the Pope's overriding message. And "merciful discretion" directs our attention to an equitable form of justice that complements and tempers the sometimes poisoning effects of formulaic, mechanistic, and amoral auditing. The finger-wagging, checklist-beholden internal auditors who mocked the Pope would have benefited from trying to understand his humane advice. Ironically, it was a religious leader who reminded scientistically inclined auditors of their profession's humanistic inheritance.

The papal view of auditing as a moral act is a valuable springboard for our exploration, in this section, of the concept of virtue in internal auditing. We understand virtue to mean moral excellence – not morality in a religious sense (though that route to virtue is available to individual internal auditors), but rather from a secular, universal perspective. A profession like internal auditing that aims to contribute to social trust and our collective well-being requires a grounding in virtue. In other words, a virtuous foundation for internal auditing is essential if internal auditing is to serve fully the public good, although the notion of the internal auditor as a "moral actor" has frequently been described as problematic in practice (e.g., in Everett and Tremblay, 2014; Nickell and Roberts, 2014).

Before delving more deeply into this topic, let us take a final, quick glance at the Pope's message to the Holy See's internal audit team. We have interpreted Francis's comments on "merciful discretion" as an appeal for a humane rather than a mechanistic approach to auditing – an approach that elevates the sensitivities of real-world considerations over the dry imperatives of a formulaic pseudo-professionalism. In addition to such secular understandings, we may consider briefly a theological aspect to Francis's comments. In everyday use, the term "scrupulous" has positive connotations of diligence, attention to detail, and conscientiousness. From a theological perspective, however, "scrupulosity" is considered a sinful, unwarranted, even pathological fear of committing sin. The Church encourages the devotion and piety of its adherents, but it repudiates a fanatical and obsessive attachment to religious devotion. The theological notion of scrupulosity is not unlike the modern, secular psychiatric disorder of obsessive–compulsive behavior. The Church takes a dim view of a fanatical devotion to prayer and piety, considering it comparable to obsessively washing one's hands far beyond the needs of what hygiene requires. Theologically, scrupulosity is considered not only to be sinful, but is often viewed as a diabolically inspired sinfulness.

Applying the concept of scrupulosity to internal auditing, a fanatical devotion to audit literalism might blind an internal auditor's judgment to the nuances and realities of everyday life. A fanatical obsession with committing sin doesn't allow a person to function properly. One might be ethically paralyzed by a fear of sinning. Similarly, an obsessive crusade to root out all possible wrongdoing through auditing may be counterproductive, as it distorts discernment and judgment. A differentiation between grave sins and lesser sins, and between sinning and not sinning, is essential for true morality. In internal auditing an excessive adherence to the stark, amoral technicalities of algorithmic testing is dysfunctional. Excessive moral absolutism is the enemy of true morality, because it distorts ethical judgment.

Let us now return to secular ethics. Virtues are "character-traits which we need to live humanly flourishing lives" (Oakley and Cocking, 2001, 18), and they are central to a wise deployment of moral agency in internal auditing. Moral agency has been defined as acting "in a manner that expresses concern for moral values *as final ends*" (Garofalo and Geuras, 2006, 3, emphasis added), and morality in this sense is intrinsic, not instrumental. In other words, the virtues are not a means to an end but ends in themselves. Professional virtue entails the transcendence of prescriptive, written, rules-based Standards which detract from the exercise of moral agency. The technique-driven, hollow formalities of modern internal auditing diminish the importance of professional character.

In assessments of the future, value judgments are almost unavoidable. For instance, in considering environmental and economic sustainability, how far should we trade off our current prosperity against the achievement of future benefits? To what extent should we sacrifice the beauty of our rural areas and the safety of birds to accommodate wind farms? Such matters go beyond technical expertise into matters of public policy, and into considerations of quality of life, and aesthetics, in which the professional expert offers only one voice among many. What is at stake here is the soundness of professional opinions, part of which depend on objective factual knowledge, and part of which depend on informed judgment. And it is on questions of judgment that the reliability of professional expertise often succeeds. Or fails.

When we refer to virtue as moral excellence, we mean an excellence of disposition or character that encourages ethical decision-making. As we suggested earlier, an understanding of ethics based on adherence to rules or standards differs from a character attuned to ethical choices. The difference between rules-based and character-based ethics has been described as follows: "Whereas deontology [i.e. a system of ethics based on rules] asks what a person should *do*, virtue ethics asks what a person should *be*"

(Neri, 2021, 53, emphasis in original). In the Western tradition, we look to classical Greece, above all to Plato and Aristotle. But a brief etymological digression is informative. The word "virtue" entered the English language through medieval French from the Latin *virtus*, which originally had broad, ancient connotations of masculine attributes like martial strength, toughness, fitness for political leadership, and moral excellence. Over time, the Latin *virtus* came under the influence of the Greek term *arete*, meaning purposeful excellence, and gravitated to a narrower focus on moral excellence. Originally, *arete*'s meaning of excellence was construed widely, in a gender-neutral fashion, as the ability to perform a function to its full potential. It covered inanimate and animate beings – for example, the excellence of a knife resides in its sharpness; the excellence of a guard dog resides in its alertness, and in its bark and bite; and the excellence of a football (soccer) goalkeeper resides in his ability to keep a clean sheet.

The focus of Greek philosophers in the Socratic tradition on *arete* as moral excellence led to the formulation of the four cardinal virtues in Plato's writings. These virtues were courage, moderation, wisdom, and justice. (The term "cardinal" here derives from the Latin word for a hinge and refers to the importance of the four principal virtues, on which all other virtues are hinged.) The four terms courage, moderation, wisdom, and justice are all rich in meaning, especially wisdom which is often understood as a kind of prudent judgment founded on sensible and practical behavior. Discussions of the cardinal virtues are widespread in Plato's dialogues, most notably in *Republic* 427e and *Alcibiades* 121e-122a (although the authorship of the latter dialogue is disputed). In *Euthyphro*, Plato seems to have considered piety as a possible fifth cardinal virtue, but his Greek successors preferred not to broaden the list beyond what we now know as the four classical, secular, cardinal virtues. (It is interesting to reflect that the Christian tradition later added the three theological virtues of faith, hope, and charity to the four classical cardinal virtues: Piety seems stubbornly to refuse to go away.)

Let us glance at one of the cardinal virtues, moderation, and its embodiment in the person of Socrates. Indeed, Socrates was so moderate in his lifestyle that he not only refused to accept bribes, but would not even charge fees for teaching his followers (Plato, *Euthyphro* 3d-e and Xenophon, *Memorabilia* I.ii.5–8 and I.ii.60). In contrast to Socrates' avoidance of fee-charging, the famous teachers of rhetoric of Plato's day were notorious for charging substantial fees for their instruction (Plato, *Alcibiades* 119a). In Xenophon's *Defence to the Jury* Socrates demonstrates his moderation and incorruptibility: "Who is there in your knowledge that is less a slave to his bodily appetites than I am? Who in the world more free, – for I accept neither gifts nor pay from any one?" And "while other men get their delicacies in the markets and pay a high price for them, I devise more pleasurable ones from the resources of my soul, with no expenditure of money" (637–663).

Socrates' indifference to money and bribes was put to the test while he languished on death row, at the age of 70, awaiting an execution that was a consequence of speaking truth to power. Socrates' friend Crito suggested bribing the jailors, to allow Socrates to escape to a comfortable life in exile. Socrates declined the offer, and informed Crito that his understanding of justice and his loyalty to Athens required him to pay the ultimate price. Essentially, Socrates refused to engage in one type of injustice, bribery, to counter another injustice, his unfair execution. (Crito's offer is set out in Plato's *Crito* 44a-46a, and Socrates' justification of his acceptance of his premature death is set out in both *Crito* and *Phaedo*, passim.) Beyond his restraint with money, Socrates also curbed his sexual appetites (Plato, *Symposium* 215a-291e), and led a life simple to the point of frugality, from which the Stoics – who considered their philosophical inheritance to be Socratic – took inspiration. By holding his appetites in check, Socrates clearly exhibited the virtue of moderation. And, crucially, Socrates used his powers of reasoning to control his appetites: In *Phaedrus* (246a–254e) Plato uses the allegory of a charioteer who handles two horses, one of which is passionate and unruly, and the other calm, to symbolize the role of reason in self-control and moderation.

Much energy has been devoted to the question of the unity of the virtues. There is a good reason for this focus on the virtues' alleged unity – it matters in terms of how we understand living well. The basic question is whether or not a hierarchy exists among the four cardinal virtues. Or are they all aspects of a unified concept of moral excellence? Socrates (or, more accurately, Plato's Socrates) was sometimes ambiguous on this point. In *Protagoras* 329d-e, Socrates uses analogies of the human face and gold to consider the unity of the virtues – are the virtues identical in their essences, like the individual fragments of a gold nugget that has been shattered into pieces? Or are they interrelated but distinct parts of a whole, in the way that the mouth, nose, eyes, and ears relate to the entire face? The matter was left unresolved by Plato in *Protagoras*. And Xenophon also left the question of the unity of the virtues unclear (*Memorabilia*, III.9.4-6 and IV.6.1-11). But in the *Republic*, Plato (or Plato's Socrates) made a bold statement on the unity of the virtues and, as this topic is relevant to our modern predicament, it is worth exploring further.

In the *Republic*, Plato linked the four cardinal virtues to both the social classes of the ideal city-state of Callipolis and to human faculties, providing a striking, comparative perspective on the unity of the virtues. Socrates distributed the three virtues of wisdom, courage, and moderation between the three main groups of Callipolis's inhabitants, so that (1) the ruling class, through its *wisdom*, creates just laws, (2) the soldiers defend the city and its laws with *courage*, and (3) the working class creates wealth through its *moderation* and productive ways of living. The fourth virtue, justice, emerges naturally from the harmony of the three other virtues, in the way that a triad chord in music is constructed from three individual notes. A division of labor and of responsibilities therefore leads to a unity of the virtues. In other words, the city is (1) wise as a whole because of its wise rulers, (2) brave as a whole because of its brave soldiers, (3) moderate as a whole because of its moderate workers, and it is (4) just as a whole because of the harmonious combination of the three preceding virtues. Justice is therefore simultaneously a derivative yet crowning public virtue. In Socrates' words: "in establishing our [utopian] city, we aren't aiming to make any one group outstandingly happy but to make the whole city so, as far as possible. We thought that we'd find justice most easily in such a city" (*Republic*, 420b).

Socrates goes beyond a harmonious distribution of the virtues among the social classes of the ideal state. He suggests a comparable co-existence of the same three virtues in the individual's soul (or, if we prefer, the individual's character or consciousness). At the level of the individual, a person who satisfactorily displays the three virtues of (1) wisdom, (2) courage, and (3) moderation will also be a just person. Socrates therefore draws a parallel in the *Republic* between justice in the city, arising from the harmonious distribution of virtues within its tripartite social structure, and justice in the individual, arising from a similar distribution of virtues within the tripartite soul or character.

Plato's remarkable vision of the cardinal virtues in the *Republic* has three aspects that we should hold in mind as our arguments progress. First, Socrates identifies justice not as an isolated virtue, but as one arising from and dependent on the harmony of the other virtues. This summoning of justice from the harmony of wisdom, courage, and moderation achieves a unity of the virtues. Second, Plato's vision suggests that society is the human individual writ large. Or, in reverse, that the individual is a microcosm of the social community. From either point of view, a harmonious unity of the virtues conquers moral confusion and disorder in both individuals and in society at large. Third, Plato's vision is secular and universal. It is not necessarily based on any post-mortem rewards in an afterlife for good conduct (though it may be). It is understood as inherently desirable in our worldly arrangements.

What can internal auditors learn from the *Republic*'s concepts of individuals at peace with themselves and with others, through an internal, justice-generating harmony of the virtues? We shall argue that for internal auditing to contribute to society its professional activity should be founded on the classical virtues, and demonstrably so. Let us consider the ways in which the individual virtues and their collective unity might relate to internal auditing.

We may start with wisdom, which arises at the intersection of relevant, abstract knowledge; practical expertise; and a commitment to the public good. Wisdom involves the type of sound judgment that cannot be learned from a book or from a code of conduct. Nor is it available for consultation in a set of written standards. Wisdom is generally gained slowly, over many years, through the often painstaking process of learning through error. Wisdom involves a mastery of one's emotions, and a firm but nuanced sense of right and wrong. Internal auditors need a space in their daily work in which to gain wisdom, but our age of increasingly amoral proceduralism and algorithmic auditing does not seem auspicious for the inculcation of wisdom. (Chapter 5 covers the topic of wisdom in more detail, linking it to critical thinking and qualitative judgment.)

In terms of courage, an internal auditor may be courageous in bringing to light unpopular audit findings. It might take an act of serious bravery to report a finding that could lose a financial auditor her contract with a client, or might place an internal auditor's job in jeopardy, or that might simply cause complications that the auditor would prefer to avoid. Nonetheless, courage may be deemed a necessary but insufficient attribute of an internal auditor. With a nod to the concept of the unity of the virtues, we may affirm that difficult audit-related decisions require wisdom (and perhaps also moderation) to deliver a virtuous outcome. For example, an over-hasty reporting of a potential problem, without a comprehensive and wise assessment of the related evidence, might lead to the invalid reporting of a matter. It is necessary to subject a potentially tricky audit finding to corroborative testing and the application of wise judgment. Courage without the restraint of the other virtues can amount to recklessness, like a crazed soldier from Plato's Callipolis charging at the enemy without regard for safety precautions, thereby placing himself and his comrades in danger. A focus on a single virtue may therefore lead one astray, if that focus is not tempered by the harmonious unity of the cardinal virtues.

Turning now to moderation, what can we make of the relevance of the Socratic/Platonic view of moderation, especially in matters of money, to modern internal auditing? We saw, in Section 3.1, that the effects of freewheeling greed on the financial auditing profession from the early 1990s led to the catastrophic demise of the audit firm Arthur Andersen in 2002. A once venerable firm became a symbol for the greed and corruption that the public associated with external auditing. An avalanche of global legislation and regulatory activity followed the Arthur Andersen debacle, and it rescued a profession that had become a laughingstock. A ruthless obsession with the billable hour came close to permanently destroying the credibility of financial auditing, and its long, slow recovery was hard fought. We would not expect auditors of any specialty who are subjected to the financial pressures of modern life to undertake their professional work *pro bono*. However, we might expect auditors to carefully restrain the extent of their commercial activities.

We shall develop the topic of moderation in financial matters for internal auditors at Section 4.4. But the virtue of moderation goes beyond money matters. Moderation implies self-control across a range of topics, and perhaps the overriding implication for modern internal auditing is for its practitioners to restrain temptation toward conceitedness and hubris. Internal and external auditors both frequently overpromise on what their activities can achieve. Not least among the expectations generated by modern auditing rhetoric is the achievement of the control of risks. The corrective impact of Michael Power's concept of the "audit society" (discussed in Chapter 3) should convince prudent auditors to have reservations over setting foot on the wilder shores of internal auditing. If auditing and risk management, as Power has suggested, frequently act as little more than a social palliative, through the issuance of hollow assurance, internal auditing should aim to solidify its basic activities before trying to capture new ground. One can understand the desire of auditors, especially internal auditors, to keep their activity relevant, and to acquire and retain an advisory seat at the top table of their organizations, but the aspirations of internal auditors to take the lead in providing assurance on a range of new topics, from social justice to environmental concerns, seems unrealistic at present. A more temperate approach to the expansion of internal auditing into new fields is likely to safeguard internal auditing's professional credibility. If our concept of revolutionary changes in the distribution of accountability and social trust (outlined in Chapter 2) is correct, internal auditors of a moderate disposition should reflect carefully on internal auditing's future positioning in an era of fluid, piecemeal assurance.

The fourth of the cardinal virtues, justice, is particularly important for internal auditing. The findings, opinions, and judgments of internal auditors should do justice to all those impacted by auditing, including stakeholders (construed in the widest sense). An internal auditor who omits crucial testing from an audit, deliberately or negligently, is not doing justice to the stakeholder who might rely on the audit's findings. An auditor who overlooks or discards awkward findings, to keep a lucrative audit client (in external auditing) or to bolster their job security (in internal auditing) has failed in terms of justice. He has also failed in terms of courage (as we have already seen), and he has failed to display moderation by not tempering a greedy desire for money or status. He has also shown himself to be unwise, by repudiating a common sense approach to life that allows one to weigh the costs and benefits, and the rightness and wrongness, of certain courses of action. Again, we may note the tendencies of the four cardinal virtues to coalesce into an aggregated, justice-generating unity. We tend to isolate the virtues at our peril. And although Plato, in the *Republic*, suggested that justice might materialize quasi-automatically once the three other virtues are established, the internal auditor would benefit from reflecting independently on justice. The cardinal virtues provide modern internal auditors a more trustworthy path to understandings of social justice and the equitable treatment of individuals than the deceptive, polished *shtick* of the hustling consultant motivated by the maximization of his billable hours.

We argue, therefore, that the cardinal virtues are not an anachronism. They are timeless signposts to moral excellence. Any professional framework that dampens down an individual's flourishing through the acquisition and display of the classical virtues is unfit for purpose. Of course, Plato's treatment of the virtues is far richer than space has permitted us to illustrate. For the purpose of filling out our presentation, we should note that late in his life Plato modified some of his arguments in the *Laws*, in which Plato's ideal city of Magnesia is less utopian and less authoritarian than Callipolis. Magnesia is governed not by autocratic philosopher-kings, but by impartial law, and it is far closer to what we would recognize today as a reasonable political dispensation. Despite this, the Plato of the *Laws* is no less interested in morality and the virtues than the Plato of the *Republic*. For example, Plato approached the topic of corruption as follows:

> Members of the public service should perform their duties without taking bribes. Such a practice must never be extenuated by an approving reference to maxims like 'One good turn deserves another'. It is not easy for an official to reach his decisions impartially and stick to them, and the safest thing he can do is to listen to the law and obey its command and to take no gifts for his service.
>
> *Laws XII, 955c-d*

Timeless wisdom of this nature resonates today in our narrowing, algorithmic social environment.

We ignore ancient wisdom at our loss: Plato was writing at a time of crisis in Athens' institutions, perhaps reflecting the crisis we face today in the deterioration of our traditional institutions. But it should be remembered that the Greeks' cardinal virtues are not to be understood as similar in nature to the biblical Ten Commandments. The Greek virtues were character traits rather than rules to be followed. Putting this another way, the virtues are not a list of commands – they are more a state of being, or a disposition that drives behavior. And it was Aristotle who developed the habit-forming concept of virtue in striking ways.

Before we discuss Aristotelian views of virtue, however, the author wishes to offer two important clarifications. First, he apologizes in advance to the reader who might think that he gives Aristotle's virtue ethics short shrift in this book. Plato is often portrayed as a precursory, warm-up act before Aristotle took virtue ethics to a higher level of sophistication. The approach we shall take does not take such a view of developmental progression between the two great philosophers. The author believes that the discussions of the virtues in Plato's dialogues are the finest classical expression of matters of virtue relevant to the modern internal auditor. Aristotle had profound things to say on the virtues, as we shall see, but they did not necessarily supplant Platonic themes. In our arguments, Aristotle's insights accompany and amplify, rather than replace, Plato's discussions.

A second consideration before we look more deeply into Aristotelian virtue ethics is a tendency when interpreting Plato and Aristotle to follow a long tradition of perceiving Plato as impractical and mystical, in contrast to Aristotle's grounding in day-to-day reality. The *School of Athens* (*La Scuola di Atene*), a sixteenth-century Vatican fresco by Raphael (1483–1520), depicts Plato in old age, walking in conversation with his middle-aged student, Aristotle. Raphael's Plato, portrayed with a somewhat grumpy expression, points sternly to the sky to emphasize transcendental and universal abstractions. Raphael's Aristotle on the other hand gestures downward, a reflection of his allegedly more down-to-earth interests. What's more, both philosophers are carrying books – Plato is carrying a copy of *Timaeus*, his account of the ancient nature of the world and humanity, while Aristotle carries his *Nicomachean Ethics*, which brims with practical advice. Although Raphael was right to highlight Aristotle's commitment to practical ethical matters, his fresco implied an oversimplistic dichotomy between a transcendental Plato and a worldly Aristotle. Perhaps the core difference between the two philosophers was captured nicely by John Child, as follows: "Plato sought to find the basis for an ideal society ... By contrast, Aristotle was concerned to understand the world as it is, and to provide a scientific methodology for such enquiry, rather than how the world might be" (Child, 2019, 20).

While the traditional differentiation between Plato and Aristotle carries some truth, it can be heavily qualified. Plato was not obsessed solely with abstract universals: Through his portrayal of his teacher Socrates, he fought the corruption in the very down-to-earth *polis* of classical Athens. While it might be argued that other Greek *poleis* of the day displayed even greater levels of corruption, Plato is concerned primarily to challenge and reform the immediate society into which he was born. Plato's Socrates undertakes what might be described as an ethical audit of Athenian society. In an echo of future medieval England, with its culture of the unwritten "audit by ear" in manorial governance, Socrates never committed anything to writing. His inquiries into the social and cultural pathologies of Athens were entirely oral, and it was left to Plato, Xenophon, and others to commit the Socratic tradition to writing. We should therefore be clear that Plato's concerns and his forms of the classical virtues were intended as a very practical type of knowledge, to be applied to the heart of social interaction. As one scholar has expressed this: "We misread Plato disastrously when we read him in light of a Gnostic otherworldliness that pictures the forms as resident in a place far, far away from ours, rather than as the principles of the intelligibility of this ... world" (Kosman, 2007, 136–137).

Having set out these preliminary comments, the author shall focus briefly on several aspects of Aristotle's teachings that seem to him most relevant to our discussions of internal auditing. Aristotle made a distinction between virtues of character, like courage, and virtues of the intellect, like practical wisdom. He assessed correct behavior as possessing neither an excess nor a deficiency of individual virtues. The correct "measure" of virtue was determined by context, and to be found on a continuum between extremes: Aristotle's "Golden Mean" posited the existence of an appropriate position on a continuum between the excess or deficiency of a virtue. The "Golden Mean" recalls the Buddhist "Middle Way". Siddhartha Gautama, the founder of Buddhism, advocated moderation after a life of extremes – a youth of luxurious living and later experiments with severe asceticism. The "Golden Mean" might also be seen as an application of the Platonic concept of moderation: Plato warned in *Laches*, 193d, that courage can be weakened or undone by "foolish daring", and an application of the Aristotelian "Golden Mean" to courage would suggest it belongs somewhere between reckless bravery and cowardice.

Aristotle considered the purpose of human life to be the achievement of *eudaimonia*, often unhelpfully translated as happiness but meaning something closer to a holistic, virtuous attainment of self-fulfillment. In keeping with the established classical Greek view of a virtuous life, *eudaimonia* does not arise from following rules or commands, but rather from a more generalized "activity of the soul in accordance with excellence" (*Nicomachean Ethics*, 1098a16), especially a matching of excellence of character with excellence of intellect. This suggests the development and cultivation of virtuous habits: The notion of character-forming habits exposes the limitations of prescriptive, rules-based professional standards, as it gives prominence to the cultivation of virtuous character traits rather than the following of rules. However, Aristotle considered the virtues necessary but insufficient for self-fulfillment: He emphasized the importance of other, external "goods" such as friends, good looks, and wealth in a truly self-fulfilled life. He therefore doubted whether true *eudaimonia* is feasible for an individual blighted by having, for instance, "totally depraved children or friends" (*Nicomachean* Ethics, 1099b3–8).

Aristotle famously called the human individual a political animal (*Politics*, I,1:1253a2). He might have focused exclusively on humans as social animals, which even today remains a common platitude, but he chose to emphasize humanity's political nature. The implication of Aristotle's characterization of us as political animals is that we are required by our existence to come to terms with the state's formal governance structures. Political governance, for Aristotle, is not an artificial framework unnaturally imposed on us, but rather a universal manifestation of human nature: We therefore must learn to flourish in a political context.

The significance of Aristotle's views for internal auditing may be summarized in a question: How can we make internal auditing a *eudaimonic* profession? If we follow Aristotle's lead, we would ensure that professional frameworks encourage habits that inculcate the virtues of both character and intellect, in order that we can best meet the socio-economic and political demands of our profession, through a rigorous commitment to serve the public good. For this to occur, professional standards should be principles-based, not rules-based. Just as the classical virtues were founded on habit and character rather than on obedience to rules, our professional activities should be founded on habit-forming principles. Unfortunately, internal auditing standards have degenerated into rules and checklists. They might contain some principles, but the preponderance of the standards tells us what we may and may not do.

Let us pull together the overall themes of our review of the relevance of the classical virtues to modern internal auditing. We have already referred to a preference for principles-based, rather than rules-based, standards. More generally, we have argued in favor of a reversal of the current path toward an over-emphasis on prescriptive expertise, at the cost of character-based judgment. Internal auditing is not alone in experiencing a retreat from virtue and character: Other professions have been similarly damaged. But the harm to internal auditing has been particularly severe. Modern internal auditing today promotes inferior thought through simple-minded, algorithmic logic with little humanistic resonance: In contrast, the exercising of virtue-based judgment would encourage understandings that transcend algorithmic facts and mechanistic decision-making.

Questions of professional virtue therefore reach far beyond superficial technicalities into profound ethical considerations. We may, for example, condemn unreservedly "white collar" acts of corruption like bribery and embezzlement among corporate executives. But can we apply the same judgment to a low-paid clerk pocketing a can of sardines from an organization's stocks to feed her starving family? This is a question of degree, not of kind, and it requires sensitive judgment. Another example: The internal auditor may feel a strong sense of loyalty to her organization, and this loyalty may on occasion come into conflict with a duty to serve the public interest. Should an auditor blow the whistle on institutional criminality, thereby flagging it to the wider community, or should she merely report it internally, for discreet, in-house handling? The auditor's dual loyalties are in conflict in such a situation. Larry Sawyer (1911–2002), known in the IIA as "the father of modern internal auditing", emphasized the "crucial dilemma" facing internal auditors in such circumstances, as they struggle to reconcile loyalties to both "employers or profession, in situations of conflict" (Sawyer, 1987). In facing a sliding scale of judgments between such extremes, the auditor's thoughts are pushed to levels of inquiry that no checklist or algorithm can satisfy.

What are the dangers of a virtue-less profession? At its extremes, the deployment of bureaucratic professional practices in the service of evil has been well documented. The warnings of Polish-born sociologist Zygmunt

Bauman (1925–2017) of the dangers of Holocaust-era bureaucratic practices shredded of moral considerations continue to haunt us: "Technical responsibility differs from moral responsibility in that it forgets that ... action is a means to something other than itself ... *the result is the irrelevance of moral standards for the technical success of the bureaucratic operations*" (Bauman, 1989, 10, emphasis in original). In less extreme cases, forms of internal auditing devoid of ethical dimensions are, we argue, a betrayal of the social purposes of auditing. Obedience to rules is not the same as the exercise of moral agency, and modern internal auditing is increasingly inculcating a perilous mindset of obedience to its virtue-dampening, written standards.

A final comment and a note of caution on our brief summary of the classical virtues. Our review of this complex area has of necessity been somewhat cursory, but we have made a case for the importance of the classical virtues as enduring components of human life, and therefore of professional activity. But we should always be a little cautious when applying concepts from the ancient world to today's contexts. Although Platonic and Aristotelian notions of virtue address perennial questions of morality and the public good, they were developed in a different setting. To consider just one example, in Aristotle's time there was no concept comparable to modern theories of probabilistic risk. Instead, Aristotle thought along the lines of necessity and contingency, in which events tend to follow necessarily from defined causes, but in which unexpected events may on occasion interrupt the normal flows from cause to effect. Aristotle provides (in *Metaphysics*, Book Delta, 30) an example of a contingent interruption to normal cause-and-effect flows – a farmer unexpectedly finds buried treasure as he digs a trench as part of his routine agricultural work. The farmer's discovery of the treasure suggests two unrelated chains of causation: (1) A hoarder burying the treasure and (2) a farmer digging to plant a crop becomes suddenly enriched by stumbling on the treasure. For Aristotle, there is nothing probabilistic about the occurrence of such an event. It is simply a case of chance causality. One can only speculate on what Aristotle would have made of our modern culture of amoral risk algorithms and our intellectual surrender to probabilistic risk theory and rulebooks. Professional virtue entails the transcendence of formulaic frameworks of behavior. The algorithmic de-personalization of virtue fosters complacency and detracts from understanding, and it is perhaps one of the greatest threats to internal auditing today.

4.4 INTERNAL AUDITING: TRADE OR PROFESSION?

We have seen in Section 4.3 that an appropriate place for money in our hierarchy of interests is an important aspect of Socratic and Platonic concepts of the virtue of moderation. Plato made it clear that

> the pursuit of money should come last in the scale of value. Every man directs his efforts to three things in all, and if his efforts are directed with a correct sense of priorities he will give money the third and lowest place, and his soul the highest, and his body coming somewhere between the two.
>
> *Laws, V, 743e*

We should not conclude from this that money is unimportant. Instead, we should conclude that money is important as a means to an end and not as an end in itself.

The relevance of this Platonic insight to modern professional life is significant. We discussed in Section 4.1 the sociological critique of rent-seeking professionals who allegedly rig markets and manipulate supply and demand for their services. The relationship between the professions and money has long been of public interest and has at times been ambivalent. For instance, the notion of professionals advertising their services is a relatively recent development. It comes as a surprise to many to learn that before 1986 it was illegal for lawyers in England to advertise their services. In that year, the Law Society of England and Wales first gave its members the permission to advertise, and it was a development that encountered widespread public concern. Although such advertising now seems perfectly normal (although some lawyers still continue to oppose it, even today, on principle), it had been assumed that advertising would shatter the English legal profession's decorum, distract lawyers from their professional responsibilities, and give rise to a generation of ruthless ambulance chasers.

Our example from the United Kingdom might seem attributable to the crusty, conservative traditions of the British legal system, but it is worthwhile recalling that only from 1977, with the Supreme Court decision in *Bates v State Bar of Arizona*, have attorneys in the United States been permitted by law to freely advertise their services (Roberts, 2021, 18). To be more precise, the *Bates v State Bar of Arizona* decision provided constitutional protection for attorney advertising. This meant that professional regulation was not entirely precluded, for example in cases of alleged false, misleading, or deceptive advertising. Nonetheless, the barriers to attorney advertising were torn down in 1977, and nobody has credibly suggested rebuilding them.

The 1977 Supreme Court decision on advertising had implications beyond the legal profession, impacting other professions with advertising bans. The American Institute of Certified Public Accountants changed its rules to permit its members to prohibit only false, misleading, or deceptive advertising. The large external audit firms subsequently took to advertising with gusto. They enthusiastically embraced aggressive marketing techniques for auditing and other services that culminated, in the 1990s, in the culture of immoderation and greed which diminished the public credibility of external auditing. Initially, the firms with forceful marketing techniques were seen as unprofessional *parvenus* in the external audit sector, but such approaches to maximizing billable hours soon became commonplace (Picard, 2016). An observation of a former Arthur Andersen insider from those years is revealing:

> The managers and others who worked in my group were one step below me in the food chain, and they, like fish gasping for oxygen, needed work in order to bill the hours that would ultimately give them a raise or a promotion.
>
> *Toffler and Reingold, 2003, 111*

In our day, the iron imperatives of maximizing billable hours again seem to be underpinning a significant amount of internal auditing activity. Many ambitious, young internal auditors aspire to sit in elegant offices in towering skyscrapers, enriching themselves through the hustle to source new contracts. For consultants in the large advisory firms, an ability to pull in new business is often high on the list of hiring and performance criteria.

Internal auditing is diminished by the tendency of the large consulting firms to commodify it. An internal audit is not like an item on a superstore shelf or, perhaps more aptly, like an item in an online store. An internal audit is not a mere service like a haircut, a commodity to be bargained and purchased from the cheapest or slickest provider. To express these sentiments is not to attack market forces, which can be highly beneficial to internal auditing. It is reasonable to expect hard-working internal auditors who deferred prosperity to study and acquire certifications to be well compensated: It is a well-deserved return from an investment of years of training. And high incomes for internal auditors attract talented individuals to the profession. Another advantage of competitive markets is to place downward pressures on the costs of internal auditing, with obvious benefits to those being audited. However beneficial such market traits might be, an excessive commodification of internal auditing services fits uneasily with internal auditing's moral purpose. We may accept the valuable role of market forces in internal auditing while recognizing where the writ of the market ends. Wherever one draws the line between reasonable professional remuneration and aggressive commercialization, a line has to be drawn somewhere.

There is nothing inherently wrong with consulting and advisory services: Throughout history, advisory services have been important, and kings, emperors, and Popes have all relied heavily on their advisors (McKenna, 2006, 10–11). Consultants provide valuable services to internal auditing by providing flexible options of temporary, outsourced, or co-sourced personnel; by sharing knowledge and expertise; and by undertaking market research activities that keep a check on the pulse of professional developments. The consulting industry can therefore be seen as a valuable helping hand. Too frequently, however, internal auditing is overdependent on the large consulting firms, who often appear to offer guiding rather than helping hands, coaxing the internal auditing profession down avenues that primarily serve their commercial interests.

An internal auditor who attends conferences, training courses, and networking events, will come away with a collection of business cards that offer ways of "helping" internal audit functions with a range of "innovative" approaches, involving both standardized and customized "deliverables". This is part and parcel of the hustle that surrounds modern internal auditing. Powerful consulting interests thrive in a culture of hype, relentlessly promoting "innovations" that may still be at modest stages of development.

Although consultants bring expertise, knowledge, and skills to their clients, the extent to which such capacities are permanently transmitted to clients is questionable. The consultant's "deliverables" tend to focus on the *application*, rather than the *transfer*, of knowledge. Institutional learning is an incremental process that the transactional nature of consulting services rarely fulfils. On the contrary, the consulting industry has been accused of using "proprietary information, awe-inspiring technology, and linguistic tricks" (Mazzucato and Collington, 2023, 3) to convey a façade of legitimacy while ruthlessly maximizing revenue opportunities, all the while withholding the transmission of knowledge. The negative effects of consulting therefore include a hollowing out or de-skilling of recipient organizations, who effectively outsource creativity and expertise to external parties. The end result is a damaging of clients' policy-making capacity and originality of thought.

The IIA has had an ambivalent relationship with the steady flow of consultants drawn by the scent of opportunities for the lucrative billable hour. Ambivalent, that is to say, for the notion of giving primacy to serving the public interest. Among those prominent in supplying consulting services to internal auditing are the Big Four external auditing and professional services firms. The Big Four and other large consulting firms are adept at seeking new avenues for profit, and at discovering or creating fresh approaches to auditing and accounting activities. In suggesting sometimes-questionable new areas of activity and advocating sometimes-questionable new approaches to already established areas within internal auditing's purview, the more aggressive consultants act like a powerful tail wagging the compliant internal auditing dog.

When a large consulting firm produces a glossy brochure, sometimes coauthored with the IIA, that sets out an "innovative" new topic or a "pioneering" new internal auditing methodology, allegedly arising from its peerless "thought leadership", with exhortations to the reader to take up the consulting firm's "help", the internal auditor's skepticism is warranted. The consultants' quest for maximizing billable hours may encourage internal auditors to chase red herrings, thereby hampering the ability of internal auditing to fully serve the public good. For example, the prominence in today's auditing context of Environmental Social and Governance (ESG) considerations has been a market-driven bonanza for the consulting industry. It is perfectly reasonable for internal auditors to consider matters like the polluting effects and social damage caused by the organizations they audit, but ESG has taken on urgent, quasi-messianic overtones, while efforts to establish universal, measurable criteria for ESG topics have faltered. The slow take-up by global corporations of the World Economic Forum's "Stakeholder Capitalism Metrics" project suggests a resistance to the harmonization of measurement methodologies widely agreed to be necessary for ESG to prosper in the corporate world. Competing ESG frameworks promulgated by consulting firms have undermined universal standards for comparability purposes, while lining consultants' pockets. Notably, the characterization in 2021, by Blackrock's former sustainable investing chief officer, of ESG as a "dangerous distraction" that amounts to "a giant societal placebo where we think we're making progress even though we're not" (cited in Mazzucato and Collington, 2023, 232) suggests that more careful thought is needed to address questions of assessing the physical and social environment for the public good.

A call for a more prudent approach to determining the best ways to address assurance over environmental and social issues is not to advocate procrastination on issues of pressing importance. However, the moral panic over ESG in the early 2020s has worked to the commercial advantage of the large consulting firms. The topic of ESG should be tempered by a more measured approach that is less driven by commercial exhortations to sell "solutions" and "frameworks" and "deliverables". The emergence of piecemeal assurance (covered in Chapter 2) involves emerging and yet-to-emerge assurance mechanisms to address questions of accountability and social trust at and beyond organizational boundaries, and we are still working through these challenges. Perhaps we have barely started to address them. A measured approach arising from virtues like moderation and wisdom should take precedence over a stampede to solutions drummed up by consultants with an eye to surging billable hours. Lenz and Jeppesen (2022) have encouraged a concept of internal auditing as a "gardener of governance", suggesting a measured and careful evolution of internal auditing practices: The horticultural metaphor implies the inadvisability of periodically ripping out healthy plants, and replacing them with new, untested ones. It is far better to nurture the evolution of the internal auditing profession's existing strengths by prudent and wise handling, rather than by greedy slash and burn methods.

In defense of the large consulting firms, it would be misleading to portray internal auditing as a helpless, under-developed profession under attack from aggressive consultants. If internal auditors lacked the appetite for consulting services, the market for them would not exist. The current appetite of internal auditors for consulting services suggests a void in conceptual and intellectual leadership at the heart of the internal auditing profession: Nature abhors a vacuum, and consultants are sucked in to fill the void.

The topics of greed, power, money, and the public good are far from exclusive to internal auditing – they are inherent in the human condition. In Section 4.1, we considered the lessons for modern internal auditing to be found in Richard Wagner's *Die Meistersinger von Nürnberg*. The same composer's most well-known work, *Der Ring des Nibelungen*, first performed in 1876, also has connotations valid for our discussion here. The *Ring* is an epic tale, drawing on mythology, of the perennial struggle between money and love, and between power and selfless devotion. Alberich, chief of the goblin-like Nibelungs, renounces love in order to steal the powerful gold of the river Rhine from its guardians, the aquatic Rhine Maidens. He uses the gold to create a ring that endows its wearer with the ultimate mastery of worldly power, but he soon has the ring taken away – he then curses the ring and a complex struggle for its possession is unleashed. Alberich never recovers the ring, and he is ultimately defeated by the power of the love he renounced, the tale culminating in Brünnhilde's restoration of the gold to its guardians in the Rhine. After restoring the gold, Brünnhilde's subsequent self-sacrifice by immolation purges the world of Alberich's curse. Of course, the purge can only be temporary. The destruction of the gods at the end of the *Ring* makes way for human society to face the endless struggle between altruism and the curse of money-obsession.

There are many interpretations of the *Ring*, but prominent among them is the notion that the sacredness of our humane inheritance is corrupted by an obsession with money and power. The implications for a profession's proclaimed objective to serve the public interest is evident. The Wagnerian depiction of the struggle between power and love is not merely an oddity of nineteenth-century German romanticism: Michael Ewans has convincingly demonstrated the durability of the *Ring*'s themes by a careful comparison with the themes of Aeschylus' *Oresteia* (Ewans, 1982). The struggle to keep greed at bay is at the heart of our condition as fallible beings with a brief, worldly existence. Internal auditing cannot, collectively, avoid this struggle.

Our discussions have indicated that internal auditing is both a trade and a profession. Keeping these two elements in balance is not easy, but the pendulum in internal auditing may already have swung too far to the trade end of the spectrum. Internal auditing as a commercial activity is in rude health. But as a professional service in the public interest it is in difficulty. Internal auditing's commitments to the public good risk being swamped by commercial interests, to the disquiet of many practitioners who sense that something has gone wrong. As we saw in Section 3.1, the craze for billable hours almost destroyed the external auditing profession through cut-throat competition in the 1990s. The billable hour is rapidly becoming a unit of currency in the hustle and bustle of today's freewheeling internal auditing market. How long can internal auditing tolerate brash commercialism without denaturing its professional commitment to serve the public interest? Or have we already gone beyond that point? It is important not to lose sight of the reasons why we undertake internal auditing: Our financial rewards are a by-product, not the main aim, of internal auditing activities. Our focus should be, always, on enriching the public good.

A profound reorientation of internal auditing is therefore needed toward a clearly articulated vantage point of public service, so that both internal auditors and auditees are viewed as citizens in their communities, rather than as market actors like providers, consumers, or clients. The ravenous commercialism that dominates modern internal auditing risks bringing internal auditing into disrepute.

Chapter 5

Numbers, wisdom, and folly

5.1 INTERNAL AUDITING IN THE "ALGORITHMIC SOCIETY"

Internal auditing is increasingly characterized by the application of algorithms to analyze and "solve" problems. Internal auditors are tending to downplay or drop nonmathematical considerations, including ethical matters, that are not readily amenable to quantification. This is the "algorithmic society" in action, in which we are subjected to "the replacement of human, legible and accountable judgments with 'black-box' algorithms" (Peeters and Schuilenburg, 2021, 1). The algorithmic society covers not only the use of algorithms, but the networks in which they are disseminated, the individuals who are compelled to use them, and the individuals who create and deploy them. The rampant spread of the algorithmic society represents a victory, of sorts, for technological progress, but it is the type of progress that is accompanied as much by loss as by gain. In this chapter, we shall review some of the follies of self-deception arising from our faith in algorithmically based technological progress. These follies include the de-personalization and de-moralization of important social decisions, amounting to new forms of governance (Shore and Wright, 2015) from which human agency is banished, and through which the opacity of algorithmic parameters damages transparency. In Mustafa Suleyman's words, we are in danger of finding ourselves "at the mercy of algorithms that we don't understand" (Suleyman, 2023, 3–4). (We have already reviewed the misuse of algorithms for predictive purposes in Section 2.3, in the context of "surveillance capitalism".)

Before proceeding, let us consider an example of the development of the algorithmic society in an important aspect of our lives – banking and finance. In the 1960s and 1970s, the author's father managed a small bank branch in the north of England. In that era, the banks had vast networks of branches to ensure a close proximity to their customers. A careful familiarization with the bank's customers was an important part of my father's responsibilities: He was closely aware of their circumstances and banking

DOI: 10.1201/9781032664880-5

needs. He assisted elderly customers to open, transfer, and close their accounts; his opinion on customers' credit worthiness was an important component in lending decisions; and his hands-on oversight of the evening closing procedures ensured that any malfeasance by employees was soon spotted and resolved. The customers appreciated his advice. Farmers would often express their appreciation through gifts of cartons of eggs; a local professional footballer (soccer player) occasionally offered him two complimentary tickets to high profile matches; a senior police officer would invite my parents to black-tie social events; elderly ladies would present him with Christmas gifts like a home-knitted scarves; and elderly gentlemen would hand him an occasional bottle of a traditional Irish liqueur.

My father's world of banking has vanished. The branch he managed is long-closed, and the slightly larger branch to which its operations were transferred in the 1980s has also been closed. Along with the rationalization of bank branches, the bank itself – the Midland Bank – has disappeared, its sorry and impoverished remnant acquired (or, perhaps more accurately, rescued) by HSBC bank in 1992. Reputed at one point, just after the First World War, to be the world's largest bank in terms of the aggregated value of customers' deposits, the Midland Bank's fortunes diminished in the twentieth century along with the United Kingdom's post-imperial decline. A particularly harmful blow to the Midland's fortunes was its ill-advised and mis-handled acquisition of the ailing, California-based Crocker National Bank in 1981.

Today, in line with general trends in commercial banking, customers in the small town in which my father worked have to travel a long distance to their nearest branch for face-to-face customer service. The banks now prefer their customers to engage in online or telephone banking. (In February 2024 the British press reported that the closure of the last bank branch in the town of Leiston, in Suffolk, left the townsfolk with a near 50-mile round trip to that bank's nearest branch.) Moreover, credit decisions in commercial banking are reached not judgmentally, through a close knowledge of the customer's individual circumstances, but algorithmically, through the completion of online questionnaires – except for the wealthiest customers, who still receive personalized attention. The small gifts from satisfied customers to bank employees that were common in my father's day are, I am told, extremely rare today. And any such gifts would probably be scrutinized zealously by internal auditors for compliance with codes of "ethical" conduct: The present day interpretation of gift-giving as an unethical social practice contrasts with traditional perceptions of small gifts as the natural consequence of healthy social interaction.

The author of this book is by no means a Luddite. It makes economic sense for the banking industry to rationalize its operations through the opportunities provided by technology and algorithmic decision-making. Nonetheless, de-personalized banking has led to the loss of important elements of our collective social life. The human contact between bank and customer has all but vanished, except for the very rich. The kinds of small gifts my father received from satisfied customers were tokens of appreciation and an integral part of a small town's social life, but they would now be deemed unacceptable "conflicts of interest" by literalist, checklist-wielding internal auditors. My father was accountable for his credit-worthiness decisions in ways that credit checking algorithms cannot be held accountable. In short, social trust in our banking arrangements has largely evaporated. A world of humanistic interaction has become a world of the online algorithm, the all-powerful formula, and the impersonal checklist.

The example we have reviewed is not to suggest that the banking industry is somehow villainous. In recent decades, large areas of socio-economic activity have drifted away from individual judgment toward an algorithmic approach, to the extent that the algorithmic society is riddled with depersonalized, formulaic ways of interacting with individuals. The use of "Big Data" and digitalized algorithms can achieve efficiency in many areas, from establishing loan eligibility to performing complex actuarial calculations for the purposes of determining insurance premiums and establishing the funding requirements for pension schemes. In addition, algorithms may eliminate human bias in areas like gender-based prejudice against female loan applicants.

The dangers and dysfunctions of formulaic methods of reasoning arise in part from an algorithm's limited scope for encouraging judgmental inferences. By privileging knowledge acquired from algorithms over the types of knowledge that come from practical experience, an excessive reliance on algorithms deforms our reasoning capabilities. An algorithm, by and large, is only as useful as the interpretative abilities of the people who deploy it. In 2013, an unfortunate citizen of the United Kingdom who suffered from gallstones was killed by a reliance on algorithmic assessment. The individual called an emergency assistance number for an ambulance. Despite his descriptions of agonizing abdominal pains, the responder informed him that his symptoms did not meet the formulaic requirement for an ambulance and advised him to seek non-emergency treatment. An out-of-hours doctor confirmed this decision. The patient was dead within days. It was reported that a routine operation to address his gallstones problem would have saved his life: "Instead of an individual, he was treated as an abstract statistical point in a population" (Scherz, 2022, 144), a victim of the reductionist dangers of the algorithmic society. As one commentator has warned us: "For decisions that matter, algorithmic reasoning may not rise to the desired standard of wisdom" (Porter, 2020, viii). Overall, a dehumanizing, over-dependency on algorithmic ways of thinking and acting has little room for considerations of moral agency, judgment, and creativity.

The widespread use of algorithmic governance raises additional concerns beyond incorrect decision-making. We hinted above that algorithms and data analysis may eliminate human bias. The use of DNA matching has helped to solve many criminal cases where police guesswork has fallen short. However, algorithmic practices and data analysis have been described as a "double-edged sword" (Sinnreich and Gilbert, 2024, xi), providing both solutions for and creating problems of bias. For example, facial recognition technology has been used in attempts to reduce criminality, but the questionable reliability of facial detection among some ethnic groups has led to bias and a distorting of objectives (Cheney-Lippold, 2017, 15–17). The ostensible amorality of quantification and algorithms does not therefore necessarily guarantee impartiality. The use of bell curve analysis to portray the "normal" distribution of traits in a population of data may suggest a problematic or undesired "deviance" from the norm – "eugenics sought to shift the characteristics of the population shown in the normal distribution by sterilizing the lower end of that distribution" (Scherz, 2022, 98). As Sinnreich and Gilbert warn us, "the premise of statistical objectivity serves to justify, amplify, and obscure a multitude of subjective opinions, often in the exercise of social power" (Sinnreich and Gilbert, 2024, 27 and 69). In other words, quantification might carry overtones of value judgments, and even provide the pretext for abuses of power. In the absence of moral judgment and qualitative explanation, the ostensible amorality of the algorithmic society is misleading.

A further problem in the algorithmic society is the use of algorithms for binary decisions – to accept or reject an application for a loan, or to send or withhold an ambulance service to an individual. In reality, human activities often have more than one objective, and sometimes competing objectives that require judgment and wisdom to navigate through the necessary trade-offs. Algorithms that lack complete or precise parameters may result in harmful decisions, as we discussed above in relation to the dangers of facial detection technology.

There are also wider social downsides to algorithmic governance. The move away from humanistic to algorithmic activities hollows out our social relations. Returning to our banking example, the small English bank branch was a microcosm of the local society, a meeting place in which more than merely financial matters were transacted. The branch was a social hub where individuals of differing social strata rubbed along on a basis of mutual needs, and built a sense of community. My father was a multi-tasker well before the term became popular: He did several things at once, processing banking transactions, keeping cash secure, holding conversations, and maintaining a friendly, congenial atmosphere that encouraged customers to return. The closing of that small bank branch damaged the social environment of the local town by eliminating an important space for the sharing of news and gossip, and for strengthening the bonds of social cohesion and social trust. Moreover, with the loss of the branch came a loss of social knowledge and information. Who in that small town now has an overarching view of the financial health of the local community, individually and collectively?

A more recent example of a loss of knowledge caused by a shift toward algorithmic activities was presented to the author days before writing this chapter. During a ride hailing service in Washington D.C., the driver lamented the disappearance of a way of life. He had spent 30 years as a taxi driver, before switching to an online ride-hailing service, and he recalled fondly the daunting tests of local routes and maps that had been required in past times from all taxi drivers. Now such knowledge is almost redundant – the traditional taxi industry has been almost completely wiped out by firms like Uber and Lyft that use Global Positioning Systems (GPS) technology. We exchanged thoughts on the implications of these changes. While the marvelous technological advances associated with GPS have improved the efficiency of road transport and navigation a generation's intimate knowledge of local streets has vanished. This does not greatly matter most of the time – until the GPS glitches and we flounder, helplessly lost.

Beyond the collective societal worries originating in the algorithmic society, concerns have been expressed for our individual well-being amid the deconstruction (or reconfiguration) of our identities. For example:

> companies like Google use their algorithms and our data to produce a dynamic world of knowledge that has, and will continue to have, extraordinary power over our present and futures. And as we also continue to be well filled with data, this algorithmic logic produces not just the world *but us*.
>
> *Cheney-Lippold, 2017, 11, emphasis added*

As we saw with surveillance capitalism in Section 2.3, the algorithmic society carries dangers of reducing us to manipulable numbers.

No activity displays the dispiriting impact of a surrender to algorithmic ways of thinking more than auditing. The modern external auditor's imagination is crimped by materiality limits: Discussions with external auditors often tend to revolve around whether a topic fits a specific audit's materiality criteria and therefore merits review. The algorithmic materiality assessments of items in financial statements remove significant judgment from external auditing. For internal auditing, it is sometimes difficult to detain the auditor's attention to matters beyond data analytics, dashboards, and statistical sampling. Floods of information and number-crunching have their purposes, but they may have reached the point at which they have become a substitute for creative thinking. Expertise in auditing is increasingly reduced to the deployment of formulaic solutions.

Just as the lending departments of large banks rely decreasingly on familiarization with the circumstances of customers, in favor of algorithmic processes, often delivered facelessly and online, modern internal auditing is similarly characterized by impersonal algorithmic activities transmitted through hollow, boilerplate language. Internal auditing's present-day malaise may be explained away as simply a reflection of the broader social trends that squeeze questions of virtue, character, and judgment out of public life. Yet internal auditing's unique mission perhaps requires it to act as an antidote to the wider de-personalization of social life and other socially regressive trends. The march of technology continues, from Artificial Intelligence to the Internet of Things to the proliferation of algorithmic decision-making. Internal auditing's embrace of technology should be treated as a means to an end, and not as an end in itself. The modern style of formulaic internal auditing can respond only with difficulty to the reality it encounters. Algorithms tend to renounce real discourse and leave little room for critical thinking. We arguably acquire the most valuable knowledge and practical sensibilities from immersion in face-to-face internal auditing, rather than from behind algorithms and other veils of false scientific insight.

The all-conquering thirst for algorithms in modern auditing reflects a broader over-reliance on technological solutions. One is reminded of the Zen parable of the philosopher pointing at the moon while her disciples are fixated on her finger rather than on the moon. The moon in this parable represents knowledge, or self-knowledge, or perhaps a realization of the contingencies of our existence, but an unwarranted focus on the finger blocks any such insights. Similarly, internal auditors are focused more and more on technology (the finger, in our analogy) rather than on the aims of the technology (the moon). Technology has little interest in our moral matters, through which we make ourselves accountable to others.

We have more to discuss on the topic of quantification. In the next section, we shall turn our attention to an unwarranted faith in the power of numbers that seems as old as civilization itself.

5.2 THE SORCERY OF NUMBERS

A meticulous handling of numbers has always been expected from auditors. Any specialty of auditing uncomfortable with handling and interpreting numbers would be hollow, insubstantial, and lost in the modern world. Despite this, internal auditing involves far more than merely number-crunching. We have argued in Section 5.1 that the algorithmic society has exacerbated our increasing collective obsession with quantification, but something deeper than our present-day submission to algorithmic governance is at play. For the duration of recorded history, it seems that numbers have held a grip on our imagination, and often to an unwarranted degree. If a respected colleague leans across a table to address you, his brow furrowed and his voice deepened to emphasize the importance of his message, and he insists that you cannot rate an audit finding without numbers to back up your assessment, you are in the presence of this enduring faith in numbers. Those who crave numerical justifications and data-driven evidence to the extent of distrusting qualitative assessment are heirs to a lengthy tradition of numberphilia, and internal auditing is not immune from these broader cultural tendencies.

Although quantification can be reliable, the seeming objectivity of numbers can be misleading. Simplification through quantification can slide into over-simplification as we impoverish complex realities by boiling them down to quantifiable analysis. Quantification has been described as a "system for throwing away information" (Espeland, 1998, 25). Exercises in quantification can therefore reduce as well as promote knowledge and understanding. One way to envision the problematic process of simplification arising from quantification is through the analogy of a map. A map is a way of simplifying a territory or patch of land (Nigam and Trujillo, 2016, 525): Ambiguous or incomplete cartographic choices may result in an unreliable or misleading map. Quantified analysis, like a map, chops down complex realities into easily understood abstractions, thereby sacrificing some of the detail and significance of the matter under analysis. In internal auditing we should be careful that our quantification activities do not sacrifice too much important information accessible through alternative evaluative choices. Judgment and bias in the gathering and handling of data may distort an analysis by quantification. An over-reliance on number-crunching is perilous.

A part of our enduring fascination with numbers is that they amount to more than a mere list of signifiers and counting tools: An individual number possesses a unique character and structure. We can sense the individualized "personality" of numbers through a consideration of prime numbers. Indeed, primality reveals profound information about individual integers. A prime number is an integer with only two factors (i.e., divisors), the number 1 and itself, rather than two smaller numbers. An example of a prime number is 3 – it is a product of only two factors, 1 × 3 (which can of course also be expressed as 3 × 1). The initial ten prime numbers are 2, 3, 5, 7, 11, 13, 17, 19, 23 and 29. (The number 1 tends to be excluded from the prime numbers because it has only one factor – itself.) Non-prime numbers are designated as composite numbers, as they can be factorized by two numbers smaller than themselves. The number 4, for example, is composite because it is a factor of 2 × 2, but the number 6 is often considered to be the first "authentic" composite number as it is the product of two different factors (2 × 3 or 3 × 2).

Primality has important applications in many areas of mathematics, and prime numbers can be considered as the "building blocks" of our counting systems. Some believe that prime numbers help to explicate the scientific structures underpinning our world. For example, in North America there are three types of cicada with life cycles of 7, 13, and 17 years. Is it merely a coincidence that 7, 13, and 17 are all prime numbers, or does it point to some profound biological regularity or ratio (Wilson, 2020, 20–21)?

Primality is not the only source of our fascination with the insights of numbers into the structure of the world. The preponderance of Fibonacci numbers in patterns of flower petals has struck many as significant for understanding the deep structures of our botanical and wider biological environments (Stewart, 1995, 135–143), while the use of Fibonacci numbers in the analysis of market trends and commodity prices is common. (In the Fibonacci sequence, the numbers are the sum of the two preceding numbers: Thus, 0, 1, 1, 2, 3, 5, 8, 13, 21, 34, 55.)

The more we think about the properties of numbers, whether individually or in sequential patterns (or even in geometric patterns), the more we seem to be sucked into a world of fascination. Let us glace at some instances of number curiosities. Irrational numbers, i.e., numbers that cannot be expressed precisely as a ratio of two integers, have long captivated our collective imagination. Examples of irrational numbers include *pi* (π), the ratio of a circle's circumference to its diameter (approximately 3.14) and *phi* (φ), the "golden ratio" (approximately 1.62) – these numbers are irrational in the sense that they are incommensurable, meaning they can never be resolved exactly. The number zero has a unique position in number theory, and has been described as a "very interesting, singular, and thought provoking sign ... intimately connected to the idea of nothing, emptiness, the void" (Botman, 1987, 1).

We could dwell on the familiar yet strange qualities of individual and sequential numbers, because it is a topic that is inherently enthralling. Nonetheless, for our purposes it is enough to note the grip that numbers, as abstract objects, hold on our imagination. We shall see in due course how people attach mystical significance to individual numbers, but it is the *reliability* and *unambiguity* of numbers as mathematical objects that concern us initially. A contrast with words helps to explain the reliability of numbers. Terminology tends to evolve over time, with words acquiring more nuances. At any point in time, words may be equivocal with a range of meanings. This can cause confusion. In contrast to the equivocal nature of everyday language, numbers appear to enjoy univocal, timeless, and unchangeable qualities that eliminate (or drastically reduce) ambiguity. For example, the word "bank" in English can refer either to an institution that keeps our money or lends us money, or to the sloping land at the edges of a river. In contrast, the number 3 refers always to the integer that falls sequentially between 2 and 4.

Numbers therefore seem to offer, in addition to their utility in counting, measurement, and arithmetical operations, a safe haven of unambiguity in an often-confusing world in flux. A further attraction of numbers is their abstractness. By abstract, we mean "existing outside place and time" (Kouremenos, 2019, 17, n19). We may therefore describe numbers as non-spatiotemporal objects. Of crucial importance is the fact that these objects exist "independently of us" (Balaguer, 1998, 5). The abstract nature of numbers implies precision and logic, at least in the practical, everyday use of numbers. Combining the elements of permanence and abstraction, it is not difficult for us to look beyond the contingencies of various systems of numerals (i.e., the diverse writing conventions used around the world to portray numbers) to the universality and consistency of numbers. The English mathematician G.H. Hardy famously argued for the enduring truths of numbers and mathematics: "Greek mathematics is 'permanent', more permanent even than Greek literature", and "immortality may be a silly word, but probably a mathematician has the best chance of whatever it may mean" (Hardy, 1940, 81).

The aforementioned characteristics of numbers have encouraged both rational philosophical inquiry and mystical interpretation. In the Platonic hierarchy of reality, numbers seem to have held an intermediate metaphysical position, close to the abstract, immaterial forms, yet also reaching into our physical, tangible world in which numbers are manipulated as mathematical objects. To be more precise, the numbers up to and including 4 were considered by Platonists to be natural objects and therefore closer to the ideal truth, while larger "arithmetical" numbers were considered less pure because, as the results of constructions from smaller numbers, they seemed closer to the physical world (Nikulin, 2013, 15ff). The Platonist sees numbers as a bridge between our everyday world and the divine, a metaphysical notion of degrees of numerical perfection that has not lost its potency over the millennia.

Prior to Plato, Pythagoras (c.570–c.495 BCE) and his followers had attributed both practical and mystical powers to numbers. The Pythagoreans explored the role of numbers in structuring (or, perhaps, reflecting the structure of) our experience, from musical scales to astronomical observations. They also speculated on the mystical significance of numbers (Dudley, 1997). Pythagoras and Plato remind us that rational inquiry into the significance of numbers has long co-existed with mystical speculations. Today, many individuals believe that numbers symbolize, contain, or are channels for magic, and for luck (good or bad), and that they possess extraordinary spiritual powers or divine insight. For such individuals, numbers have an inward or esoteric significance, as well as a *prime facie*, exoteric meaning. Others delude themselves that numbers, through the "fog of mysticism", have an occult power over human events, rather than over hyper-imaginative human minds (Dudley, 1997, 17). The French mystic Simone Weil, for example, had strong beliefs in numerology: The universal truths of numerology are to be found

> in the ancient mythologies; in the philosophy of Pherecydes, Thales, Anaximander, Heraclitus, Pythagoras, Plato, and the Greek stoics;

> in Greek poetry of the Great Age; in the universal folklore; in the Upanishads and the Bhagavad-Gita; in the Taoist texts and in certain Buddhist schools; in the remains of sacred Egyptian scriptures; in the dogmas of the Christian faith and in the writings of the greatest Christian mystics, especially John of the Cross; in certain heresies, especially the Cathar and Manichaean traditions.
>
> *cited in Nirenberg and Nirenberg, 2021, 126*

Looking closer at the esoteric significance of individual numbers, one might take the example of the number 7, which has traditionally been of supernatural importance in many cultures. Among other things, it tallies with the number of planets known to the ancient Greeks; the 7 days of the week (and the account of creation in the Hebrew Bible's book of *Genesis*); the 7 notes of the musical octave; the 7 colors in the visible light spectrum; the 7 hills on which Rome was built; and the 7 chakras of kundalini yoga. One could write an entire book about the mystical symbolism of the number 7! Or the number 3. Or, indeed, any of the first ten numbers, plus a handful of the larger numbers. Perhaps the most notorious example of numerical mysticism with contemporary power is the phenomenon of *triskaidekaphobia*, i.e., fear of the number 13 (Schimmel, 1994, 203), which is surprisingly commonplace around the world.

In addition to the esoteric powers attributed to individual numbers, some identify esoteric meaning in recurring patterns or sequences of numbers. For instance, some view odd numbers as masculine and even numbers as feminine. There are also well-established, ambitious, holistic systems of numerology, like the mystical assignment of numbers to alphabetic letters to reveal deeper meanings beyond literal, linguistic interpretations. In the Pythagorean tradition, mystical insights were sought through the practice of *isopsephy*, in which the values of the numbers assigned to Greek letters in a word or phrase were added together. The use of a similar system, *gematria*, in Judaism's Kabbalistic tradition to interpret sacred texts has been adopted by some Muslim and Christian mystics, with widespread use continuing to the current day. Some Christian proponents of biblical inerrancy have dwelled at length of the significance of 666, the number of the apocalyptic beast in the New Testament book of *Revelation*, 13:18. The mystically inclined George Ivanovich Gurdjieff (c.1867–1949) included in his eclectic teachings, known by various terms like the "The Fourth Way" and "The System", the enneagram – a star-like, nine-pointed symbol with metaphysical significance and complex numerical allusions (Dudley, 1997, 263–269).

In short, some people find numbers fascinatingly mysterious. This fascination can extend beyond numbers to numerals, i.e., the shapes of written numbers. There are also striking artistic dimensions to the fascination with the "strangeness" of numbers. In some of his musical compositions, Olivier Messiaen (1908–1992) applied the qualities of different prime numbers into unpredictable interactions of rhythm and pitch. The haunting otherworldliness of his *Quatre Études de Rythme* (1949–1950) can only be appreciated through listening. Descriptive words seem to fail when this music "speaks".

What does all this suggest for the practice of internal auditing? A preliminary observation is that numbers provide many individuals with a sense of comfort and stability in a world subject to social upheaval and change. To many, therefore, numbers are synonymous with science, accuracy, and permanence. A colleague who insists that you cannot reliably rate an audit finding without a quantifiable, numerical basis is not necessarily a maverick or a crank – he is part of a long tradition of suspicion of qualitative judgment. A second observation is that the objective reliability of numbers coexists with, or overlaps with, a mystical streak in humanity's relationships with numbers. Individuals are often attracted by the esoteric and enigmatic qualities of numbers, with the dangers of embracing irrationality.

Throughout this book we have argued that internal auditing has been impoverished by an excessive emphasis on quantification. To be called "calculating" is not usually a compliment – it suggests a "cold, fish-like and completely self-interested" obsession with measurement, without necessarily understanding the reality behind the numbers (Boyle, 2000, xi). Number obsession has more troubling implications: Humans and their activities are rarely reducible to numbers, or only in the extremely dangerous service of de-personalization and de-humanization that leads to the obscenities of genocide and slavery. (Chilling examples of the dehumanizing use of numbers are given by Funnell, 1998; Rodrigues et al., 2018; Rosenthal, 2018).

Peter Bernstein (1998, 7) warned us that our lives "teem with numbers but we sometimes forget that numbers are only tools. They have no soul; they may indeed become fetishes". Under such circumstances, internal auditors should discern carefully between the contexts in which quantification is a help or a hindrance, and seek a difficult-to-define point of equilibrium between the alternatives of quantification and qualification. This discernment requires experience and expertise, which we discussed in our review of professional standards at Section 4.2. In our pursuit of a more controllable cosmos, we have perhaps extended our trust in numbers to too many aspects of human life (Porter, 2020), with a danger that we might forget what it means to be human. In Section 5.3, we shall see that the current passion for quantification and our obsession with numbers may have some of their roots in cerebral asymmetry.

5.3 CEREBRAL ASYMMETRY AND THE ENTRENCHMENT OF LEFT-HEMISPHERIC THINKING

The brain is the zone of the body where matter meets consciousness. Or, expressed differently, the brain is the embodiment of the mind. It is of little surprise that the workings of the brain have long fascinated both scientists and philosophers, and not least among brain-related topics has been the existence and significance of cerebral asymmetry. In this chapter, we shall perhaps encounter, in discussions of the dual-hemispheric brain, an overarching explanation for many of the troubling tendencies of internal auditing (and for wider society) toward algorithmic thinking, a detail-obsessed building-block mindset, and a corresponding struggle with holistic, "big picture" thinking. The work of philosopher-neurologist Iain McGilchrist (born 1953) on the structural and functional differences between the brain hemispheres, described in his *The Master and his Emissary: The Divided Brain and the Making of the Western World* (2009, revised 2019), comes close to providing an overall explanation for the various manifestations of the distressed condition of modern auditing we have considered throughout this book.

A preliminary word of caution is in order. The subject of cerebral asymmetry has had a checkered history, littered with falsehoods and half-truths. For example, some have talked of a masculine left hemisphere balancing a feminine right hemisphere, while others have promoted the notion of a rational, clinical left hemisphere in contrast to an emotional, gullible right hemisphere. Far above such facile representations of brain lateralization, a remarkable book, *The Origin of Consciousness in the Breakdown of the Bicameral Mind*, published in 1976 by Princeton psychologist Julian Jaynes (1920–1997) offered a fascinating perspective on the role of brain lateralization in the development of introspective self-awareness. Jaynes enriched our understanding of the importance of metaphor in consciousness, especially in the ages of Homeric Greece and the Hebrew Bible. Unfortunately, for our purposes, his overall argument on brain lateralization was almost the opposite of McGilchrist's. Jaynes argued that a breakdown of the bicameral brain has been in progress, the two hemispheres converging as they increasingly work together, but McGilchrist's more persuasive arguments posit a tendency for the brain, at the present time, to become more and more asymmetrical, with a harmful over-dependence on the left hemisphere.

McGilchrist has indicated that his decades-long investigations into cerebral asymmetry arose from his initial "neuroimaging research on the loss of normal brain asymmetry in schizophrenia" (McGilchrist, 2019a, xi). Indeed, it is through brain impairment that the impact of cerebral asymmetry is often revealed and studied. In a healthily balanced brain, the two hemispheres cooperate. But the functions of the two hemispheres are different, in areas like the treatment of language and conceptual understanding, and their interrelations are complex. In McGilchrist's words: The left hemisphere offers

> a valuable but intermediate process, one of 'unpacking' what is there and handing it back to the right hemisphere, where it can be ... integrated into the experiential whole, much as the painstaking fragmentation and

analysis of a sonata in practice is reintegrated by the pianist in performance at a level where he or she must no longer be aware of it.

McGilchrist, 2019b, 25

Or, more succinctly, and in relation to animals as well as humans, the left hemisphere yields "narrow, focussed attention" while the right hemisphere yields "broad, vigilant attention" (McGilchrist, 2019a, 27).

These comments on cerebral asymmetry suggest that the left hemisphere plays a useful role in the analysis of details, while the right hemisphere synthesizes fragmented information into coherent, "big picture" perspectives. If, for any reason, the right hemisphere is inhibited or impaired, the mind over-relies on the left hemisphere, and its focus remains fixated on fragmented details rather than on coherent overall perspectives. An example of a left hemispheric perspective was provided by the French novelist Marcel Proust (1871–1922), in his *À la recherche du temps perdu* (*In Search of Lost Time*), published between 1913 and 1927. The narrator, in a distressed state of mind, experiences a vertiginous disorientation in Venice. His experience portrays characteristic viewpoints of the left hemisphere:

> The town I saw before me had ceased to be Venice. Its personality and name seemed to be deceptive fictions I no longer had the courage to impress on its stones. I saw palaces reduced to their constituent parts, lifeless heaps of marble with nothing to choose between them, and the water as a combination of hydrogen and oxygen, external, blind, anterior and exterior to Venice.
>
> *translation based on O'Hear, 2001, 83*

Here, the narrator's mind apprehends the building blocks and structural elements of Venice, the lumps of marble and stone of the buildings, and the splashing of water molecules against canal walls, but a larger, integrated perspective of the city slips from his mind.

In modern society, McGilchrist argues, we are all increasingly tending to see Venice in the manner of the Proustian episode. More and more, we are collectively in thrall to an over-dependency on left hemispheric thinking.

> [Y]ou could say, to sum up a vastly complex matter in a phrase, that the brain's left hemisphere is designed to help us to *ap*-prehend – and thus manipulate – the world; the right hemisphere to *com*-prehend it – see it all for what it is.
>
> *McGilchrist, 2021, I: 3, emphasis in original*

An excessive left hemispheric focus has a reductionist outlook. We should prefer a richer outlook that permits us to discern overarching meaning: The use of the right hemisphere prevents our world from becoming mechanistic and shallow. As indicated in the title of his book *The Master and his Emissary* (McGilchrist, 2019a), McGilchrist portrays the left side of the brain as a good servant but a poor master. The right hemisphere's function of interpreting our world in an integrated, holistic, "big picture" manner not only makes use of the left hemisphere's analytical powers – interpretatively, it transforms them.

McGilchrist suggests that three characteristic aspects of right hemisphere functions are "the capacity to read the human face, the capacity to sustain vigilant attention, and the capacity to empathise", and he warns that the behavior of children is increasingly indicating a collective deficit in right hemispheric functions:

> between a quarter and a third of children aged as old as five to seven are now having to be taught how to read the human face, something that until recently would have been necessary only in the case of children with autism ... a third of all children now have difficulty carrying out tasks that a decade ago virtually every child in a mainstream school would have been able to do easily – tasks that depend on sustained attention ... [and] research suggest[s] that young people today are less empathetic than children thirty to forty years ago.
>
> *McGilchrist, 2019a, xxii*

McGilchrist's arguments, if correct, have immense and troubling consequences. The dispositions of one's consciousness determine one's encounters with the world. The functional asymmetries arising from the bi-hemispheric structure of the brain do not therefore amount merely to a question of fragmented versus consolidated perspectives, because such differences "are not different ways of *thinking about* the world; they are different ways of *being in* the world" (McGilchrist, 2019a, 31, emphasis in original). If we have been correct in our assessment that internal auditing today focuses too much on the building blocks of information, to the detriment of synthesizing details into "big picture" perspectives, and that internal auditing's algorithmic, numbers-obsessed, and checklist-oriented mindset has tended to marginalize internal auditing's humanistic and ethical aspects, it is not difficult to connect our findings to McGilchrist's portrayal of excessive left hemispheric thinking. Modern internal auditing's reductive, narrow-sighted, and mechanistic focus is a textbook example of such thinking.

Throughout this book, we have argued that internal auditing today displays an impoverished, detail-obsessed mindset that has wrought havoc on trust, virtue, and wisdom. A balance of both brain hemispheres' functions is needed for healthy individuals and healthy societies and, indeed, for healthy internal auditing. Instead, an over-reliance on the left side of the brain is hampering pluralistic assessments in internal auditing by over-emphasizing an analytical and quantitative focus on fragmentary details, to the detriment of integrative, synthetic forms of judgment. What is missing from internal auditing's impoverished perspective is a countervailing sense of the whole.

McGilchrist has suggested that the left hemisphere's

> mode of thinking prizes consistency above all and claims to offer the same mechanistic models to explain everything that exists. This thinking is common to those who espouse naïve reductionist science ('scientism'), enthusiasts for technological solutions to what are complex human problems, and designers and implementers of bureaucratic systems.
>
> *McGilchrist, 2019a, xxiii*

These comments fit our analysis of the malaise of modern internal auditing: We have discussed in this book auditing's scientistic surrender to technological innovations (like data analytics), at the cost of humanistic judgment, and its increasingly checklist-based, bureaucratic approach to its activities. A hindrance of right hemispheric thinking may therefore be a contributor to the lack of creativity we have identified at the root of modern internal auditing's malaise. In McGilchrist's words:

> Creativity involves a number of elements in which the right hemisphere is superior to the left: breadth of vision, the capacity to forge distant links, flexibility rather than rigidity, a willingness to respond to a changed, or changing, context, a tolerance of ambiguity, and an ability to work with knowledge that is, for the most part, inherently both imprecise and implicit.
>
> *McGilchrist, 2021, 1:304*

Looking beyond internal auditing to the wider social picture, we discussed in Chapter 2 the decay of traditional institutions that is afflicting many parts of the modern world, accompanied by a steep decline in social trust. This topic too can be captured by McGilchrist's theory – McGilchrist considers that in classical Athens "the two hemispheres worked in harmony as never before or since" and that much of subsequent history, from the decline of the Roman Empire through the Renaissance, the Enlightenment and the Industrial Revolution, represents "a power struggle between these two ways of experiencing the world" and he suggests that we have now "ended up prisoners of just one – that of the left hemisphere alone" (McGilchrist, 2019b, 27). If this is true, it suggests that the dismal condition of modern internal auditing is simply a reflection of wider patterns of deteriorating thought processes arising from an over-reliance on left hemispheric thinking. In this sense, the degradation of internal auditing into an unimaginative focus on fragmented building blocks of information may be considered as inevitable. Regrettable, certainly, but part of a wider and unavoidable pattern of cultural decline – "societal changes that are stifling our capacity for big thinking" (Bhaskar, 2021, 187). Therefore, if the older patterns of social organization in bureaucratic, command-and-control organizations are giving way to horizontally distributed accountability among digital networks, it is perhaps unsurprising that internal auditing has failed to keep pace with such changes. Internal auditing is patterned into the fabric of society and is a victim of broader social trends.

Nonetheless, we have argued in this book that internal auditing should be an antidote to the dysfunctional effects of wider, cultural pathologies. Instead, modern internal auditing has to date been far from an antidote – it is part of the dehumanizing trends of many social activities. One may protest that, as individuals, we are not reducible to our brains, just as society as a whole is not reducible to a collection of brains. However, McGilchrist's richly nuanced arguments relating to cerebral asymmetry provide a plausible, overarching, big picture understanding of why modern internal auditing is struggling to comprehend big picture perspectives.

The findings of modern neuroscience were anticipated by earlier reflections on the problem of apprehending big picture perspectives by avoiding nitpicking, mathematical detail. The Anglo-Irish satirist Jonathan Swift (1667–1745), in his *Battle of the Books* (1704), contrasted ancient and modern literary and cultural traditions through a fable-like analogy of a spider and a honeybee. Swift was addressing an echo in the Anglophone world of the French Enlightenment debate known as the *Querelle des Anciens et des Modernes* (the Quarrel of the Ancients and the Moderns). The *Querelle*'s argument centered on the relative literary and artistic merits of classical Greek and Roman civilization on one hand, and contemporary French language and literature on the other. The Ancients argued for the superiority of antiquity, while the Moderns proclaimed that the current culture surpassed classical achievements.

Swift made his spider a Modern, his bee an Ancient. Swift's mathematically obsessed spider argues with the bee, and denounces the honey-making insect as a mere pollen collector, "a vagabond without house or home .... Your livelihood is a universal plunder upon nature; a freebooter over fields and gardens". In contrast, the spider claims intellectually autonomy: His web is "built with my own hands, and the materials extracted altogether out of my own person". The bee retorts that he possesses authentic creativity: "I indeed visit all the flowers and blossoms ... but whatever I collect from thence enriches myself without the least injury to their beauty, their smell, or their taste". According to the bee, the spider's web-spinning is destructive, turning all into "excrement and venom" and producing nothing but "flybane and a cobweb". (The reference to excrement seems to refer to the belief current in Swift's time that cobwebs were made of spiders' digestive refuse, rather than from silk). In contrast, the bee "by a universal range, with long search, much study, true judgment, and distinction of things, brings home honey and wax". (All quotations from Ross and Woolley, 2008, 111–112.)

Swift is suggesting that calculative expertise is insufficient without the access to accumulated wisdom derived from a broad cultural foundation. The bee offers a profound wisdom arising from the accumulated experience recorded and transmitted by our inherited culture: It offers a deeper reservoir of knowledge and wisdom than the spider's mathematical equations and logic-chopping. The bee draws on centuries of accumulated sagacity and insight, but the spider is restricted to the observation of the flux of daily events. The bee enjoys creative imagination applied to his daily observations, while the spider is limited to dry number-crunching in the impoverished world of the here and now. In McGilchristian terms, Swift's allegorical spider represents left hemispheric thinking, the bee right-hemispheric thinking. In more general terms, Swift was well aware of the traditional cultural associations of the honey bee: An ancient Greek legend had it that bees, "as agents of Apollo's servants the Muses, sat on baby Plato's lips and filled his mouth with honey, as a token of his future eloquence and erudition" (Waterfield, 2023, 1).

Of course, Swift, as a satirist, is not being fair to his spider in his portrayal of two different and competing types of knowledge. We might conclude that the best approach would be to combine the best aspects of the spider and the bee – tight empirical observation enriched by a deep cultural understanding. In terms of cerebral asymmetry, we might favor a balance of brain hemispheric activity. And applying the Swiftian analysis to auditing, we might say that auditing is much a creative, humanistic art as a dry, numbers-based science. At the very least, we may say that internal auditing falls between the humanities and the sciences, having borrowed from both. However, modern internal auditors increasingly resemble Swift's spider, spinning webs of formulaic checklists and algorithms, rather than his bee, with its creative cultural cross-pollination. A Swiftian would say that we are losing a vision of auditing as a humanistic combination of science and art. Calculating, algorithmic individuals tend to avoid individual creativity and avoid interpretative judgment. In contrast, individuals schooled in the humane traditions of give and take welcome and accept creative judgment.

Chapter 6

Toward a renaissance of internal auditing?

6.1 HEGEL'S OWL OF MINERVA IN A POST-BUREAUCRATIC AGE OF PIECEMEAL ASSURANCE

The philosopher G.W.F. Hegel (1770–1831), in his *Grundlinien der Philosophie des Rechts* (*Elements of the Philosophy of Right*) of 1820, warned us that "the Owl of Minerva spreads its wings only with the coming of dusk". In other words, *eureka* moments of wisdom, understanding, and interpretation (symbolized by the Roman goddess' owl) tend to come to us late in the day. Usually, too late in the day. Hegel's owl suggests that understanding and discernment tend to arise only with hindsight – by the time we have gained a grasp of the challenges we face, it tends to be too late to change the course of events. This interpretation of Hegel's metaphor of the Owl of Minerva chimes with our own experience. As we age, we look back at our foolish errors, and regret that it is too late to reverse our mistakes. Our past mistakes become *faits accomplis*.

As it flutters through the dark forest and flits between twilit branches, the Owl of Minerva sees (and, by extension, we see) history receding through a metaphorical rearview mirror, beyond our control. Additionally, in the darkness of the forest we, as observers, are able to make out only the owl's outline and not its details, suggesting that the wisdom we belatedly obtain is likely to be somewhat obscure. We can only stumble, constrained by darkness, toward understanding the significance of the owl's semi-occluded image.

All these interpretations of Hegel's Owl of Minerva point to a difficult-to-grasp wisdom that arrives too late to be reversed: Our fleeting wisdom falls short of adequately shining its reformist light on our predicament. Applying this insight to our inquiries into modern internal auditing, it suggests that it might be too late to remediate internal auditing's flat-footed response to the assurance demands arising from the increasing fragmentation of accountability and social trust. It also suggests that it might be too late to reform internal auditing's tendencies toward clockwork routines and checklist-based methodologies.

 DOI: 10.1201/9781032664880-6

However, we need not necessarily despair. Hegel's owl is probably the most contentious and disputed bird in the history of philosophy, and it is open to many interpretations. A more promising approach to our cryptic and elusive owl was suggested by English philosopher Mary Midgley (1919–2018), who argued that Hegel's metaphor counsels us that wisdom "comes into its own when things become dark and difficult rather than when they are clear and straightforward" (Midgley, 2005, x). In other words, we should look for wisdom not only when and where it is easy to do so, but at times and in places that are dark and troubling. This approach, one might argue, has underwritten the purpose of this book – we have sought out internal auditing's challenges in some less-than-obvious recesses of our culture, such as the liminal spaces on the peripheries of our organizations, and even in extra-mural spaces beyond organizational boundaries. Midgley's interpretation suggests that it is never too late to try to propose remedies to internal auditing's malaise.

Up to this point in the book, we have been clearing the ground ahead of the articulation of solutions. If we perceive internal auditing's current trauma not as a puzzle to be contemplated, but as a problem to be solved, the next logical step after clearing the ground is to pursue pragmatic improvements. In modern internal auditing we face a balancing act, navigating and interpreting continuities and ruptures between the older approaches we have inherited and the newer approaches we contemplate. Even if one is inclined to gradual reform over radical change (Berman and Fox, 2023), accelerated, significant change is sometimes warranted. Modern internal auditing's problems do not seem to be self-resolving aberrations: We have arrived at a fulcrum moment in the history of internal auditing, and an exhaustive re-thinking of policy and practice is demanded to define a program of reform. The following eight suggestions are offered in this spirit.

6.2 SUGGESTION 1: PRINCIPLES-BASED PROFESSIONAL STANDARDS

We encourage the Institute of Internal Auditors, and other professional associations responsible for issuing internal auditing standards, to move toward principles-based standards that promote individual judgment and critical thinking. The IIA's *Global Internal Audit Standards* (GIAS), published in 2024, provide an adamantine framework of prescriptive rules and requirements that encourage conformity, consistency, and the predictability of processes, but at the cost of eroding professional judgment. Principles-based standards would provide an overarching structure for the exercise of individual judgment, both technical and ethical. Such a change of emphasis from rules to principles in internal auditing standards might encourage a renaissance of trust, virtue, and wisdom in internal auditing.

Technical expertise does not guarantee wise judgment if it is based on rigid rules and mechanistic checklists that dampen interpretative thought.

In Section 4.2, we welcomed the injection of principles into the GIAS. The GIAS arranges its 52 standards under 15 guiding principles, gathered in turn into five domains (although the first domain consists of only a "purpose of internal auditing" statement and contains neither principles nor standards). However, the standards as a whole were not *revised into principles*, but rather *rearranged by principles*. The apparatus of the standards has therefore changed in the direction of principles, but the principles serve largely as category-markers for a bloated inventory of judgment-suppressing rules.

At present there is little evidence that prescriptive professional standards orient internal auditors toward serving the public good to the fullest extent. Indeed, internal auditing is a stark example of how a professional activity declines after it has scorned virtue. Too many internal auditors have been forced into hectic professional lives, their increasingly hollow assignments amounting to little more than fungible commodities forged by mechanical processes in the service of an efficient, "data-driven" consistency. Without a radical overhaul in favor of nurturing a professional space for ethical judgment, and for rehabilitating internal auditing from its current formulaic, amoral, and clockwork methodologies, the GIAS will remain inadequate to pass on to future generations the inheritance of internal auditing as an authentic moral activity. And modern internal auditing, if unreformed, may experience a hemorrhage of talent as new generations turn away from a profession perceived as little more than the formulaic operation of data analytics, information dashboards, and empty, mechanistic routines.

As internal auditors, our principal loyalty and accountability is to society at large. In other words, internal auditing owes an allegiance to something beyond itself – to the public good. Without the exercise of judgment and discernment through reasoning, we conduct our internal audits in a moral vacuum in which accumulations of rules and checklists banish ethical understanding and moral explanation. Internal auditing is as much a moral as a technical undertaking, and we should remain vigilant to the ethical blindness typically inculcated by a checklist-wielding culture. The professional repudiation of virtue encapsulated in and communicated through the GIAS has eroded the moral authority of internal auditing. To reverse the de-moralization of internal auditing, we should seek to re-moralize its written standards.

In Chapter 4, we considered professional virtue in the light of our ethical inheritance from the ancient Greek philosophers. Virtue in internal auditing is to be found less in committee-driven written standards than in the capacity of practitioners to apprehend the broader truths that stand in judgment over such standards. These broader truths encompass ethical considerations at levels of inquiry that no written rule or checklist can satisfy.

6.3 SUGGESTION 2: AN ABSTRACT BODY OF KNOWLEDGE

We noted in Section 4.2 that the concept of professional expertise invokes the notions that

> (1) the expertise derives from a largely abstract body of knowledge, (2) the possessor of the abstract knowledge is capable of applying that knowledge in practice, and (3) professional knowledge is cumulative: it is not merely a matter of mastering a fixed body of knowledge at a single point in time, but rather of mastering a foundation of knowledge upon which further experience and learning accumulate.
>
> *Lenz and O'Regan, 2024*

The existence of an abstract body of knowledge is both anterior to and a pre-requisite for written professional standards, in which knowledge overlaps with expertise.

We also suggested in Section 4.2 that the Institute of Internal Auditors' "common body of knowledge" (CBOK) does not amount to an abstract body of knowledge. Instead, it consists of an ongoing project that has generated a suite of reports summarizing the opinions of practitioners and stakeholders. The CBOK therefore comprises, not abstract reasoning, but a preponderance of opinions on the value of existing practices. Internal auditing therefore suffers from a slippery, elusive, and rather arbitrary knowledge base, and the obvious solution to this problem is to increase the CBOK's abstract elements, and to reduce its opinionated content. The development of a CBOK founded on abstract reasoning would fortify the reliability of the knowledge base of the IIA's vision of internal auditing, reduce the scope for opinionated elasticity, and provide a clear pathway toward the articulation of non-prescriptive, written standards.

6.4 SUGGESTION 3: "BIG PICTURE" PERSPECTIVES AND THE IMPORTANCE OF HISTORY

The British political scientist Matthew Goodwin (born 1981) has identified two types of social science researcher. By extension, we may use his description to pinpoint two types of internal auditor: On the one hand, we have "parachutists who survey the landscape from great heights" and, on the other, "truffle hunters who immerse themselves in only a small piece of territory" (Goodwin, 2023, xii). The parachutists are "big picture" individuals with a bird's eye perspective of the terrain they survey. The truffle hunters are those happy to plunge into the details of a topic, sniffing out the building blocks of information without ascending to the parachutist's all-encompassing perspectives. Goodwin's dichotomizing metaphors set out two fundamentally different approaches – the most reasonable solution for internal auditing is to balance the two perspectives. With an excessive focus on the big picture, we lose our grasp of the detail. Conversely, too much truffle hunting sacrifices the larger perspective.

We have suggested throughout this book that internal auditors increasingly resemble Goodwin's truffle hunters rather than parachutists. Internal auditing involves abstractions of our understandings of reality, and if internal auditing's abstractions remain at the level of the truffle-hunter's details, our overall interpretations will be simple-minded. A focus on details crowds out and cuts us off from understandings of a deeper, holistic reality. Only "big picture" abstract judgments derived from a synthesis of details can reach reliable, overarching conclusions.

The answer to this problem is for internal auditors to be trained in grasping "big picture" perspectives. The technical education of internal auditors already covers the analysis of details, and perhaps excessively so. To inculcate a tendency to look for wider frameworks of meaning, educational curricula for internal auditing should encourage the synthesis of scattered details into holistic understandings. One way of achieving this goal would be the incorporation of the study of auditing history into internal auditing education. The study of history is not merely of antiquarian interest: It encourages us to see large trends and to identify the interconnectedness of social, economic, and political themes on a global scale. Auditing's rich and sophisticated development is relevant to its current condition, and provides evidence of auditing's perennial adaptability. Familiarity with the development of auditing would illuminate for internal auditors the profile of professional auditing, and encourage the raising of the internal auditor's gaze from the here-and-now to overarching perspectives. The study of auditing's history would initiate new generations of internal auditors into a shared but fragile inheritance of public service. It would offer the advantage of a radical break from the ahistorical emphasis of modern internal auditing curricula, by introducing internal auditors to the broad, long term perspectives that are inseparable from service to the public good.

Internal auditing should amount to more than a toolbox of expert tricks and cost-containing algorithms. The study of auditing's past developments contributes to the internal auditor's overall ability to approach broad perspectives by encouraging the ability to abstract broad frameworks of understanding from reality. Those with an aversion to mandating the study of auditing's history in the IIA's educational curricula might seek alternative methods of encouraging "big picture" thinking, such as the study of systems thinking and mind-mapping. However, we advocate history as the best tool for inclusion in internal auditing education. (For those interested in the approach of philosophical hermeneutics taken by the author to interpret the material covered by this book, Appendix A sets out the importance of historical awareness to our inquiries.)

6.5 SUGGESTION 4: QUALITATIVE ASSESSMENT

In internal auditing, the expectation of a meticulous handling of numbers and a rigorous treatment of quantification is unquestionable. It is rightly taken for granted that internal auditors excel in these matters. Yet internal auditing, we have argued throughout this book, is not a value-free activity, and ethical considerations abound. To audit is to undertake a moral act. The current over-emphasis in modern internal auditing on numbers "exiles moral considerations" because it understands calculative activities as purely technical matters, devoid of ethical considerations (Williams, 2018, 167). Quantification does not always succeed in helping us to interpret evidence in the fullest sense, and it might circumscribe our ability to engage with the reality around us. For example, complex considerations of risk "are mistakenly conceived as machine-like problems of risk analysis" (Power, 2007, 14) and therefore tend to deteriorate rapidly into the quasi-scientific use of quantification techniques.

In Chapter 5, we suggested that the current over-reliance on quantification in internal auditing derives from two, deep-rooted sources – an unwarranted faith in the unambiguity of number-driven explanations, and an irrational, mystical belief in the metaphysical power of numbers. An unquestioning faith in numbers can at times lead to inappropriate judgments. The solution to this problem is to encourage internal auditors to embrace qualitative techniques in the evaluation of audit evidence. An emphasis on non-quantitative skills will therefore be needed in auditing education and practice to rebalance the core rigidities of an internal auditing culture conditioned so profoundly by algorithmic logic.

6.6 SUGGESTION 5: THE IMPORTANCE OF SKEPTICISM

Throughout this book, we have noted a craving for innovation by many internal auditors. This is an understandable reaction to the threats arising from a fast-moving environment. Some internal auditors talk of "steadily marching forward to a drumbeat of change" (Chambers and Pérez, 2024, 5), and internal auditing's propensity to perceive itself as an endlessly emergent phenomenon leads frequently to a commitment to innovation and self-reinvention (e.g., Ridley, 2019). A search for innovation and relevance in internal auditing has legitimate grounds. Nonetheless, modern internal auditing often resembles a barracuda zipping beneath the ocean's waves, unwilling to come to rest, betting its very survival on a need to relentlessly move ahead, attempting to carve out a new future for itself amid new sources of food, and rarely taking a rest. The problem is that the innovations typically sought by internal auditors often do not address the problems we outlined in Chapter 2 of this book – the revolutionary shifts in patterns of accountability and social trust, and the emergence of new, creative forms of assurance that threaten to marginalize traditional internal auditing.

The remorseless interest in innovation for innovation's sake in internal auditing sometimes hints at a mild identity crisis, and it might lead to a premature embracing of newfangled fads and buzzwords. Internal auditing is based on timeless considerations of honesty, truth, and logic. Such qualities provide an enduring compass with which to steer through fickle trends in socio-economic and political accountability. As such, internal auditing should be informed and shaped by our inherited stock of knowledge and morality, so as to resists fads and the exhortations of special interests.

Internal auditing sometimes turns into a battleground for special interests. The propagators of social and political grievances are incentivized to create new markets for their services and, as never before, internal auditing is forced to navigate a rocky terrain of over-hyped new topics and misplaced innovation. A healthy skepticism in auditing is likely to favor a prudent pattern of evolution rather than radical, risky revolution. As suggested in the influential metaphor of the internal auditor as a "gardener of governance" (Lenz and Jeppesen, 2022), it is careful evolution rather than abrupt revolution that is likely to yield the best results. In the words of Onora O'Neill, "[p]lants don't flourish when we pull them up too often to check how their roots are growing: political, institutional and professional life too may not flourish if we constantly uproot it to demonstrate that everything is transparent and trustworthy" (O'Neill, 2002, 19). A careful, skeptical approach in internal auditing is a good antidote to the risks of reckless innovation.

6.7 SUGGESTION 6: THE PRIMACY OF LOGIC IN INTERNAL AUDITING

A streak of irrationality runs through human nature. Internal auditing is embedded within our social environments, and it should therefore come as no surprise that our discussions have identified streaks of irrationality running through internal auditing. The technological prowess of modern internal auditing coexists with superstitious mumbo jumbo. We looked (in Section 5.2) at the ways in which a quasi-superstitious faith in the power of numbers to provide reliable abstractions of reality has settled over internal auditing, and (in Sections 3.4 and 3.5) we suggested that unwarranted levels of faith in risk control models and probabilistic prediction are often as effective in "managing" risks as the placing of a horseshoe over one's front door. Such flights from reason may be mitigated by a rigorous application of traditional logic to auditing.

Judgment in auditing is at constant risk from cognitive bias and heuristic thinking, for which logic is the best antidote. We are not referring here to the logic of computer programming, nor to symbolic, mathematical logic: We do not suggest that auditors need learn how to master Boolean equations. Instead, it is traditional, Aristotelian logic that we have in mind – the type of logic that uses, and copes with, the ambiguities and complexities of everyday language. Logic based on everyday language can offer surprisingly high levels of precision, and it captures qualitative elements of auditor judgment. In contrast, symbolic logic contains a kind of ghostly emptiness, its symbols resembling chess pieces: A king in chess is a game piece with permitted moves and powers, but it has nothing in common with a real, flesh-and-blood king, like the British monarch Charles III. Symbolic logic suffers from a formulaic detachment from the realities of traditional, language-based logic.

Many commentators have recognized the centrality of logic to auditing. It has been argued that "[p]hilosophy is important in identifying the goals of the audit and logical reasoning is, or at least should be, used in justifying how well those goals are achieved" (Smieliauskas et al., 2021, 23). Mautz and Sharaf (1961, 192–193) judged that external auditing "has its primary roots in logic, not in accounting", and it has also been suggested that of equal importance to evidence as "the foundation upon which all audits must stand" are the logical processes auditors bring to bear on evidence (Ratliff and Reding, 2002, 377).

Despite the centrality of logic to auditing's inferential processes, auditors usually have no explicit training in logic (Nelson et al., 2003). Perhaps the only exception to this trend is the implicit deployment of inductive logic in statistical sampling. It is rare to see an explicit documentation of logical analysis (beyond statistical sampling), in either symbolic or everyday language form, in internal audit work papers. Nonetheless, logic underpins auditors' reasoning, often in a tacit, informal, non-explicit manner. (A rare example of overt references to formal logic in an internal auditing textbook can be found in Ratliff and Reding, 2002.) Expertise in auditing is not merely familiarity with a list of facts and techniques, but rather the application of reason and logic to those facts. But modern internal auditors are increasing tunnel-visioned, their powers of judgment buffeted and diminished by a mindset conditioned by formulae, checklists, and prescriptive standards.

A knowledge of basic, traditional logic is a regrettable gap in the Institute of Internal Auditors' syllabi, and its remediation would be of benefit to internal auditors. In particular, the use of inductive logic (that provides outcomes in terms of degrees of probability, rather than certainty) is central to auditing. An extension of an internal auditor's knowledge of inductive logic beyond areas like statistical sampling into qualitative assessments of evidence would likely enhance the effectiveness of the ways in which conclusions are inferred from audit evidence. The opinions of auditors should always be based on cogent reasoning, and this demands – explicitly or implicitly – inductively strong arguments, supported by unambiguous terms and warranted premises. The alternative, as we are currently experiencing, is to rip internal auditing away from its moorings in logic, and to let it float on the wild seas of opinion.

6.8 SUGGESTION 7: CURTAILING THE COMMODIFICATION OF INTERNAL AUDITING

Commercialization has suffused internal auditing to such an extent that the motivations of acquiring money may usurp the public interest. In Section 3.1, we reviewed the way in which external auditing was brought to the brink of ruin by the greed of the large audit and advisory firms around the turn of the millennium. In Section 4.4, in considering where best to position internal auditing on the continuum between a profession and a trade, we encouraged a dampening of the commodification of internal auditing. The professional ethos of internal auditing may be undermined by an aggressively commercialized approach. In practical terms, we suggested measures such as restricting the role of the consulting industry to the sidelines of internal auditing, from where it may offer a helping hand with expertise and flexible staffing resources. Too often, consultants offer guiding rather than helping hands.

Anticipating the discussion of cultural differences in Section 6.9, understandings of the role of money in relation to professional morality might be culturally conditioned. This concern extends beyond internal auditing: Visitors to the United States are often surprised to see the focus on money within the learned profession of divinity, where frequently "the relation of a preacher to his congregation can take a business-like form" (Scruton, 2007, 560). We should therefore be attentive to the dangers that the hype-driven market logic underpinning the role of powerful advisory firms in internal auditing in the English-speaking countries may not be universally shared.

To promote internal auditing as a profession whose primary purpose is to serve the public interest, rather than as a trade with lucrative ambitions, a fundamental reorientation is needed so that internal auditors and auditees are viewed as flesh and blood citizens in their communities, rather than reduced to providers, consumers, clients, or other participants in a trade. By curtailing the commodification of internal auditing, we will place a protective shield around internal auditing's professional ethos.

6.9 SUGGESTION 8: UNIVERSALITY AND SUBSIDIARITY IN INTERNAL AUDITING

Forms of modern internal auditing have been traced back to the 1880s in the United Kingdom's railway sector (Matthews, 2006, 68), but it was not until 1941 that the Institute of Internal Auditors, an association with universal, professional aspirations for internal auditing, was formed in the United States. The IIA has developed into the main, global association for internal auditing. However, there is a question mark over the IIA's universal claims to represent global internal auditing. The basic issue at stake is the inherent tension between universalism and subsidiarity.

Universalism is a trend toward "affirming the moral unity of the human species and according a secondary importance to specific historic associations and cultural forms" (Gray, 1986, x). The term subsidiarity derives from the context of canon (ecclesiastical) law, particularly as it was used in the 1929 papal encyclical *Divini illius Magistri* (*That Divine Teacher*) of Pope Pius XI, and it was formally adopted into the law of the European Union in the 1992 Treaty of Maastricht. It refers to socio-administrative arrangements in which decisions on important matters should be taken at the level closest to those whose interests are likely to be most affected by the decisions. This implies that decentralized, localized decisions should take precedence, where appropriate, over remote, centralized decisions. In other words, subsidiarity involves – at least in theory – a devolution of decision-making powers and accountability, both geographical and hierarchical. In practice, however, subsidiarity in the European Union sits uneasily with the top-down *acquis communautaire*, the overarching body of rights and obligations contained in the European Union's laws and policies. The conflict between subsidiarity and the *acquis* was at the roots of Brexit, the United Kingdom's decision to leave the European Union: Many Britons were of the view that the weight of the *acquis* suffocated the local initiative essential for subsidiarity. Brexit was essentially a political decision in favor of re-establishing local autonomy, decision-making, and sovereignty.

There may be lessons for internal auditing in the events that led to Brexit. The IIA, headquartered in the United States, claims authority over the definitions and standards of internal auditing worldwide. This notion sits uneasily with the principles of subsidiarity. The IIA's activities and pronouncements often display a somewhat provincial flavor, favoring the interests and predilections of North American culture. Matters that seem uncontroversial in the United States may appear problematic elsewhere. For example, in Sections 4.4 and 6.8 we noted that large consulting firms sometimes play a prominent role in the IIA's policy directions, acting more as guiding than helping hands, and that the market logic of such activities does not necessarily sit comfortably round the world.

No one country is predestined for permanent global dominance in internal auditing. It is not written in the stars that internal auditing is to be forever institutionally headquartered in Orlando in the United States. One can envision a future, multipolar internal auditing world, in which several centers of excellence emerge that satisfy local demands, in line with the subsidiarity principle. We might expect to see the allegiance of global internal auditors to the remote rigidities of the IIA become increasingly fragile, and the emergence of competing authorities for internal auditing, especially in the Global South. Such pressures are likely to come from the initial member states of the BRICS organization (i.e., Brazil, Russia, India, China, and South Africa). For example, India already possesses competing written standards for internal auditing. The Board of Internal Audit and

Management Accounting of the Institute of Chartered Accountants of India promulgates *Standards on Internal Audit*, while the Internal Auditing and Assurance Standards Board of the Institute of Cost Accountants of India has developed *Internal Audit and Assurance Standards*. Both institutes have also published supplementary guidance for specific industries and technical matters. The Indian standards rub shoulders locally with the IIA's *Global Internal Audit Standards*, with the result that three sets of internal auditing standards issued by different professional associations are currently circulating in India. It is not inconceivable that the energy and creativity Indians have invested in developing internal auditing standards will spill over from the subcontinent to offer their attractions to the rest of the world. The Institute of Chartered Accountants of India or the Institute of Cost Accountants of India, separately or together, might one day decide to develop an international version of India's internal audit standards, in a bid for global technical and moral leadership in internal auditing. The Indian internal auditing standards are already written in English, facilitating their potential amendment and adoption for international use.

The notion of Indian international leadership in internal auditing is not preposterous. The suggestion of Brexit once also appeared preposterous to those in the European Union who viewed a political rejection of the *acquis communautaire* as inconceivable. India possesses an ancient pedigree in auditing: Kauṭilya's ancient treatise on statecraft and public administration, the *Arthaśāstra*, dates to the fourth century BCE and the treatise includes a sophisticated treatment of auditing and compliance (Mattessich, 1998; Olivelle, 2013). In the author's view, India's *Standards on Internal Audit* and *Internal Audit and Assurance Standards* represent authentic Indian auditing traditions – they are not simply echoes of North American concepts of internal auditing, or watered-down imitations of the IIA's standards, as some would have us believe. With the increasing economic power of the Global South, it is possible that India, the world's largest country by population size, and the world's largest democracy, may one day rival, if not eclipse, the United States as the world leader in internal auditing.

When the French writer Pierre Loti (1850–1923) visited India, he avoided interaction with the British Raj – his perspective of India was conveyed in his 1903 account of his subcontinental journeys as *L'Inde sans les Anglais* (*India without the British*). The future of Indian internal auditing will likely remain as *L'Audit interne sans les Américains* (*Internal Audit without the Americans*). The technical and moral authority of India's *Standards on Internal Audit* and *Internal Audit and Assurance Standards*, and their supporting literature, remind us that the IIA's current universalistic claims should be tempered by an openness to local empowerment.

In terms therefore of its universal aspirations, the IIA is like a powerful juggernaut that is missing some of the gears needed for its optimal functioning. One of those gears is an attunement to the principle of subsidiarity, under which internal auditing should respond to local needs rather than being channeled through a globalist vision that overrides localism and cultural diversity. As a modern commentator of the concept of subsidiarity has suggested, the advantage of "humane localism" resides in the safeguarding and promotion of local traditions and cultures (Mitchell, 2019). The IIA is not necessarily central to future evolutions of internal auditing. Perhaps the IIA's dominating role in internal auditing was only a time-bound experiment that has run its course in terms of creativity and innovation. Indeed, North American concepts of internal auditing seem already to have passed the high tide mark of their creativity, and the time may have arrived for alternative visions to emerge, not least from the Global South. Internal auditors everywhere should welcome a healthy competition of ideas in internal auditing theory and practice. Monolithic or monopolistic control of the official discourse of internal auditing dampens originality: Decentralization is an antidote to innovation-suppressing uniformity and homogenized ways of thinking. In other words, internal auditing will likely flourish as a humane, creative endeavor if we encourage a plurality of competing ideas.

Chapter 7

Concluding thoughts

Our inquiries into the malaise of modern internal auditing have taken us over wide terrain. We have surveyed the implications for both the present and the future of internal auditing through reflections on Greek virtue ethics, neuroscience, the sociology of the professions, numerology, authoritarian digital surveillance, widespread institutional decay, and ongoing redistributions of accountability and social trust. Although the material in this book has been eclectic, our lines of inquiry have focused on a unified theme: A search for possible solutions to modern internal auditing's struggles of adaptation and reform.

Before considering where our journey through modern internal auditing has left us, the author hopes that the reader has shared his enjoyment of the journey itself. Along the way, our exploration of various aspects of our collective social existence has confirmed some understandings and dispelled some misconceptions. Moreover, we have identified multifaceted, prolific, and occasionally startling interconnections between the elements of our review. For example, we have suggested linkages between the irrationalities of a quasi-superstitious faith in numbers (Section 5.2) with unrealistic expectations of taming risk (Sections 3.4 and 3.5), overly prescriptive, written professional standards (Section 4.2), the rise of the "algorithmic society" (Section 5.1), and an excessive focus on the building blocks of information arising from cerebral asymmetry (Section 5.3). While it is sometimes difficult to disentangle the individual strands that connect our diverse materials, the broad strokes of our arguments have been clear.

Our review has been critical in tone, in the sense that it has not taken official narratives for granted. A tacit assumption that the range of modern internal auditing's activities is both deepening (in terms of quality) and expanding (in terms of scope) underwrites current professional discourse. Our inquiries indicate, however, that both assumptions are open to doubt. The questions we have posed throughout this book have their origins in perplexities not only inherent in internal auditing but also deeply entrenched in the ways we perceive internal auditing – does it embody a credible foundation of

DOI: 10.1201/9781032664880-7

abstract knowledge, or is it a mere "ragbag of tasks and routines in search of a unifying role or idea" (Power, 2000a, 18)? Do the enduring methods of applied logic bind together the evolving elements of internal auditing's knowledge base? Is, as the critical theorists might put it, internal auditing primarily a mechanism for perpetuating inequitable socio-economic power? An attempt to settle such matters definitively is beyond the scope of this book. We should, however, acknowledge that internal auditing is a complex mixture of some or all of these considerations.

Modern internal auditing faces the twofold challenges of adaptability and reform. The challenge of adaptability arises from ongoing redistributions of accountability and social trust, away from traditional, hierarchical institutions of the bureaucratic, command-and-control variety toward diffuse, horizontal, and largely digitalized networks. The emerging re-arrangements of accountability and social trust represent a paradigm shift. The new patterns tend to be clustered at the peripheries of organizations or scattered throughout extra-mural networks. In addition, they tend to be splintered; elusive to identify; recorded in digital rather than tangible formats; and difficult to evaluate.

Internal auditing has developed in bureaucratic organizations in which delegations of authority run down vertical lines, and accountability flows upward in the opposite direction. The prevailing outlook of internal auditing, preoccupied with bureaucratic patterns of authority and accountability, is incompatible with the assurance demands arising from horizontally distributed, networked accountability located on or beyond organizational boundaries. Internal auditing's cousin, external auditing, is similarly constrained by its activities among the remnants of hierarchical, vertical accountability relationships embodied in financial statements and underpinned by cycles of periodic, historically focused assurance. External auditing faces a future of marginalization, as it has little to contribute to the emerging demands for flexible patterns of contemporaneous assurance over peripheral and extra-mural accountability.

Although internal auditing's elastic objectives and looser knowledge base seem to offer, at first sight, greater potentialities of adaptation to the shifting patterns of accountability, internal auditing is likely to remain tethered to the inner regulatory spaces of organizations. After years of expanding its scope of activities, the long arm of internal auditing may turn out to be not so long after all – it seems to stop at institutional boundaries, the very point at which the most challenging and significant aspects of the newly patterned paradigm of accountability commence. The inner workings of organizations, peripheral activities, and extramural activities are three hitherto independent worlds now increasingly interconnected. Internal auditing remains focused on institutional inner workings, distanced from the requirements of accountability and social trust arising from the other two areas.

Internal auditing therefore is facing a future not dissimilar to that of external auditing – a limited, marginalized future, with a focus on the remnants of accountability and social trust that will remain within bureaucratic walls. As internal and external auditing continue to stagnate in their intra-mural activities, fresh forms of assurance are emerging, in a piecemeal manner, to address the more significant peripheral or extra-mural assurance demands. The forms of the new assurance mechanisms that will likely emerge may reflect some of the characteristics of the auditing methods deployed at present to address supply chains, outsourcing arrangements, franchising networks, and consortia agreements. But entirely original prototypes of extra-mural, audit-like mechanisms are likely to emerge, mirroring the semi-formal, fast-moving, temporary, flexible, and contingent horizontal networks over which they will seek to provide assurance.

Meanwhile, while new assurance demands arise, and new mechanisms develop to address them, internal auditing is likely to remain entangled in the inner workings of traditional institutions. There will always be a demand for this kind of assurance, but we have argued that the center of gravity of accountability and social trust is already moving toward and beyond organizational boundaries. Internal auditing is facing a future of increasing marginalization within traditional, bureaucratic organizations while the real action on accountability moves elsewhere.

The second challenge facing internal auditing is one of general reform. In recent decades, internal auditing has become increasingly mechanical, algorithmic, and rules-based, with a disastrous narrowing of humane, moral, and creative horizons. Internal auditing's creative potential has been hampered by its tendency to reduce its activities to checklists, number-juggling exercises, and clockwork routines, and by the resulting abstractions of reality into impoverished, simple-minded patterns. The repudiation of judgment and the reduction of wisdom to technique continue to deny internal auditing the creativity through which its shortcomings might be corrected. The Institute of Internal Auditors has failed to maximize the conditions for creative and innovative thinking, and has therefore stunted internal auditing's moral imagination.

Harm flows from the fallacy that we are superior in intelligence and logic to our predecessors. Internal auditing continues at a frantic pace, confusing technological means with logical ends, absorbing vast amounts of time and money, and diverting energy and talent away from more creative uses. It is often vigorous rather than rigorous. The bluster of internal auditing masks a thinned-out inner experience. Humanistic understandings of internal auditing, that promote creativity over pedantic literalism, and critical thinking over adherence to algorithms, are rapidly disappearing. The result is a dampening of the internal auditing profession's ability to respond imaginatively to both the emerging patterns of extra-mural accountability and the ethical demands that require the exercise of moral agency.

The twofold challenges of adaptability and reform facing internal auditing are turning into crises of authority and credibility. Even internal auditing's well-established position as the pre-eminent channel for assurance within the inner workings of the traditional, command-and-control organization might also be placed in jeopardy, in the absence of meaningful reform. Without an overhaul of its concepts and practices, the Institute of Internal Auditors' brand of internal auditing will probably experience a large degree of labor substitution by Artificial Intelligence and machine processing. Algorithmic, mechanistic auditing is ideal material for automation. Therefore, as we move deeper into a digital operating environment in which professional judgment is increasingly subordinated to algorithms, many of the de-personalized, repetitive processes commonly used for internal auditing are at risk from a takeover by technology.

Indeed, internal auditing's decline has been intertwined with the development of powerful technological tools: The conceptual substance of internal auditing has never been weaker, while the information technology tools at its disposal have never been stronger. Some modern auditors equate information technology developments with a false sense of progress. They eagerly embrace data analytics, risk assessment scores, and data sorting tools, treating them almost as ends in themselves rather than as means to ends. And they fail to discern that internal auditing might be devoured by the information systems whose power they seek to harness. An ever-more mechanized internal auditing is becoming the domain of skilled technicians rather than accomplished professionals.

Even more troubling, internal auditing techniques might be deployed in the service of authoritarian, technocratic surveillance. The "audit society" might develop into the "surveillance society", with internal auditing co-opted into authoritarian imperatives. Perhaps the question we face is not to assess the extent to which internal auditing will be automated, but to what ends and for what purposes the automation of internal auditing will be deployed. And, if internal auditing does become an instrument of social control, whose interests will it serve? Radical reform along the lines of our suggestions in Chapter 6 might reduce the dangers of the potential misuse of auditing for authoritarian purposes.

A further consideration should internal auditing remain unreformed will be the rise of competitive challenges to the universal ambitions of the Institute of Internal Auditors. As we saw in Section 6.9, an inherent tension between universality and subsidiarity in internal auditing is building in intensity. Subsidiarity refers to social arrangements in which decisions on important matters should be taken at the level closest to those whose interests are likely to be most affected by the decisions. This implies that decentralized, localized decisions should take precedence over centralized, remote decisions. In other words, subsidiarity involves a devolution of powers both geographical and hierarchical, and subsidiarity thereby sits uncomfortably with the notion of the Institute of Internal Auditors governing internal auditing worldwide from its base in the United States. We might expect to see the emergence of competing authorities for internal auditing, especially in the Global South, from countries like India or other member states of the BRICS organization (i.e., Brazil, China, Egypt, Ethiopia, Iran, Russia, South Africa, and the United Arab Emirates). The Institute of Internal Auditors' ambitions for global dominance in defining the practices and written standards of internal auditing are therefore likely to be increasingly punctured by alternative voices.

Some might object that our arguments in this book amount to overblown scaremongering, and that we should not be gripped by pessimism. They may dismiss the anxieties afflicting internal auditing today as simply a local reverberation of a general malaise running through our modern societies, and through many of our institutions and professions. For example, the effects of the "algorithmic society" reach far beyond internal auditing into our wider social structures: Mark Jones has warned us of "a crisis of well-being, distress, and dysfunction that has afflicted the legal profession and other professions in recent years" (Jones, 2021, 3). However accurate this may be, in this book we have envisioned internal auditing as a corrective or antidote to broader social pathologies. Quite simply, internal auditing is, or should be, different. In Mustafa Suleyman's words, auditing can be "critical to containment" when it comes to the technological dangers facing humanity (Suleyman, 2023, 245). And we have suggested that there are grounds for thinking that internal auditing may yet surprise us, not only by succeeding in adapting to the new world of fragmented, horizontally distributed assurance, but also by reforming its prevailing clockwork methods. Yet any success of this type is likely to be a slow, frustrating process, akin to groping one's way into a heavy, damp haystack.

Let us wrap up our evaluation of modern internal auditing. Our inquiries have indeed sought to be an evaluation, in the literal sense of assessing internal auditing's *value* in serving the public interest, and for safeguarding accountability and social trust. We have tried to unpeel the onion of modern internal auditing's problems, to find evidence of its ability to meet the challenges of adaptability and reform, and to steer it away from its potential abuse in authoritarian surveillance before it slips into a crisis of legitimacy.

We have concluded that modern internal auditing needs a restoring hand, to release it from its current intellectual exhaustion and monotony of thought. Beneath the surface fizz of technological progress and the superficial bluster of feverish activity, a bleak, creativity-inhibiting uniformity has taken hold of internal auditing. As we noted in Section 2.1, public perceptions of auditing generally tend to be somewhat negative. Perhaps the concept of auditing as a vexatious feature of our socio-economic and political life may reflect the traditional alignment of internal auditing (and, for that matter, external auditing) with command-and-control forms of bureaucracy that have been so maligned and lampooned in cultures around the world. Or perhaps it is a consequence of perceptions of what auditing, especially internal auditing, has become in recent decades – a mechanistic assurance tool of limited humanistic character. We should be unafraid of confronting the orthodoxies of our day. Modern internal auditing is crying out for creativity over pedantic literalism, and critical thinking over algorithmic logic. The checklist-wielding auditor must be replaced by the wise auditor. Let us restore what is enduring about auditing and resist being mesmerized by what is ephemeral, so that internal auditing (and other categories of auditing) might enrich us rather than suffocate our freedom and prosperity.

In Section 5.3, we considered the argument that an increasing cerebral asymmetry, in particular a tendency to over-rely on left-hemispheric thinking, is damaging at both individual and society-wide levels. Iain McGilchrist has warned us of this social tendency in no uncertain terms:

> We should be appropriately sceptical of the left hemisphere's vision of a mechanistic world, an atomistic society, a world ... curiously stripped of depth, colour and value ... [that] displaces and renders inaccessible the vibrant, living, profoundly creative world that it was our fortune to inherit.
>
> *McGilchrist, 2019a, xxvi*

Internal auditing has been caught up in these trends. Will the internal auditing profession realize the "unlimited horizons" evoked in the title of a well-known history of the discipline, Victor Z. Brink's *Foundations for Unlimited Horizons: The Institute of Internal Auditors* (Brink, 1977)? Or will internal auditing squander its priceless inheritance?

The French philosopher-mystic Simone Weil (1909–1943) suggested that the answers to the most puzzling perplexities of our existence are out of easy reach, and that our best option is to contemplate such problems, patiently, for as long as it takes, waiting for insight to manifest itself (cited in O'Hear, 2020, xi). Nonetheless, in this book we have refused to wait, Weil-like, for insight, and we have proposed in Chapter 6 several practical suggestions for the future amelioration of internal auditing.

The suggestions set out in Chapter 6 are premised on the assumption that internal auditing's problems are not intractable, and that we still perhaps have time to reverse the corrosion of trust, virtue, and wisdom in internal auditing. Such aspirations may, however, amount to little more than wishful thinking. We do not have the luxury of future decades in which to inconclusively tinker around with written standards and to undertake cautious, incremental steps toward reorienting the purpose of internal auditing toward the public good. When a professional community chooses to feel good about itself rather than to question itself, and to measure itself against low levels of aspiration, it is a community in decline. Pursuing the public good, extracting principles from the daily bluster of events, and thinking abstractly about the purposes of our activities are necessary preliminaries to a renaissance of internal auditing. And it is essential to recognize that a commitment to the public good is not merely an optional part of internal auditing. It defines it. And it requires careful nurturing.

This book perhaps resembles an extended love letter. Tinged with melancholy, it is a letter to a once-adored profession now assailed by wrecking balls largely of its own creation. The author hopes that his thoughts and suggestions resonate with a receptive readership, and that they play a role in defining both the adaptation and the reform of internal auditing needed in our age of increasingly depleted social trust.

A final thought. We have seen (at Section 3.6) that, even in its most seemingly debased conditions, internal auditing's ritualistic tendencies may contain the seeds of a future renaissance. A ritualization of internal auditing offers not merely consolation amid decline. Rituals preserve and transmit enduring values of substance. They also symbolize a belief in the enduring distinctions that internal auditing implicitly authorizes – the differences between error and accuracy, corruption and honesty, and falsehood and truth. We lose sight of these distinctions at our peril.

Appendix A

Philosophical notes

[Note to the reader: Appendix A addresses the foundations of my approach to the arguments in this book. I have included it for reasons of completeness. It contains a certain amount of philosophical theory and terminology: The reader who finds this information obstructive or uninteresting may skip this Appendix without losing any understanding of the book's arguments.]

This book records my reflections on modern internal auditing. More specifically, it documents an extended meditation on the nature and purposes of internal auditing; its claims to knowledge and expertise; the roots and implications of its current malaise; and the likelihood of its adaptability to the modern era's transformations in patterns of accountability and social trust. My inquiry is interpretative in intention, and it has little in common with the traditional methodologies of the social sciences. Indeed, the path I take in this book is fundamentally at odds with the standard social science approach, for the reasons discussed in the following paragraphs.

To the extent that my reflections emphasize my experiences over more than three decades of immersion in internal auditing, this book might be described as an exercise in autoethnography, which links personal experiences to broader socio-economic, political, and cultural frameworks. Autoethnography deploys hindsight to the interpretation of past events, employing different levels of consciousness. It has been described as "self-as-datum", and it consists of "reflecting on – and making scholarly sense of – our own experiences" (Vine, 2021, 13: see also 99–115). It is a means of capturing "localized little stories" (Llewellyn, 1999). However, although some parts of the book may be considered autoethnographical, I would place my approach in this book within a broader and more eclectic hermeneutical endeavor, grounded somewhere between the phenomenology of the later writings of Edmund Husserl (1859–1938) and the philosophical hermeneutics of Hans-Georg Gadamer (1900–2002), especially the latter's *Truth and Method* (published, initially in German, in 1960). My interpretivist approach differs from that of the social sciences in its rejection of the notion that an adequate understanding of social phenomena like internal auditing can be satisfied purely by positivist social science methods (including surveys, experimental behavioral tasks, and quantitative data analysis). It also differs in its view that a cognizing subject cannot be detached from the phenomena it observes.

Central to Husserl's phenomenology is his notion of the *Lebenswelt* – the lived world of intentionality, human agency, and meaning. From the *Lebenswelt* we gain knowledge from our observations of the surface of life. It is the most immediate level of our shared world of experience in which intelligibility is possible. Husserlian phenomenology differs significantly from scientific understandings, yet the two ways of understanding coexist and complement each other. In the *Note on methodology* we gave the example of a smile: The *Lebenswelt*-inhabiting phenomenologist interprets the smile in terms of humanistic intentionality, based on surface appearances and the truth of experience, while scientific realism tends to understand the smile in terms of deeper, biological structures and processes.

A phenomenological interpretation is objectively valid, and no less so than the objectivity of scientistic understanding. They represent two types of interpretation: The full meaning of a smile is not reducible to a biological explanation, but phenomenological ontology does not contradict the laws of nature. In contrast to the scientistic approach, the phenomenological approach seeks to understand the human condition in human terms, without reducing it to scientific structures or laws.

Gadamer's philosophical hermeneutics were grounded in Husserlian phenomenology and concepts of intentionality applied to the *Lebenswelt.* Gadamer's approach involved distinct characterizations of the ways in which information is received, deciphered, interpreted, and subsequently communicated. In contrast to the tendencies of modern concepts of knowledge to posit a self and its consciousness disengaged from the surrounding world, Gadamer's hermeneutics rejected a sharp division of a knowing subject from the objects of its knowledge. To arrive at knowledge and understanding is therefore not achieved through isolated or subjective acts of consciousness; it is, rather, the outcome of both a participation in events and an encounter between the mediating role of tradition and the historically formed (and historically informed) self. Understanding and interpretation occur in a fusion of self-awareness with awareness of the world, and are therefore grounded in a pre-existing context. According to Gadamer, any understandings derived from participation in the fusions of horizons are not only guided by but, crucially, limited by language. Knowledge, therefore, is linguistically mediated. Wittgenstein had already suggested as much, in section 5.6 of his *Tractatus Logico-Philosophicus*: "The limits of my language mean the limits of my world".

The hermeneutic ideal of knowledge and our perceptions of the world have been characterized as differing from the general trends of modern epistemology in the following ways: "Not distance but involvement, not impersonal observation but personal interaction" (Zimmermann, 2015, 53). Unlike some later advocates of philosophical hermeneutics, Gadamer sees tradition as something to be embraced in the interpretative process, rather than undermined or repudiated.

One of Gadamer's aims in *Truth and Method* was to overcome the traditional dichotomy between subject and object. In showing that our minds are correlated to objects in the world, and by arguing for a close engagement between subject and object, Gadamer's path to understanding has narrowed differences between epistemology and ontology. Indeed, his hermeneutics imply a narrowing of the strict binary positions not only of subject and object, but also of essence and contingence, the self and the other, the timeless and the historical, and the empirical and the normative.

Gadamer built on a tradition in modern German-language philosophy that first flowered fully in the work of Wilhelm Dilthey (1833–1911) – a differentiation between interpretative understanding (*Verstehen*) and scientific proof and causal explanation (*Erklären*). Social scientists have borrowed from laboratory scientists the process of formulating a hypothesis, identifying a body of discrete data, and using that data to test the hypothesis. In so doing, in Gadamer's view, social scientists are merely dressing up their activities in scientific clothes, and Gadamer's inquiries purposely "seek the experience of truth that transcends the domain of scientific method" (Gadamer, 2004, xx–xxi). As with Husserlian phenomenology, this does not imply that there are two social realities, but rather two ways of trying to understand one social reality. Humane understanding is different from, and irreducible to, scientific understanding. Put differently, humanistic rationality is different from scientific rationality, but it is nonetheless rational. (Owing to these differences, it is frequently suggested that we inhabit two cultures, in which scientists criticize the lack of scientific knowledge of humanists, while the latter bemoan the ahistoricism and philistinism of scientists.)

Arguing in *Truth and Method* that the truths of social life cannot be accessed solely through scientific methodologies, Gadamer indicates that they are best accessed through a kind of *dialogue*. This dialogue, in Roger Scruton's words,

> involves listening to the voice of history as enshrined in traditions and to the voice of a culture ... Much of the alienation and disorientation of modern society stems from the attempt to replace the natural tendency to enter into dialogue with the world with an unnatural obsession with scientific inference.
>
> (Scruton, 2007, 267)

A type of broad metaunderstanding is nourished by the dialogical space inherent in Gadamer's hermeneutics. The approach I have taken in this book is therefore a philosophical path to knowledge which, in Gadamer's words, addresses "not what we do or ought to do, but what happens to us over and above our wanting and doing" (Gadamer, 2004, xxv–xxvi).

Just as Gadamerian hermeneutics emphasizes the importance of historical horizons, I have in this book aimed to take the past into account in interpreting contemporary conditions – the ahistorical auditor is at a disadvantage in trying to interpret the world around her. A study of history inculcates many skills, including information gathering, problem solving, and the presentation of arguments. But it offers more than marketable skills: An ahistorical or uncultured mind is an impoverished mind with restricted abilities to understand and interpret our social life. A fusion of horizons assumes an understanding of those horizons as a prerequisite for their mutual dialogue.

According to Gadamer, therefore, understandings of social reality may be explained by philosophical inquiry as much as by social science methodologies. The norms of social science therefore have little or no place in the arguments of this book, although I sometimes evoke the findings of social scientists as illustrative examples. I consider the meaning of internal auditing to be irreducible to algorithmic testing, checklists, or clockwork sampling techniques. My view is that modern internal auditing has gone too far down the scientific route, and that we have impoverished internal auditing by repudiating the notion of it as a social reality accessible equally well through phenomenological considerations.

The reader who considers the philosophical outline, up to this point, to be overly Euro-centric might be heartened to learn that I have also found guidance in a non-Western tradition of epistemology and logic, the traditional *Nyāya* school of India. Gadamer was not prescriptive in terms of hermeneutic methodologies, leaving to the discretion of the individual the precise methodology of arriving at knowledge and understanding. *Nyāya* emphasizes a need for epistemological clarity, and I have found *Nyāya* both helpful and reconcilable with the aims of philosophical hermeneutics.

Western views of India are often tinged with orientalist conceptions of Indian culture as other-worldly and meditative, with Indian thought directed primarily at a unity of existence far above earthy concerns. But India has in fact a strong philosophical tradition based on rigorous attempts to understand down-to-earth ontological and epistemological questions. *Nyāya* is one of Hinduism's major *āstika* (orthodox) philosophical traditions: Its origins are uncertain, but they clearly predate its oldest extant text, the *Nyāya-sūtra*, of CE200, attributed to the sage Akṣapāda Gautama. (The Gautama of *Nyāya* is, of course, not to be confused with Siddhartha Gautama, the founder of Buddhism, who lived in the sixth or fifth centuries BCE.) Developments in the school's philosophy over the subsequent centuries were summarized and rationalized by Gaṅgeśa Upādhyāya in his monumental fourteenth century text *Tattva-chintā-maṇi* (Phillips, 2020).

Post-Gaṅgeśa *Nyāya* is often referred to as *Navya-Nyāya* (neo-Nyaya) to differentiate it from the older tradition.

In its search for epistemic clarity, *Nyāya* envisions cognitive events as moments of consciousness in which knowledge is apprehended, and it provides strict guidance for verifying the doxastic (belief-forming) processes that arise from the accumulation of cognitive events (Phillips, 2012, 24–32). *Nyāya* accepts four paths to reliable and valid knowledge. These paths, in order of decreasing importance, are (1) perception (i.e., direct experience), (2) inference, (3) analogy, and (4) testimony. The *Nyāya* system therefore prioritizes experiential knowledge as the first and most important path to knowledge. Perception has been defined by Iain McGilchrist as "the capacity of each of the senses to make discriminations, and thus help us to bring about a world of experience" (McGilchrist, 2021, 1:105). Although perception is *Nyāya*'s principal path to knowledge, our senses can deceive us, and *Nyāya*'s remaining three paths provide safeguards against misperception. The three remaining paths may be considered "lines of defense" that help us to identify errors of perception, thereby to banish scarecrows of our imagination. The notion of sensory experience providing access to reality is not unrelated to our phenomenological approach based on the Husserlian *Lebenswelt* – both are rooted primarily in experience.

Nyāya's emphasis on perception is not, therefore, a simple, naïve empiricism, as it is complemented by the paths of inference, testimony, and analogy. The second path to knowledge, inferential logic, requires the epistemic agent to infer the meaning of perceived objects and events. *Nyāya* demands a significant inferential effort by epistemic agents, and inductive, deductive, and abductive reasoning all form part of *Nyāya*'s system of logic. Indeed, *Nyāya* is admired as much for its logical sophistication as for its epistemology: One commentator has claimed that Aristotle is the "only other logician whose influence on a long and continuing logical tradition is comparable" to that of Gautama (Chakrabarti, 1977, introduction).

Analogy is *Nyāya*'s third path to knowledge, and I have made liberal use of analogy throughout this book. As a form of reasoning, analogical arguments do not provide the certain conclusions of deductive logic (in the manner of the Aristotelian syllogism). They may provide, perhaps, the degrees of probability of the conclusions of inductive logic. Certainly, they offer degrees of *plausibility*. Notwithstanding such limitations, the power of analogy is cemented in the metaphors that run through our cultural and literary traditions. As with the role of tradition, history, and culture in Gadamerian hermeneutics, analogies in *Nyāya* evoke understanding through imaginative, perspective-enlarging comparisons. They bring unfamiliar things into sharper view through a proximity to the familiar. *Nyāya* possesses well-defined requirements for the validation of sound analogies – for example, structural analogies are stronger than those based on superficial similarities, and multiple analogies supporting the same conclusion are viewed as more argument-strengthening than isolated or non-recurring analogies.

Regarding the fourth and least important path, testimony, the references section of this book provides a multitude of witnesses to the book's themes. They have guided and refined my thoughts as I have weighed the testimony of my senses and inferential abilities against the testimony of others. According to *Nyāya*, testimony is a relatively straightforward path to knowledge: It relies on those who have mastered knowledge and transmitted it to us. Therefore, if the source of the testimony is trustworthy, little subsequent analysis is needed, beyond a prudent assessment of the degree of consistency of testimonial with non-testimonial evidence, which in any case rarely reaches the level of absolute consensus. Our cognitive existence would grind to a halt if we had to learn all disciplines anew, or if our skepticism dismissed all evidence from third parties, so a prudent reliance on testimony is evitable in our daily lives. However, an overreliance on testimony is risky, leaving us at the mercy of epistemic authorities who might turn out to be untrustworthy. In summary, coherence between experience and testimony is only suggestive of truth, and in no sense guarantees it (Olsson, 2005), and for this reason testimony is the least important of *Nyāya*'s four paths to knowledge.

We have discussed the influences on the approach taken in this book of the Western traditions of phenomenology and philosophical hermeneutics, and the epistemology of the Indian system of *Nyāya*. Readers may also detect an eclectic range of other philosophical influences in the text – the notion of a collective bond or partnership between the living, the dead, and the unborn developed by Edmund Burke (1729–1797); the *Tractatus Logico-Philosophicus* (first published, in German, in 1921) of Ludwig Wittgenstein (1889–1951); the mystical Platonism of Eric Voegelin (1901–1985); the mystical anti-Platonism of Jonathan Sacks (1948–2020); the value of tradition articulated by Roger Scruton (1944–2020); the liberal iconoclasm of Conor Cruise O'Brien (1917–2008); and the implications of cerebral asymmetry in the writings of Iain McGilchrist (born 1953).

A few words on Plato are in order, as he appears prominently in the discussions in Chapter 4. As is well known, interpreting Plato can be controversial. Some prefer a literal reading of Plato's dialogues and letters, while others tend to allegorize his writings. Some dispute the authenticity of most or all of Plato's letters, and some of the dialogues. Some view the entirety of Plato's corpus of work as internally consistent, while others consider that Plato developed his views throughout his lifetime. Even those who advocate a developmental progression in the Platonic corpus frequently disagree about the chronology of the writings. In addition, some claim that Plato had unwritten or esoteric doctrines (the *ágrapha dógmata*) that supplemented or even underpinned his publicly available, exoteric writings.

It is therefore appropriate that I provide a brief summary of my approach to Plato. I have taken a developmental approach to Plato's writings, as indicated, in Chapter 4, in the contrast between the character of the pragmatic city of Magnesia in *Laws* and the earlier, utopian city of Callipolis in the *Republic.* I agree with the general consensus among scholars of Platonism on the chronology of Plato's works. I see no reason to doubt the authenticity of the letters, especially the crucial Seventh Letter. I have sympathy with the arguments in favor of Plato's "unwritten doctrines", partial testimonies of which have survived in a fragmentary manner. This line of interpretation – that Plato's "writing remains basically reliant on oral supplementation by 'things of greater value' (*timiôtera*)" (Szlezák, 1999, 79) – has been associated in the modern era initially with the German *Tübinger Platonschule* (centered on the University of Tübingen), followed by the emergence of a related school of thought in Italy, centered around Giovanni Reale (1931–2014). The joint German/Italian tradition is sometimes described, in Italian, as a consolidated *Scuola di Tubinga-Milano*. The significance of the inner-Academy *timiôtera* are vigorously disputed, but I find compelling the modern arguments in favor of the unwritten doctrines (in, for example, Nikulin, 2013; Reale, 2008; Szlezák, 1999).

Beyond this eclectic range of influences, the three "acts of the intellect" of Aristotelian logic frame this book. The acts of the intellect are (1) the apprehension of terms, (2) the judgment of propositions, and (3) the reasoning of arguments, and their respective objectives are (1) clarity, (2) truth, and (3) validity. The slipperiness of many auditing terms appears to be attributable as much to language conventions as to the nature of auditing, and in the *Auditor's Companion* (O'Regan, 2024), a dictionary of auditing, I address the first of the three acts – the clarification of auditing's terms, or at least an attempt to reduce their ambiguity. I have addressed the remaining two acts of the intellect in the present book, in which I set out judgments and arguments in a search for truth and validity. An argument is good if it is valid (deductively) or strong (inductively); based on premises whose truth is warranted; clearly stated; and relevant. Although both the *Companion* and the present book stand independently as self-contained works, they also together constitute a two-part project to apply the three objectives of traditional logic to modern auditing.

And now some reflections on the eclecticism of the book's intellectual and conceptual frameworks. I think of the multiplicity of these approaches as *Rashōmon*-like changes of perspective rather than changes of direction, akin to the viewing of a statue from various angles to obtain a rounded aesthetic appreciation. Perhaps the *Rashōmon* analogy implies a greater ambition than this book aims for. The camera of Akira Kurosawa (1910–1988) acted as the "eye of God" (Ganeri, 2021, xii) in *Rashōmon*, not only displaying but pulling together the film's various perspectives into an integrated narrative. My aim in approaching internal auditing through a multiplicity of perspectives is more modest – I have sought to achieve what Robert K. Merton (1920–2003) described as "disciplined eclecticism", understood as "the controlled and systematic use of complementary ideas drawn from different orientations" (Merton, 1976, 169). I have used several conceptual perspectives in a capacious phenomenological manner, drawing from personal experience, common sense observations, testimony I consider reliable, and inferential conclusions. I have scrutinized my findings using both factual and counterfactual considerations. And I hope that the use of complementary frameworks may subsume the risks of individual anomalies of judgment within an integrated range of counterbalancing judgments.

Social scientists have two main avenues to approach matters like internal auditing and social trust. First, they use opinion polls and academic surveys, but individuals often tell pollsters what they want to hear, and the ways in which pollsters phrase their questions can lead to biased responses (O'Neill, 2002, 9–10). That said, this text contains a handful of survey findings. I offer these – in line with the spirit of philosophical hermeneutics – as illustrative examples, not as argument-clinchers. The second, scientistic approach to studying social phenomena is the laboratory-based experiment, such as "trust games" to assess individuals' responses to challenges and dilemmas. Sometimes social science experiments take place on the streets: A well-documented example is the "wallet drop test", in which wallets are dropped on the streets and the extent to which passers-by return the wallets to their owners is taken as an indication of social trust.

In contrast to such behavioral manifestations of trust, my focus is more on epistemic trust. The approach of philosophical hermeneutics places less emphasis on methodologies like social science experimentation and the accumulation of examples than on creative reflection and the discernment of "big picture" patterns derived from experiences in the *Lebenswelt*.

The application of Gadamerian hermeneutics to questions of auditing has been relatively rare. One such rare example (Francis, 1994) has suggested that "scientism and technocratic rationality" deform humanistic understandings of auditing, and that "highly structured audit methodologies" have a damaging effect on auditing's judgmental character. These suggestions correlate to the broad findings of this book, as does Francis's concern that, as a result of scientistic and prescriptive trends in auditing, "auditors may lose their capacity for moral and critical reasoning and hence for moral agency with respect to their actions". No applications of *Nyāya*'s epistemic concerns to internal auditing are readily available. While the links between Gadamer's thought and Indian philosophy have been explored (e.g., Frazier, 2009), my application of an eclectic Gadamerian/*Nyāya* framework to the analysis of auditing seems to be a novel interpretative approach.

Appendix A has, in a highly compressed manner, set out the eclectic philosophical approach on which my inquiries into internal auditing are grounded. Within this eclectic framework, I have tried through my arguments to craft fresh constellations of connections and areas of emphasis within auditing's social mission. But I have not ventured very far, in Appendix A, beyond a description of the philosophical framework to a systematic defense of it. To document that defense in detail, however pleasurable a task, might require another full-length book to do it justice. I therefore hope that the relevance of the outcomes of my inquiries will provide at least some indirect indications of my eclectic methodology's validity. It is for the reader to assess whether my approach has adequately served its purposes.

Appendix B

Aphoristic wisdom and internal auditing

Detailed explanations are often a blunt tool in aiming to understand, interpret, and communicate complex matters. To balance the narrative explanations in this book, the author has compiled a selection of 50 ancient and modern aphorisms relevant to the book's themes. Aphorisms are compact and concise statements of truth that reach out to the reader for interpretation. These fragments of compressed wisdom can stimulate one's imagination and creative understanding: Appendix B is therefore an important part of this book. The aphorist Nassim Nicholas Taleb (2015, xiii) has suggested that no more than four aphorisms should be reflected on in one sitting. This may or may not be good advice, but Taleb's suggestion of not overloading oneself with too many aphorisms at any point in time is sound. Some of the following citations appear in the main body of the text – most do not.

On the nature and fragility of social trust:

1. "What is trust? A confident relationship with the unknown" (Botsman, 2017, 2).
2. "The audit society is a less trusting society" (Power, 2000b, 117).
3. "When it is not necessary to write everything down, citizens and society save a lot of time and a lot of trouble" (Svendsen, 2014, 21).
4. "Distrust comes easily because it can be built on a limited bit of behavior by the distrusted. Trust, however, requires too rich an understanding of the other's incentives for it to come easily to many people" (Hardin, 2002, 91).

On the dangers of over-auditing:

5. "Plants don't flourish when we pull them up too often to check how their roots are growing: political, institutional and professional life too may not flourish if we constantly uproot it to demonstrate that everything is transparent and trustworthy" (O'Neill, 2002, 19).

On philosophy and logic in auditing:

6. "Philosophy is important in identifying the goals of the audit and logical reasoning is, or at least should be, used in justifying how well those goals are achieved" (Smieliauskas et al., 2021, 23).

On the difficulty of recognizing profound social changes:

7. "The unprecedented is necessarily unrecognizable" (Zuboff, 2019, 12).

On postmodernism:

8. "The general tenor of postmodern thought derides essences and universal claims" (Stephenson, 2015, 12).
9. "Just as we are being told that grand narratives are dead in the postmodern world, it may be that they are alive and well, have vacated academia and now reside in conceptions of managerial practice" (Power, 2007, viii).

On the transformative effects of auditing:

10. "Many audit processes are not neutral acts of verification but actively shape the design and interpretation of 'auditable performance'" (Power, 2000b, 114).
11. "Concepts of performance and quality are in danger of being defined largely in terms of conformity to auditable process" (Power, 1994a, 48).

On expertise:

12. "It is by knowledge that one ought to make decisions, if one is to make them well, and not by majority [opinion]" (Plato, *Laches*, 184e).
13. "Wisdom and knowledge are ... the most powerful forces in human activity" (Plato, *Protagoras*, 352d).
14. "The first requirement for the authority of auditors is competence. Audit competence requires both knowledge and skill, which are the products of education, training and experience" (Flint, 1988, 48).

On the public good and professional decay:

15. "If the public interest is well served, rather than the private, then the individual and community alike are benefited" (Plato, *Laws*, 875a).
16. "A society with decaying professions will itself surely decay" (Anderson, 1998, 9).

On the dangers of over-relying on quantification:

17. "Those who live only by the numbers may find that the computer has simply replaced the oracles to whom people resorted in ancient times for guidance in risk management and decision making" (Bernstein, 1998, 336).
18. Our lives "teem with numbers but we sometimes forget that numbers are only tools. They have no soul; they may indeed become fetishes" (Bernstein, 1998, 7).
19. "The death of one child is a tragedy; the death of a million is a statistic" (popular aphorism, cited in Taleb, 2010, 304).

On the importance of qualitative judgment:

20. "Professional knowledge is eclectic. Professional problems are variegated and fluid. Professionalism requires an imaginative and probing mind" (Kultgen, 1988, 271).
21. "I feel it, and cannot understand it; I cannot hold on to it, nor yet forget it;
    and if I grasp it wholly, I cannot measure it!
    But then, how should I grasp what seemed to me immeasurable?"
    Hans Sachs, in Act Two of Richard Wagner's *Die Meistersinger von Nürnberg* (1868).

On illusions of progress:

22. "In science progress is a fact, in ethics and politics it is a superstition ... The illusion [of progress] is in the belief that it can effect any fundamental alteration in the human condition. The gains that have been achieved in ethics and politics are not cumulative. What has been gained can also be lost" (Gray, 2004, 2).
23. "Not ignorance, but ignorance of ignorance, is the death of knowledge" (McGilchrist, 2021, I:44).

On the risks of excessive quantities of data:

24. "O accumulation of information!" (Buber, 2023, 21).

On algorithmic bias:

25. "[V]irtually every form of [Artificial Intelligence] and algorithm you've ever interacted with, knowingly or not, displays ... tendencies to reproduce the racism, sexism, homophobia, and other forms of bias that plague human societies worldwide" (Sinnreich and Gilbert, 2024, 69).

On interpretation:

26. "Fortunate is the person capable of learning the causes of things" [*felix qui potuit rerum cognoscere causas*] (Virgil, *Georgics*).
27. "Sometimes, a cigar is just a cigar" (attributed to Sigmund Freud, probably apocryphal).
28. "Never in our lifetimes, it seems, has there been greater uncertainty about the future – and greater ignorance of the past" (Ferguson, 2021, 1).
29. "The question is not what you look at, but what you see" (Henry Thoreau, cited in McGilchrist, 2019a, xxvi).
30. "[W]earing glasses can sharpen your eyesight; but they only work if you have eyes" (McGilchrist, 2021, I:44).

On brain asymmetry and the loss of "big picture" perspectives:

31. "If a neuropsychologist had to choose three things to characterise most clearly the functional contribution of the right hemisphere, they would most probably be the capacity to read the human face, the capacity to sustain vigilant attention, and the capacity to empathise" (McGilchrist, 2019a, xxii).
32. [In the context of music and improvisation] "An algorithm is what the left hemisphere wants; the recognition that it's got to be free of any algorithm, yet not at all random, is characteristic of the understanding of the right hemisphere" (McGilchrist, 2021, I:15).
33. "Why do we ... tend to see the pennies instead of the dollars? Why do we keep focusing on the minutiae, not the possible significant large events, in spite of the obvious evidence of their huge influence?" (Taleb, 2010, xxiii).

On the importance of avoiding trivialities:

34. "Small things capture small minds" [*parva leves capiunt animas*] (Ovid, *Ars Amatoria*).

On the nature and importance of organizations:

35. "We are born in organizations, educated by organizations, and most of us spend much of our lives working for organizations. We spend much of our leisure time paying, playing and praying in organizations Most of us will die in organizations, and when the time comes for burial, the largest organization of them all – the state – must grant official permission" (Amitai Etzioni, cited in Vine, 2021, 99–100).

36. "Along this tree / From root to crown / Ideas flow up / And vetoes down." (A senior corporate executive at Unilever, reported by Peter Drucker in the 1970s, and cited in Child, 2019, 93).

On the inevitability of change:

37. "If we want things to stay as they are, things will have to change" (Giuseppe Lampedusa, cited in Berman and Fox, 2023, 7).

On avoiding procrastination:

38. "Time, that devours everything" [*tempus edax rerum*] (Ovid, *Metamorphoses*).

On the stubborn uncontrollability of risk:

39. "Only that shall happen which has happened, only that occur which has occurred: there is nothing new beneath the sun" (*Koheleth / Ecclesiastes* 1:9).
40. "Though on the sign it is written: 'Don't pluck these blossoms'—it is useless against the wind, which cannot read". (Japanese proverb, cited on the tombstone of writer Richard Mason, 1919–1997.)

On the modern neglect of virtue ethics and moral agency in professional life:

41. "It's a virtue to take responsibility" (Russell, 2013, 2).
42. "Like spells against witchcraft, complaints about 'character' are thought to belong to a bygone era" (Bosworth, 2014, 3).

On internal auditing and opportunity costs:

43. "The cost of a professional internal audit department should not be calculated as the cost of hiring one but as the cost of not having one" (Luaces Calpe, 2024, 40).

On the limitations of checklists:

44. "A good auditor does not just follow checklists without reflection" (Luaces Calpe, 2024, 49).

On the scope and boundaries of science:

45. "[S]cience can just as well serve oppression as freedom" (Gray, 2023, 68).

46. "We find in the history of science as many fashions, crazes and schools as in the history of literature or interior decoration" (Koestler, 1964, 248).
47. "[E]xplaining social phenomena in general and management phenomena in particular requires imagination (e.g., using counterfactuals) and intuition (e.g., drawing on experience). Thus, more often than not, the endeavor is not just a scientific activity but also an art" (Tsang, 2023, 31).

On the nature and importance of philosophical analysis:

48. "True philosophy entails learning to see the world anew" (Maurice Merleau-Ponty, cited in McGilchrist, 2021, 1:377).

On the value of analogy:

49. "Without analogy there might be no knowledge: the perception of analogies is a first step towards classification and generalization" (Bunge, 1973, 125).
50. "Only the [brain's] right hemisphere has the capacity to understand metaphor" (McGilchrist, 2019b, 115).

References

Notes on ancient references:

References to Plato provide Stephanus Numbers and the translations collected in John M. Cooper's edition of the complete works (Cooper 1997), with occasional emendations. All citations from Xenophon's *Memorabilia* are taken from the Loeb Classical Library edition (vol. 168, Cambridge, MA, 2013, rev. ed.). For Aristotle, Bekker references are provided, and translations from the *Nicomachean Ethics* are taken from Christopher Rowe's translation (Broadie and Rowe, 2002). Translations from the Hebrew Bible are taken from the Jewish Publication Society's editions available at the time of writing.

Abbott, Andrew. 1988. *The System of the Professions: An Essay on the Division of Expert Labor*. Chicago: University of Chicago Press.

Ackroyd, Stephen. 2005. "The re-organized economy." In Stephen Ackroyd, Rosemary Batt, Paul Thompson, and Pamela S. Tolbert (eds.), *The Oxford Handbook of Work and Organizations*. Oxford: Oxford University Press: 449–461.

Anderson, Digby (ed.) 1998. "Introduction and summary" to *Come Back Miss Nightingale: Trends in Professions Today*. London: Social Affairs Unit.

Balaguer, Mark. 1998. *Platonism and Anti-Platonism in Mathematics*. New York and Oxford: Oxford University Press.

Bauer, Paul C., and Markus Freitag. 2018. "Measuring trust". In Eric M. Uslaner (ed.), *The Oxford Handbook of Social and Political Trust*. Oxford: Oxford University Press: 15–36.

Bauman, Zygmunt. 1989. *Modernity and the Holocaust*. Cambridge: Polity Press.

Beard, Mary. 2015. *S.P.Q.R.: A History of Ancient Rome*. London: Profile Books.

Bebbington, Jan, and Carlos Larrinaga. 2024. "The influence of Power's audit society in environmental and sustainability accounting." *Qualitative Research in Accounting and Management*, Vol. 21, No. 1: 21–28.

Beck, Ulrich, 1992. *Risk Society: Towards a New Modernity*. London: Sage Publications. [Originally published in German as *Risikogesellschaft*, 1986.]

Bennett, Alan. 2015. *The Lady in the Van: The Complete Edition*. London: Faber & Faber.

Berman, Greg, and Aubrey Fox. 2023. *Gradual: The Case for Incremental Change in a Radical Age*. New York and Oxford: Oxford University Press.

Bernstein, Peter L. 1998. *Against the Gods: The Remarkable Story of Risk*. New York: Wiley.
Bhaskar, Michael. 2021. *Human Frontiers: The Future of Big Ideas in an Age of Small Thinking*. London: Bridge Street Press.
Black, Robert A. 2019. "Accounting and the auditing function in economic history: Transaction costs, trust, and economic progress." *Journal of Markets & Morality*, Vol. 22, No. 1: 41–65.
Bloom, Allan. 1987. *The Closing of the American Mind: How Higher Education Has Failed Democracy and Impoverished the Souls of Today's Students*. New York: Simon & Schuster.
Bok, Sissela. 1978. *Lying: Moral Choice in Public and Private Life*. New York: Pantheon.
Bosworth, David. 2014. *The Demise of Virtue in Virtual America: The Moral Origins of the Great Recession*. Eugene, OR: Front Porch Republic Books.
Botman, Brian. 1987. *Signifying Nothing: The Semiotic of Zero*. Stanford: Stanford University Press.
Botsman, Rachel. 2017. *Who Can You Trust? How Technology Brought us Together and Why it might Drive us Apart*. New York: Public Affairs.
Bottausci, Chiara and Keith Robson. 2023. "'He Hears': An essay celebrating the 25 year anniversary of The Audit Society." *Critical Perspectives on Accounting*, Vol. 97, December.
Boyle, David. 2000. *The Tyranny of Numbers: Why Counting Can't Make Us Happy*. London: HarperCollins.
Brink, Victor Z. 1977. *Foundations for Unlimited Horizons: The Institute of Internal Auditors 1941–1976*. Altamonte Springs, FL: Institute of Internal Auditors.
Broadie, Sarah, and Christopher Rowe. 2002. *Aristotle: Nicomachean Ethics*. Oxford: Oxford University Press.
Bronner, Stephen Eric. 2017. *Critical Theory*, 2nd ed. Oxford: Oxford University Press.
Brooks, David. 2000. *BOBO's in Paradise: The New Upper Class and How They Got There*. New York: Simon & Schuster.
Buber, Martin. 2023. *I and Thou* [Centennial edition]. New York: Scribner.
Bunge, Mario. 1973. *Method, Moral and Matter*. Dordrecht: Reidel.
Burns, David C., James W. Greenspan, and Carolyn Hartwell. 1994. "The state of professionalism in internal auditing." *Accounting Historians Journal*, Vol. 21, No. 2: 85–116.
Camfferman, Kees and Stephen A. Zeff. 1994. "The contributions of Theodore Limpberg Jr. (1879–1961) to Dutch accounting and auditing". In Kees Camfferman and Stephen A. Zeff (eds.), *Twentieth-Century Accounting Thinkers*. London: Routledge: 112–141.
Chakrabarti, Kisor Kumar. 1977. *The Logic of Gotama* [Monograph No. 5 of the Society for Asian and Comparative Philosophy]. Honolulu: University Press of Hawaii.
Chambers, Andrew D. 1980. "Developments in internal auditing." *Accounting and Business Research*, Vol. 10, No. 39: 273–283.
Chambers, Richard F., with Robert Pérez. 2024. *Agents of Change: Internal Auditors in the Era of Permacrisis*, 2nd ed. Place of publication not stated: Fina Press.
Chen, Deqiu, Li Li, Xuejiao Liu, and Gerald J Lobo. 2018. "Social trust and auditor reporting conservatism." *Journal of Business Ethics*, Vol. 153, No. 4: 1083–1108.

Cheney-Lippold, John. 2017. *We Are Data: Algorithms and the Making of Our Digital Selves*. New York: New York University Press.
Child, John. 2019. *Hierarchy: A Key Idea for Business and Society*. Abingdon, UK: Routledge.
Chin, Angelina. 2022. *Recognizing and Mitigating Cognitive Biases: A Threat to Objectivity*. Lake Mary, FL: Internal Audit Foundation.
Cohen, Daniel. 2018. *The Inglorious Years: The Collapse of the Industrial Order and the Rise of Digital Society*. Princeton, NJ: Princeton University Press.
Cooper, Cynthia. 2008. *Extraordinary Circumstances: The Journey of a Corporate Whistleblower*. Hoboken, NJ: Wiley.
Cooper, John M. (ed.). 1997. *Plato: Complete Works*. Indianapolis: Hackett.
Costouros, George J. 1978. "Auditing in the Athenian state of the golden age (500–300 B.C.)." *Accounting Historians Journal*, Vol. 5, No. 1: 41–50.
Cousins, Jim, Austin Mitchell, Prem Sikka, and Hugh Willmott. 1998. *Auditors: Holding the Public to Ransom*. London: Association for Accountancy and Business Affairs.
Dalton, Dennis. 1993. *Mahatma Gandhi: Nonviolent Power in Action*. New York: Columbia University Press.
Davis, Harry Zvi. 1981. "Note on the First recorded audit in the Bible." *Accounting Historians Journal*, Vol. 8, No. 1: 71–72.
Davis-Floyd, Robbie, and Charles D. Laughlin. 2022. *Ritual: What it is, How it Works, and Why*. New York: Berghahn.
de Swaan, J.C. 2020. *Seeking Virtue in Finance: Contributing to Society in a Conflicted Industry*. Cambridge: Cambridge University Press.
Dierynck, Bart, and Christian Peters. 2022. "Auditor task prioritization: The effects of time pressure and psychological ownership." Available from https://papers.ssrn.com/sol3/papers.cfm?abstract_id=3450363
Dinesen, P.T., and K.M. Sonderskov. 2018. "Ethnic diversity and social trust: A critical review of the literature and suggestions for a research agenda". In Eric M. Uslaner (ed.), *The Oxford Handbook of Social and Political Trust*. Oxford: Oxford University Press: 175–204.
Dudley, Underwood. 1997. *Numerology: Or, What Pythagoras Wrought*. Washington D.C.: Mathematical Association of America.
Dunn, John, and Prem Nath Sikka. 1999. *Auditors: Keeping the Public in the Dark*. Basildon, UK: Association for Accountancy & Business Affairs.
Engelland, Chad. 2020. *Phenomenology*. Cambridge, MA: MIT Press.
Espeland, Wendy Nelson. 1998. *The Struggle for Water: Politics, Rationality, and Identity in the American Southwest*. Chicago: Chicago University Press.
Everett, Jeff, and Marie-Soleil Tremblay. 2014. "Ethics and internal audit: Moral will and moral skill in a heteronomous field." *Critical Perspectives on Accounting*, Vol. 25, Issue 3: 181–196.
Ewans, Michael. 1982. *Wagner and Aeschylus: The Ring and the Oresteia*. Cambridge: Cambridge University Press.
Ferguson, Niall. 2012. *The Great Degeneration: How Institutions Decay and Economies Die*. New York: Penguin.
———. 2021. *Doom: The Politics of Catastrophe*. New York: Penguin.
Fischhoff, Baruch and John Kadvany. 2011. *Risk: A Very Short Introduction*. Oxford: Oxford University Press.

Flint, David. 1988. *Philosophy and Principles of Auditing: An Introduction.* Basingstoke: Macmillan.

Fonfeder, Robert, Mark P. Holtzman, and Eugene Maccarrone. 2003. "Internal controls in the Talmud: the Jerusalem Temple." *Accounting Historians Journal*, Vol. 30, No. 1: 73–93.

Fox, Loren. 2003. *Enron: The Rise and Fall.* Hoboken, NJ: Wiley.

Francis, Jere R. 1994. "Auditing, hermeneutics, and subjectivity." *Accounting, Organizations & Society*, Vol. 19, No. 3: 235–269.

Frazier, Jessica. 2009. *Reality, Religion, and Passion: Indian and Western Approaches in Hans-Georg Gadamer and Rupa Gosvami.* Lanham, MD: Lexington Books.

Fukuyama, Francis. 2011. *The Origins of Political Order: From Prehuman Times to the French Revolution.* New York: Penguin.

Funnell, W. 1998. "Accounting in the service of the Holocaust." *Critical Perspectives on Accounting*, Vol. 9, No. 4: 435–464.

Gadamer, Hans-Georg. 2004. *Truth and Method*, rev. ed. London: Bloomsbury Academic. [First published in German as Wahrheit und Methode, 1960.]

Ganeri, Jonardon. 2021. *Inwardness: An Outsider's Guide.* New York: Columbia University Press.

Garofalo, Charles and Dean Geuras. 2006. *Common Ground, Common Future: Moral Agency in Public Administration, Professions, and Citizenship.* Boca Raton, FL: CRC Press.

Giroux, Gary. 2017. *Accounting History and the Rise of Civilization*, Two Vols. New York: Business Expert Press.

Goodwin, Matthew. 2023. *Values, Voice and Virtue: The New British Politics.* London: Penguin Books.

Gray, John. 1986. *Liberalism.* Milton Keyes: Open University Press.

———. 2004. *Heresies: Against Progress and Other Illusions.* London: Granta.

———. 2023. *The New Leviathans: Thoughts after Liberalism.* New York: Farrar, Strauss and Giroux.

Gustafsson Nordin, Ingrid. 2023. "Narratives of internal audit: The Sisyphean work of becoming 'independent' ". *Critical Perspectives on Accounting*, Vol. 94.

Hardin, Russell. 2002. *Trust and Trustworthiness.* New York: Russell Sage Foundation.

Hardy, G.H. 1940. *A Mathematician's Apology.* Cambridge: Cambridge University Press.

Hawley, Katherine. 2012. *Trust.* Oxford: Oxford University Press.

Hay, David, W. Robert Knechel, and Marleen Willekens. (ed.) 2014. *The Routledge Companion to Auditing.* Abingdon, UK: Routledge.

Heckscher, Charles, and Anne Donnellon. (ed.) 1994. *The Post-Bureaucratic Organization: New Perspectives on Organizational Change.* London: Sage.

Hempel, Sandra. 2007. *The Medical Detective: John Snow, Cholera and the Mystery of the Broad Street Pump.* London: Granta.

Henrizi, Philipp, Dario Himmelsbach, and Stefan Hunziker. 2020. "Anchoring and adjustment effects on audit judgments: Experimental evidence from Switzerland." *Journal of Applied Accounting Research*, Vol. 22, no. 4, 598–621.

Higgins, Peter M. 2011. *Numbers.* Oxford: Oxford University Press.

Holy See Press Office. 2023. "Audience with staff of the Office of the Auditor General." *Bulletin No. 231211a, December.*

Hopkin, Paul, and Clive Thompson. 2022. *Fundamentals of Risk management: Understanding, Evaluation and Implementing Effective Enterprise Risk Management*, 6th ed. London: KoganPage.

Hubbard, Douglas W. 2020. *The Failure of Risk Management: Why It's Broken and How to Fix It*, 2nd ed. Hoboken, NJ: Wiley.

Huxley, Aldous. 1932. *Brave New World.* London: Harper & Brothers.

Institute of Internal Auditors [IIA]. 2024a. *Global Internal Auditing Standards.* Lake Mary, FL: IIA.

———. 2024b. *Report on the Standard-Setting and Public Comment Processes for the Global Internal Audit Standards.* Lake Mary, FL: IIA.

IPPF Oversight Council (2022), *Framework for Setting Internal Audit Standards in the Public Interest.* Lake Mary, FL: IIA.

Islam, Gazi. 2016. "Rituals in organizations: rupture, repetition, and the organizational event." In Raza Mir, Hugh Willmott, and Michelle Greenwood (ed.), *The Routledge Companion to Philosophy in Organization Studies.* Abingdon, UK: Routledge: 542–549.

Jaynes, Julian. 1976. *The Origin of Consciousness in the Breakdown of the Bicameral Mind.* Boston: Houghton, Mifflin.

Jeacle, Ingrid, and Chris Carter. 2022. "Audit society goes viral: The rise of the online auditor." *Qualitative Research in Accounting and Management*, Vol. 19, No. 2: 231–240.

Jokipii, Annukka, and Antti Rautiainen. 2024. "Quo vadis, internal auditing? A vision for internal auditing in 2030." *International Journal of Auditing*, Vol. 28, Issue 1: 170–184.

Jones, Mark L. 2021. *Professions and Politics in Crisis.* Durham, NC: Carolina Academic Press.

Kahneman, Daniel. 2011. *Thinking, Fast and Slow.* New York: Farrar, Straus and Giroux.

Kallinikos, J. 2004. "The social foundations of the bureaucratic order." *Organizations*, Vol. 11, No. 1, 13–36.

King, Mervyn, and Linda de Beer. 2018. *The Auditor: Quo Vadis?* Abingdon, UK and New York: Routledge.

Knight, Frank H. 1921. *Risk, Uncertainty, and Profit.* Boston: Houghton, Mifflin.

Koestler, Arthur. 1964. *The Act of Creation.* London: Hutchinson.

Kosman, Aryeh. 2007. "Justice and virtue: Inquiry into proper difference." In *The Cambridge Companion to Plato's Republic*, edited by G.R.F Ferrari. Cambridge: Cambridge University Press: 116–137.

Kouremenos, Theokritos. 2019. *Plato's Forms, Mathematics, and Astronomy.* Berlin: de Gruyter.

Kuhn, Thomas S. 1962. *The Structure of Scientific Revolutions.* Chicago: University of Chicago Press.

Kultgen, J. 1988. *Ethics and Professionalism.* Philadelphia, PA: Pennsylvania University Press.

Kuo, Nan-Ting, Shu Li, and Zhen Jin. 2023. "Social trust and the demand for audit quality." *Research in International Business and Finance*, Vol. 65: 41–65.

Lee, Tom A. 1993. *Corporate Audit Theory*. London and New York: Chapman and Hall.

———. 1998. "A stakeholder approach to auditing." *Critical Perspectives on Accounting*, Vol. 9, No.2, April: 217–226.

Lenz, Rainer and Florian Hoos. 2023. "The future role of the internal audit function: Assure. Build. Consult." *EDPACS – The EDP Audit, Control, and Security Newsletter*, Vol. 67, Issue 3: 39–52.

Lenz, Rainer and Kim K. Jeppesen. 2022. "The future of internal auditing: Gardener of Governance." *EDPACS – The EDP Audit, Control, and Security Newsletter*, Vol. 66, Issue 5: 1–21.

Lenz, Rainer, and David J. O'Regan. 2024. "The *Global Internal Audit Standards* – old wine in new bottles?" *EDPACS – The EDP Audit, Control, and Security Newsletter*, Vol. 69, Issue 3: 1–28.

Lev, Baruch, and Feng Gu. 2016. *The End of Accounting: and the Path Forward for Investors and Managers*. Hoboken, NJ: Wiley.

Liu, Catherine. 2021. *Virtue Hoarders: The Case against the Professional Managerial Class*. Minneapolis: University of Minnesota Press.

Llewellyn, Sue. 1999. "Narratives in accounting and management research". *Accounting, Auditing & Accountability Journal*, Vol. 12, Issue 2: 220–237.

Luaces Calpe, Marta. 2024. *Internal Audit at Your Fingertips*. Middletown, DE: privately published.

Macdonald, Keith M. 1995. *The Sociology of the Professions*. London: Sage Publications.

Maldonato, Mauro and Silvia Dell'Orco. 2011. *Natural Logic: Exploring Decision and Intuition*. Eastbourne: Sussex Academic Press.

Maroun, Warren, and Jill Atkins. 2018. "The emancipatory potential of extinction accounting: Exploring current practice in integrated reports." *Accounting Forum*, Vol. 42, No. 1: 102–118.

Mattessich, Richard. 1998: "Review and extension of Bhattacharyya's *Modern Accounting Concepts in Kautilya's Arthaśāstra*." *Accounting, Business and Financial History*, Vol. 8, No. 2: 131–149.

Matthews, Derek. 2006. *A History of Auditing: The Changing Audit Process in Britain from the Nineteenth Century to the Preset Day*. Abingdon, UK: Routledge.

Mautz, Robert Kuhn, and Hussein A. Sharaf. 1961. *The Philosophy of Auditing*. Sarasota, FL: American Accounting Association.

Mayer, Colin. 2018. *Prosperity: Better Business Makes the Greater Good*. Oxford: Oxford University Press.

Mazzucato, Mariana, and Rosie Collington. 2023. *The Big Con: How the Consulting Industry Weakens our Businesses, Infantilizes our Governments, and Warps our Economies*. New York: Penguin Press.

McGilchrist, Iain. 2019a. *The Master and his Emissary: The Divided Brain and the Making of the Western World*, rev. ed. New Haven, CT: Yale University Press.

———. 2019b. *Ways of Attending: How our Divided Brain Constructs the World*. Abingdon, UK: Routledge.

———. 2021. *The Matter with Things: Our Brains, Our Delusions, and the Unmaking of the World*, 2 vols. London: Perspective Press.

McKenna, Christopher D. 2006. *The World's Newest Profession: Management Consulting in the Twentieth Century*. Cambridge: Cambridge University Press.

McNamee, David, and Georges M. Selim. 1998. *Risk Management: Changing the Internal Auditor's Paradigm*. Altamonte Springs, FL: Institute of Internal Auditors.

Merton, Robert K. 1976. *Sociological Ambivalence and Other Essays*. New York: Free Press.

Midgley, Mary. 2005. *The Owl of Minerva: A Memoir*. London: Routledge.

Mihret, Dessalegn Getie, and Bligh Grant. 2017. "The role of internal auditing in corporate governance: A Foucauldian analysis." *Accounting, Auditing & Accountability Journal*, Vol. 30, No. 3: 699–719.

Miller, Norman C. 1965. *The Great Salad Oil Swindle*. New York: Coward-McCann.

Miller, Rory. 2008. *Meditations on Violence: A Comparison of Martial Arts Training and Real World Violence*. Boston, MA: YMAA Publication Center.

Mitchell, Austin, Anthony Puxty, Prem Sikka, and Hugh Willmott. 1991. *Accounting for Change: Proposals for Reform of Audit and Accounting*. London: Fabian Society.

Mitchell, Mark T. 2019. *The Limits of Liberalism: Tradition, Individualism, and the Crisis of Freedom*. Notre Dame, IN: University of Notre Dame Press.

Mitchell, Mark T., and Jason Peters (eds.). 2018. *Localism in the Mass Age*. Eugene, OR: Front Porch Republic Books.

Mungaray, Kimberly R. (2017) "Does the formal understanding of qualitative research enhance the assessment of risk in an audit?" *American Journal of Management*, Vol. 17, Issue 2: 86–94.

Myddelton, D.R. 2004. *Unshackling Accountants*. London: Institute of Economic Affairs.

Nelson, Irvine T., Richard L. Ratliff, Gordon Steinhoff, and Graeme J. Mitchell. 2003. "Teaching logic to auditing students: can training in logic reduce audit judgment errors?" *Journal of Accounting Education*, Vol. 21, Issue 3: 215–237.

Neri, Marc Peter. 2021. "Virtue ethics and the accounting profession". In Eileen Z. Taylor and Paul F. Williams (ed.), *The Routledge Handbook of Accounting Ethics*. Abingdon, UK: Routledge: 53–66.

Newton, Kenneth, Dietlind Stolle, and Sonja Zmerli. 2018. "Social and Political Trust". In Eric M. Uslaner (ed.), *The Oxford Handbook of Social and Political Trust*. Oxford: Oxford University Press: 37–56.

Nickell, Erin Burrell, and Robin W. Roberts. 2014. "Organizational legitimacy, conflict, and hypocrisy: An alternative view of the role of internal auditing." *Critical Perspectives on Accounting*, Vol. 25, Issue 3: 217–221.

Nigam, Amit, and Diana Trujillo. 2016. "Quantification as a philosophical act." In Raza Mir, Hugh Willmott, and Michelle Greenwood (eds.), *The Routledge Companion to Philosophy in Organization Studies*. Abingdon, UK: Routledge: 525–532.

Nikulin, Dmitri. 2013. *The Other Plato: The Tübingen Interpretation of Plato's Inner-Academic Teachings*. New York: State University of New York Press.

Nirenberg, David, and Ricardo L. Nirenberg. 2021. *Uncountable: A Philosophical History of Number and Humanity from Antiquity to the Present*. Chicago: University of Chicago Press.

Oakley, Justin, and Dean Cocking. 2001. *Virtue Ethics and Professional Roles*. Cambridge: Cambridge University Press.
O'Brien, Conor Cruise and Feliks Topolski. 1968. *The United Nations: Sacred Drama*. New York: Simon and Schuster.
O'Hear, Anthony. 2001. *Philosophy*. London and New York: Continuum.
———. 2020. *Transcendence, Creation and Incarnation: From Philosophy to Religion*. London and New York: Routledge.
Olivelle, Patrick. 2013. *King, Governance, and Law in Ancient India: Kautilya's Arthaśāstra*. Oxford: Oxford University Press.
Olsson, Erik J. 2005. *Against Coherence: Truth, Probability, and Justification*. Oxford: Oxford University Press.
O'Neill, Onora. 2002. *A Question of Trust*. Cambridge: Cambridge University Press.
O'Regan, David. 2024. *The Auditor's Companion: Concepts and Terms from A to Z*. Washington D.C.: Georgetown University Press.
Peeters, Rik, and Marc Schuilenburg (eds.) 2021. *The Algorithmic Society: Technology, Power, and Knowledge*. Abingdon, UK: Routledge.
Pentland, B. 1993. "Getting comfortable with the numbers: Auditing and the micro-production of macro-order." *Accounting, Organizations and Society*, Vol. 18 Nos. 7/8: 605–620.
Phillips, Stephen. 2012. *Epistemology in Classical India: The Knowledge Sources of the Nyāya School*. Abingdon, UK: Routledge.
——— (ed.). 2020. *Jewel of Reflection on the Truth about Epistemology*, [Gaṅgeśa's *Tattva-cintā-maṇi*], 3 Vols. London: Bloomsbury Academic.
Picard, Claire-France. 2016. "The marketization of accountancy." *Critical Perspectives on Accounting*, Vol. 34: 1–98.
Porter, Theodore M. 2020. *Trust in Numbers: The Pursuit of Objectivity in Science and Public Life*, rev. ed. Princeton, NJ: Princeton University Press.
Power, Michael. 1994a. *The Audit Explosion*. London: Demos.
———. 1994b. *The Risk Management of Everything: Rethinking the Politics of Uncertainty*. London: Demos.
———. 1997. *The Audit Society: Rituals of Verification*. Oxford and New York: Oxford University Press.
———. 2000a. *The Audit Implosion: Regulating Risk from the Inside*. London: Institute of Chartered Accountants in England and Wales.
———. 2000b. "The audit society – second thoughts." *International Journal of Auditing*, Vol. 4, No. 1: 111–119.
———. 2003. "Auditing and the production of legitimacy." *Accounting, Organizations and Society*, Vol. 28, Issue 4: 379–394.
———. 2007. *Organized Uncertainty: Designing a World of Risk Management*. Oxford: Oxford University Press.
———. 2022a. "Afterword: Audit Society 2.0?" *Qualitative Research in Accounting and Management*, Vol. 21, Issue 1: 2–6.
———. 2022b. "Theorizing the economy of traces: From audit society to surveillance capitalism." *Organization Theory*, Vol. 3: 1–19.
———. 2023. Personal communication to the author, 3 May 2023.
Prasad, Ajnesh. 2015. "Liminal transgressions, or where should the critical academy go from here?: Reimagining the future of doctoral education to engender research sustainability." *Critical Perspectives on Accounting*, Vol. 26: 108–116.

Pugliese, Anthony. 2024. "New year, new standards", *Internal Auditor*, February: 8.

Rappaport, Roy. 1999. *Ritual and Religion in the Making of Humanity*. Cambridge: Cambridge University Press.

Ratliff, Richard L., and Kurt F. Reding. 2002. *Introduction to Auditing: Logic, Principles, and Techniques*. Altamonte Springs, FL: Institute of Internal Auditors.

Reale, Giovanni. 2008. *Autotestimonianze e Rimandi dei Dialoghi di Platone alle Dottrine non Scritte*. Milan: Bompiani.

Ridley, Jeffrey. 2019. *Creative and Innovative Auditing*. Abingdon, UK: Routledge.

Rittenberg, Larry, and Mark A. Covaleski. 2001. "Internalization versus externalization of the internal audit function: an examination of professional and organizational imperatives." *Accounting, Organizations and Society*, Vol. 26, Issues 7–8, October–November 2001: 617–641.

Roberts, Diane H. 2021. "History of professional accounting ethics". In Eileen Z. Taylor and Paul F. Williams (eds.), *The Routledge Handbook of Accounting Ethics*. Abingdon, UK: Routledge: 9–25.

Rodrigues, Lúcia Lima, Russell Craig, Paulo Schmidt, and José Luíz dos Santos. 2018. "Accounting and taxation practices in the operation of slavery in Brazil." In Michele Bigoni and Warwick Funnell (eds.), *The Italian and Iberian Influence in Accounting History*. Abingdon, UK: Routledge: 237–258.

Rosenthal, Caitlin. 2018. *Accounting for Slavery: Masters and Management*. Cambridge, MA: Harvard University Press.

Roslender, Robin. 2018. "Introduction". In Robin Roslender (ed.), *The Routledge Companion to Critical Accounting*. Abingdon, UK: Routledge: 3–14.

Ross, Angus, and David Woolley (eds.). 2008. *Jonathan Swift: A Tale of Tub and Other Works*. Oxford: Oxford University Press.

Rousseau, Denise, Sim Sitkin, Ronald Burt, and Colin Camerer. 1998. "Not so different after all: A Cross-discipline of trust." *Academy of Management Review*, Vol. 23, No. 3: 393–404.

Roussy, Melanie, and Marion Brivot. 2016. "Internal audit quality: a polysemous notion?" *Accounting, Auditing & Accountability Journal*, Vol. 29, No. 5: 714–738.

Rush, Fred (ed.). 2004. *The Cambridge Companion to Critical Theory*. Cambridge: Cambridge University Press.

Russell, Daniel C. 2013. "Introduction: Virtue ethics in modern moral philosophy". In Daniel C. Russell (ed.), *The Cambridge Companion to Virtue Ethics*. Cambridge: Cambridge University Press: 1–6.

Saks, Mike. 2021. *Professions: A Key Idea for Business and Society*. Abingdon, UK: Routledge.

Sawyer, Laurence B. 1987. "Professionalism," *Managerial Auditing Journal*, Vol. 2, No. 2: 7–11.

Sawyer, Laurence B., and Gerald Vinten. 1996. *The Manager and the Internal Auditor: Partners for Profit*. New York: Wiley.

Scherz, Paul. 2022. *Tomorrow's Troubles: Risk, Anxiety, and Prudence in an Age of Algorithmic Governance*. Washington DC: Georgetown University Press.

Schimmel, Annemarie. 1994. *The Mystery of Numbers*. Oxford: Oxford University Press.

Schwab, Klaus. 2016. *The Fourth Industrial Revolution*. New York: Currency.

Schwartz, Mimi, and Sherron Watkins. 2003. *Power Failure: The Inside Story of the Collapse of Enron*. New York: Doubleday.
Scruton, Roger. 1986. *Sexual Desire: A Philosophical Investigation*. London: Weidenfeld and Nicolson.
———. 1997. *A Society of Strangers: Education for Citizenship in the Post-Modern World*. London: University of London.
———. 2007. *Dictionary of Political Thought*, 3rd ed. Basingstoke, UK: Palgrave Macmillan.
———. 2015. *Fools, Frauds and Firebrands: Thinkers of the New Left*. London and New York: Bloomsbury Continuum.
Seligman, Adam B. 1997. *The Problem of Trust*. Princeton, NJ: Princeton University Press.
Sharma, Divesh S. 2014. "Non-audit services and auditor independence". In David Hay, W. Robert Knechel and Marleen Willekens (eds.), *The Routledge Companion to Auditing*. Abingdon, UK: Routledge: 67–88.
Shaw, Jack, L. G. Campbell, Mike Wright, Robert W. Scapens, J. R. Edwards, Trevor Hopper, John Perrin, Ken Peasnell, M. W. Pendlebury, Paul Collier and Michael Power. 1992. "Book reviews." *Accounting and Business Research*, Vol. 22, Issue 87: 275–288.
Shore, Cris, and Susan Wright. 2015. "Governing by numbers: audit culture, rankings and the new world order." *Social Anthropology*, Vol. 23, Issue 1: 22–28.
Sikka, Prem Nath, Anthony Puxty, Hugh Willmott, and Christine Cooper. 1998. "The impossibility of eliminating the expectations gap: some theory and evidence." *Critical Perspectives on Accounting*, Vol. 9, No.3: 299–330.
Sikka, Prem Nath and Hugh Willmott. 1997. "Practising critical accounting." *Critical Perspectives on Accounting*, Vol. 8, Nos. 1/2: 149–165.
Sinnreich, Aram, and Jesse Gilbert. 2024. *The Secret Life of Data: Navigating Hype and Uncertainty in the Age of Algorithmic Surveillance*. Cambridge, MA: MIT Press.
Smieliauskas, Wally, Minlei Ye, and Ping Zhang. 2021. *Auditing and Society: Research on Audit Practice and Regulations*. Abingdon, UK: Routledge.
Sonderskov, K.M. and P.T. Dinesen. 2014. "Danish exceptionalism: explaining the unique increase in social trust over the last 30 years." *European Sociological Review*, Vol. 30, No. 6: 782–795.
Spacek, Leonard. 1989. *The Growth of Arthur Andersen & Co., 1928–1973: An Oral History*. New York: Garland.
Spicer, André, and Bobby Banerjee. 2016. "Governance: Changing conceptions of the corporation." In Raza Mir, Hugh Willmott, and Michelle Greenwood (eds.), *The Routledge Companion to Philosophy in Organization Studies*. Abingdon, UK: Routledge: 403–411.
Stephenson, Barry. 2015. *Ritual*. Oxford: Oxford University Press.
Stewart, Ian. 1995. *Nature's Numbers: The Unreal Reality of Mathematics*. New York: Basic Books.
Suleyman, Mustafa. 2023. *The Coming Wave: Technology, Power, and the 21st Century's Greatest Dilemma*. New York: Crown.
Svendsen, Gert Tinggaard. 2014. *Trust*. Aarhus, DK: Aarhus University Press.
Szlezák, Thomas A. 1999. *Reading Plato*. Abingdon, UK: Routledge.

Sztompka, Piotr. 1999. *Trust: A Sociological Theory*. Cambridge: Cambridge University Press.

Taleb, Nassim Nicholas. 2010. *Black Swan: The Impact of the Highly Improbable*, 2nd ed. New York: Random House.

———. 2015. *The Bed of Procrustes: Philosophical and Practical Aphorisms*, rev. ed. New York: Random House.

Thielemann, Christian. 2016. *My Life with Wagner: Fairies, Rings, and Redemption–Exploring Opera's Most Enigmatic Composer*. New York: Pegasus. [First published in German as *Mein Leben mit Wagner*, 2012.]

Toffler, Barbara Ley, and Jennifer Reingold. 2003. *Final Accounting: Ambition, Greed, and the Fall of Arthur Andersen*. New York: Broadway Books.

Tsang, Eric W.K. 2023. *Explaining Management Phenomena: A Philosophical Treatise*. Cambridge: Cambridge University Press.

Uhlmann, Michael M. 1998. "From wisdom to experience: The lawyer in the USA". In Digby Anderson (ed.), *Come Back Miss Nightingale: Trends in Professions Today*. London: Social Affairs Unit: 65–76.

Ullrich, Volker. 2023. *Germany 1923: Hyperinflation, Hitler's Putsch, and Democracy in Crisis*. New York: Liveright. [Originally published in German as Deutschland 1923, 2023.]

Vine, Tom. 2021. *Bureaucracy: A Key Idea for Business and Society*. Abingdon, UK: Routledge.

Waterfield, Robin. 2023. *Plato of Athens: A Life in Philosophy*. Oxford: Oxford University Press.

Whitehouse, Harvey. 2021. *The Ritual Animal: Imitation and Cohesion in the Evolution of Social Complexity*. Oxford: Oxford University Press.

Whittington, Geoffrey. 1995. *Is Accounting Becoming Too Interesting?* Aberystwyth: University of Wales.

Williams, Paul. 2018. "Ethics". In Robin Roslender (ed.), *The Routledge Companion to Critical Accounting*. Abingdon, UK: Routledge: 164–183.

Wilson, Robin. 2020. *Number Theory*. Oxford: Oxford University Press.

Wolnizer, Peter W. 1987. *Auditing as Independent Authentication*. Sydney: Sydney University Press.

Wucker, Michele. 2016. *The Gray Rhino: How to Recognize and Act on the Obvious Dangers We Ignore*. New York: St Martin's Press.

Xygalatas, Dimitris. 2022. *Ritual: How Seemingly Senseless Acts Make Life Worth Living*. New York: Little, Brown Spark.

Zimmermann, Jens. 2015. *Hermeneutics*. Oxford: Oxford University Press.

Zuboff, Shoshana. 2019. *The Age of Surveillance Capitalism: The Fight for a Human Future at the New Frontier of Power*. New York: Public Affairs.

Index

ynes UK
ntent Group UK Ltd.
30241124
K00018B/156

9 781032 66487